Idiot Proof Archery

How To Shoot Like a Pro — Step By Step

(Even if you have a real job!)

By
Bernie Pellerite
President, Robinhood Video Productions, Inc.

Edited by
Diana LaBeau

Bernie and Jan Pellerite — Robinhood Video Productions

Idiot Proof Archery
Copyright © 2001 by Bernie Pellerite, Robinhood Video Productions, Inc. All rights reserved. Printed in the United States of America. No part of this book may be used or reprinted in any manner whatsoever without written permission. For information address Robinhood Video Productions, 1036 Arcaro Drive, Gahanna, OH 43230.

Revised and Reprinted 2002.

Design *by Steve Ruis*
Illustrations and Photos *by Bernie and Jan Pellerite, Steve Ruis, or as credited.*
Creative Punctuation *by Bernie Pellerite*
Editing *Diana LaBeau*

ISBN: 0-9712812-0-3

Author Biography

Author Bernie Pellerite

Bernie Pellerite grew up in Huntington, West Virginia. As a youth, he was a typical "over-achiever," and was on numerous sports teams including golf, baseball, bowling and basketball. He earned the rank of *Sharpshooter in the NRA* at the age of ten. He was also involved in martial arts for three years including combat judo and Okinawan karate. Upon graduation from St. Joseph High School, he attended Marshall University where he majored in Psychology and planned on becoming a criminal lawyer. As a member of *MENSA*, a high I.Q. society, he's in the top 1% in I.Q., worldwide. His personal strengths include logic, psychology, multilevel concepts, efficiency, and comparative analysis.

After leaving college, Bernie worked primarily in sales and management where he received numerous national sales awards. He then started his own direct sales company. He later married his wife, Jan, in 1981 in Columbus, Ohio, and four years later they semi-retired and moved to Honolulu, Hawaii. It was there that they started *Bullseye Hawaii*, which later became *Robinhood Video Productions*. Since then Bernie has produced, written and directed thirty seven instructional archery videos that are marketed worldwide. Bernie and Jan then moved to Ocala, Florida, where they owned and operated a successful pro shop and range for three years.

Bernie then started his writing career and has since become the most popular technical writer on the subject of archery in the U.S. Additionally, he is one of the world's most recognized authorities on target panic with eight videos, two inventions, numerous articles and industry seminars devoted to the subject.

Bernie is the inventor/distributor of an anti-panic release aid called **Bernie's Can't Punch**™. He also designed **Bernie's PanicMaster & Bow Simulator**, which is a laser-equipped multifunction retraining device to cure target panic and reprogram proper shot execution.

Bernie is presently a staff writer for three U.S. archery magazines including: *The U.S. and International Archer, National Field Archery Association's (NFAA) Archery*, and *Bow and Arrow Hunting*, and has been published in five other U.S. magazines. Bernie's articles are also translated and published in seven foreign publications all over the world.

As a bowhunter, he has put fourteen animals in the **Safari Club International's (SCI) Bowhunting Record Book**. Ten of these animals are in the "*Top Ten in the World.*" Bernie has won thirteen SCI Medallion awards. As a target archer he has captured 8 NFAA State Championships for indoor, field, and 3-D.

His coaching credentials include NAA and NFAA Instructor Certifications. Bernie is the first and only NFAA Master Coach to reach the highest plateau of "Professional Level IV." As founder and director of the *NFAA Mobile Shooter's School*, he has graduated over 1600 students in thirty five states and two foreign countries, in just five years. Shooters he has worked with have won over 800 world, national, sectional, state, and local titles, making him the most popular and successful coach for compound shooters anywhere. Bernie also designed a new 3-tiered *Certified Instructor Program* for the NFAA in 1998, and has quadrupled their instructors by certifying over 900 Advanced Level Instructors in just four years.

Dedication

I am dedicating this book to my wife, Jan, who I love with all my heart. For 20 years she's been my wife, business partner, shooting partner and best friend. I couldn't have done the shooter's school, the videos, my articles, or this book without her. She's been my sounding board for the hundreds of compulsive ideas and projects I've come up with. Even though some, I'm sure, were really ridiculous, she always listens patiently before she says, with that annoyed expression on her face, "Honey, are you nuts . . . that's really ridiculous!" But, every once in a while, I end up selling her on one, which is not easy to do because she's no dummy. She's a Master Coach who has helped me do over eighty shooter's schools, and now knows as much about archery as I do. She also knows that, whatever it is, she'll probably end up doing all the work because she understands that I'm really just a "concept person." I really don't have the patience or attention span to take most of the phone orders, make up all the packages to be mailed out, edit any of the 37 videos we produced, balance the checkbook, pay the bills, answer all the e-mails, type, edit, and retype all of my 2,500 word articles three times each, program the VCR, take the three dogs for a walk four times a day, feed the two cats and three dogs, or go grocery shopping and do the laundry and ironing. And, because "I have a bad

Jan Pellerite
Master Coach,
VP Robinhood Videos

back" . . . she also loads and unloads the motorhome when we do the shooter's school, trade shows, and tournaments *and* does half of the driving. She does all this and puts up with my obsessive-compulsive ranting and raving and, no matter what, never holds a grudge or stays mad at me for very long. I guess she does it because she loves me, believes in me, and what we are doing. Besides, I really can't do all that other stuff, because "I *really don't* have the patience" and "I *really do* have a bad back." (That's my story and I'm *stickin' to it!)*

Thanks for being there, Jan.
This book is for you.
I love you!

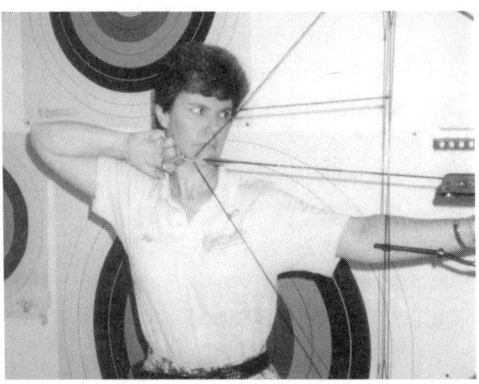

Jan's shooting career includes 7 NFAA State Championships in Indoor, Field and 3-D; 2 NFAA Sectional Championships and 2nd place in the amateur freestyle division at the prestigious Las Vegas Indoor Tournament

Preface

As with most teachers and coaches that reach any level of accomplishment or success, they learned most of what they know from others. I'm no different. When I decided back in the 1980s to try and help some fellow archers to shoot a little better, I never dreamed it would lead to "this."

Mainly because of my own hunger for knowledge, and probably my paranoia about ever being accused of "doing it wrong," I obsessively set out to survey and sometimes interrogate literally hundreds of great shooters and coaches across the country. I then proceeded to take their "tidbits" or, for some, whole volumes of information, and began to compile, coordinate, experiment, formulate, evaluate, check, analyze, scrutinize, cross-check, resurvey, theorize, recheck, acid test, double and triple check, and boil-down their sometimes contradictory information and opinions. This, in my demented mind, had to be done if I were even to possess the ultimate "bullet proof" logic and methods I needed to finally be allowed to stipulate, postulate and extrapolate, and finally pontificate my opinions on the world archery stage.

So, by the time you finish this book, I think you will find that you've discovered several basic archery truths:

1) Competitive archery is not a sport ... it's a discipline!
2) Personality usually has a lot to do with your score.
3) All new archery gadgets work ... for about three days!
4) You don't have to do it my way ... just the same way! (However, my way is easier for most people.)
5) "Bow tuning *perceived* ... is bow tuning *achieved*."
6) You're not weird if you have target panic ... you're weird if you don't.
7) There's an awful lot of luck in archery and the more you practice ... the luckier you seem to get!
8) After all, archery is really just a game ... and if you're not having fun ... you're doing it wrong!
9) And, finally, no matter what excuse you give me ... it's too late to get your money back on this book ... so you might as well *keep reading!*

You may be wondering if you have to be a *truly wise man* to write a book on archery. Well, I don't really think I'm a truly wise man; they only come around about once or twice in a generation. I think most people would say, however, that I may be a smart man. The difference is that a truly wise man *knows everything* . . . and a smart man *doesn't have to know everything* . . . he just has to have the phone numbers of the people that do!

Having said that, I need to thank those many people that helped me directly or indirectly by letting me pick their brains, question their logic, or just influenced me by their way of shooting. Among the many top shooters that contributed to what and how I teach (in no particular order) are: Ed Eliason, Darrell Pace, Terry & Michelle Ragsdale, Frank & Becky Pearson, Randy Ulmer, Larry Wise, Kirk Ethridge, Mike Leiter, Butch Johnson, Rick McKinney, Jay Barrs, Dean Pridgeon, Burley Hall, Dee Wilde, Jim Pickering, Gene Goldecker, Jim Brown, Terry Boyer, Steve Gibbs, Eric Hall, Jesse and Ginger Morehead, Jackie, Kathy, & Shannon Caudle, Larry Weir, Susan Thompson, Randy & Sonny Chappell, and many others.

Among the many archery industry people that helped, supported, or influenced me in one way or the other are: Jim Easton, Don Rabska, Pete Shepley, Ted Nugent, Andy Simo, Fred Pape, Rick Bagley, the NFAA Directors, Steve Malone, Marvin Waymack, Bruce Cull, George Ossola, Ken Rogers, Joe Bell, Marlow Larson, Jack Lyons, Stanley Hips, Myles Keller, Norb Mullaney, Don & Bobbie Metzler, Harry Hamm, Graham Weller, Tom Bishop, Norm Mallonee, Doug Walker, the late Dick Carella, Charlie Rowe, Christine McCartney, Ronnie Kimball, Patty Brady, Mike Strandlund, Paul De Lucia, Tony Altier, Byron Ferguson, Joe Angeloni, Neil Newkirk, Diana & Terry LaBeau, Ann Hoyt, the late Earl Hoyt Jr., and the late Harry Drake.

A special thanks to Arlyne Rhode, owner/Editor of **The U.S. and International Archer** Magazine for her friendship and faith in me and what I do.

Also, a heartfelt thanks to the late Bill Scott, founder of Scott Archery for his friendship, honesty, trust and his help in making **Bernie's Can't Punch Release** a quality product. And to his daughter, Melanie Scott, for her friendship, faith and integrity in continuing Bill's legacy.

And, thanks especially to Chuck Crowell, my friend and past President of the NFAA who had enough courage of conviction and "damn-the-torpedoes" blind faith to help convince the NFAA Council and Directors to let Jan and I run loose all over the country with my new, and as yet unproven, mobile shooter's school concept in 1996.

*Chuck Crowell
IFAA Vice President and Past NFAA President*

I would also like to thank my many hundreds of students that gave me my "internship" and my experience by letting me "experiment" on them. Several have stood out for their dedication, accomplishments or unshakable faith in me and what I'm trying to do. Among them are George Kong, Glenn Campbell, Ted Nugent, Myles Keller, Joella Bates, Butch Wright, Mike Martin, Dave Hryn, Gunny Benson, Jon Stephens, Cloyd Brown, Ross Pfeiffer, Jason Favella, Bruce Tajiri, Tom Lupo, the late Bill Bell, Bill Arledge, Chris Glass, Matt Setzer, Paul Arnold, Dave Martin, Bev & Bruce Chrisman, Jimmy Webb, Gilbert Schnidrig, Richard & Mary Narey, Glen Lau, Don Williams, Rob Curcio, Shawn Murray and Mark Spear.

Also among the 25 or so coaches who have helped form my opinions on what's important about equipment setup, shooting form, the mental program, and/or coaching techniques, the following people need to be acknowledged: Freddie Troncoso, Dick Tone, Bob Ragsdale, Frank Pearson, Tim Strickland, and Len Cardinale .

*Freddie Troncoso
Founder of Golden Key-Futura*

A special mention goes to Freddie Troncoso whose talent and ingenuity have benefited archery for decades. His archery career spans 60 years and covers the entire gamut. He was a top competitive shooter who also coached his wife, Eva, to six national championships in the professional women's division. His company Golden Key-Futura was the pioneer and undisputed leader in archery arrow rests and other accessories. Freddie currently holds thirty patents. I still use and recommend his TM Hunter arrow rest. Freddie is also an archery historian and was one of the first to write for **Archery** magazine, which he did for twenty-five years. His articles had a huge impact on my opinions and coaching techniques concerning the importance of (and the proper execution of) shooting form. I still use a lot of Freddie's techniques from his grip to "rotational aiming" that helps de-program target panic. Thanks a lot, Freddie, you're a credit and inspiration to archery and archers everywhere.

Frank Pearson also deserves special mention for all the things he has done and said in recent years that have definitely helped me to stay "focused and fired up." He gave me the motivation to stay "bulletproof" and stay on top. Frank also taught me that coaching archery is like playing high-stakes poker; there's two ways to do it. If you already have a "reputation" as a player, you can bluff your way through . . . for a while . . . until people start calling your bluff. But, if you don't have a big "reputation" when you start playing, you really can't bluff . . . you need to have the best hand to win! Thanks, Frank! It's guys like you that helped make me so successful!

But, by far the biggest impact on my coaching and writing has come from Len Cardinale. Len is an internationally respected coach and archery analyst who has owned and operated his own pro shop and has been coaching for over 36 years. He is a contributing writer for **Bowhunter** magazine and is a member of the Bowhunting Hall of Fame. Len has worked with the Olympic teams of four different countries. He has reached the elite status of a Level 5 NAA Master Coach and NFAA Master Coach.

Coach Len Cardinale
Belleville, NJ

Len has been both friend and mentor to me and has fueled my enthusiasm, solidified my conviction, and has given me all the key formulas and principles that I needed to build the foundation of my program. His original and profound understanding and analysis of the shot and what makes it work when it's done "excellently" (and what goes wrong when it's not!) is unique to him alone. No one I've ever talked to, heard about, or read, has such a "bullet proof" analysis of "making the shot." His methods have withstood my truly inquisitive but critical, over-analytical cross examinations. Len's dedication and love of archery have endured good times and bad as he unselfishly pours his knowledge . . . his life's blood into anyone's "cup" who is truly thirsty! From one who has gone to his "well" more than their share . . . **Thanks, Len . . . You're the Man!**

Also, a special thanks goes to Steve Ruis, Editor of **Archery Focus** Magazine, who spent a lot of time editing, scanning, taking pictures, and organizing all my incoherent ramblings into some kind of intelligible order. So thanks, Steve!

Finally, a huge debt of gratitude and THANK YOU goes to Diana LaBeau, who literally retyped and reformatted the entire book (through several drafts) and helped me and my wife edit, proofread, and scan pictures. She worked night and day for hundreds of hours, so we could finally get my ramblings to the printer. Diana was Editorial Assistant at **U.S. & International Archer** magazine for about thirteen years. As an archer she achieved the title of Collegiate All American in 1987 following "excellent coaching" from her future husband, Terry LaBeau (and Dr. Jack Pate).

Diana LaBeau former Editorial Asst., U.S. & International Archer Magazine

Terry has been involved in archery for over forty years competing in indoor, field and FITA-style tournaments. Together, they look forward to traveling, competing, and bowhunting in the future while promoting good health and wellness through the use of nutritional, magnetic, and purified water products. Their company can be reached by e-mail at DLaBeau@peoplepc.com. Diana commented, "I have chosen to work with Bernie and Jan on this book because I know that archers around the world are always looking for more information to help them succeed in archery. Although I've been privileged to meet and talk with some of the world's best archers, manufacturers and legends (thanks to Arlyne Rhode and Terry), I know that the average archer never gets that kind of opportunity. I feel it is important to give back to archery just a little for what it has done for me and my life."

Well said! Thanks again, Diana!

So, if you find what I have written entertaining and witty, or possibly invaluable, or even extremely insightful and thought-provoking, or possibly just plain brilliant, I'm glad you enjoyed it. Feel free to write or call me and please tell a friend where they can get a copy of this book.

On the other hand, if you were bored, depressed, confused, misled, or just plain mad as hell about anything at all in this book, then it was probably due to an oversight, miscommunication, foul-up, omission, misprint, or typo by "those crazy damned editors." So you can direct all of your nasty comments, critical e-mails, snide remarks, self-righteous letters, slanderous statements, crude obsenities or hate mail to our Complaint Department at *CrazyDamnEditors@. . .com* . . . and they will address your concerns as soon as they've been through ~~the shredder~~, uh, security x-ray and electronically swept and the FBI profiler has finished your background check.

Contents

Author's Biography iii
Dedication v
Preface vii
Introduction: Why You Don't Shoot Like a Pro 1
    (Or Even As Well As You Can)
Chapter 1: Equipment, Form, The Mental Game, and You! 9
Chapter 2: Your Personality ... Can you handle the truth? 17
Chapter 3: The Importance of Bow Tuning, Shooting Form,
             and Draw Length 27
Chapter 4: The Magic and Myths 49
    Of Bow & Arrow Setup and Tuning
Chapter 5: How the Pros Do It ... Part One — Aiming 81
Chapter 6: How the Pros Do It ... Part Two — Holding Steady 97
Chapter 7: The Shot Sequence ... Part One — The Defense 111
Chapter 8: The Shot Sequence ... Part Two — The Offense 143
Chapter 9: Anticipation, Programming, Back Tension &
             Your Release 153
Chapter 10: "Hi, My Name is Bernie & I've Got Target Panic" 177
Chapter 11: 44 Form Flaws —When Things Go Wrong 205
Chapter 12: Shooting Inside Your Comfort Zone 235
Chapter 13: Perfect Practice 243
    The Do's & Don'ts of an Accelerated Learning Curve
Chapter 14: Tournament Nerves, Choking Under Pressure, and
              Shooting in Adverse Conditions 255
Chapter 15: 3-D & Estimating Yardage ... "Legal & Illegal" 271
Chapter 16: Hunting With a Bow 291

Appendix
Robinhood Videos — 27 Instructional Videos 309
Bernie's PanicMaster/Bow Simulator™ 320
    Laser-equipped, multi-function retraining device
Bernie's Laz-Air Shot Trainer™ — 323
    a laser equipped, pneumatic training aid
Bernie's Can't Punch Release™ 324
    An Idiot-Proof Back Tension Wrist Strap Caliper Release

(Continued on next page)

Bernie's Missing Link Release™ — 328
    A "safe draw" back tension release
Bernie's E-Z Back Release™ — 329
    A "safe draw" back tension release
Bernie's "Control Freak™" Custom Stabilizers 330
Private Instruction with Bernie through 332
    Robinhood Advanced Archery School
NFAA Mobile Shooter's School 334
Miscellaneous Information/Archery Organizations 336
NFAA Membership Application 337

Introduction

Why You Don't Shoot Like a Pro
(or Even As Well As You Can)

If you are reading this book, I assume you are an archer who thinks you have better scores in you, but for some reason you are not making the kind of progress you think you should. Sometimes you shoot really well, then the next time you shoot, (expecting to improve even more) you get worse. You have purchased quite a few bows, arrows and accessories that should have improved your shooting, but after a short time you seem to be back in the same old pattern of "up and down" shooting. Sound familiar? It should. What you are experiencing is typical of most archers. So . . . what's wrong? Let's look at this.

Unlike golf, tennis, bowling, boxing, baseball, football, and basketball, which are all sports that have had many decades to perfect their game, their equipment, and most importantly their techniques, archery seems to be in a constant state of change. In the last few years, we have reached (in a lot of peoples' opinion) the limits of bow technology vis a vis arrow speed. In the last ten years, we discovered the popularity of 3-D archery, which has dominated our sport and the archery manufacturing industry ever since. But in recent years we have seen 3-D starting to decline in popularity. Why does archery popularity seem to run in cycles? I believe our biggest stumbling block is our overall inability to disseminate knowledge to the average archer, about the proper technique or form necessary to be competitive on a long term basis. Although for the masses of ordinary shooters like you and me, we are rightfully taught that the mental aspects of archery are

◉ **Key Point #1**

The mental aspects of archery are the real key to top competitive archery, but they only come into play after technique/form becomes constant and is no longer a variable.

the real key to top competitive archery, or any sport for that matter. However, the mental aspects only come into play *after technique/form becomes constant and is no longer a variable.* Therefore, in the beginning and intermediate stages of archery, *form is the biggest variable,* because the archer can't duplicate shot execution from arrow to arrow. At this point, form becomes key and the mental programming becomes secondary.

Most golfers know that it is really difficult to hit a ball 250 to 300 yards straight down the middle of the fairway consistently. They all realize that driving a golf ball depends on the duplication of form and timing. They know when they slice or hook the ball right or left, or shank the ball, or top it . . . *why* they did it wrong. They realize they didn't hit it squarely or smoothly and they know that usually the only way to hit it straight is to adopt the universally taught and accepted swing which can be provided to them by the local golf pro. (Golf, I'm told, has over 11,000 teaching pros in the U.S.) As in tennis, bowling, baseball, and most other sports, there are a few personal variations of technique, but there is usually only one "accepted way" that is taught in each sport, because after 50 to 100 years of playing those games, the less consistent and less effective ways of doing it fell by the wayside and the more successful forms prevailed. These sports

Shooters getting serious with Bernie in the National Field Archery Association (NFAA) Shooter's School that he created.

recognize that superior form or technique will better perpetuate the sport and, therefore, have set up and support large systems to teach proper technique to its participants.

The teaching pros and coaches created by these sports generally teach technique the same way and withhold nothing from students. After many years supported by these various systems, the average participant knows most of the "secrets" of that sport. For example, most people have a pretty good idea why they slice a golf ball, get a 7-10 split in bowling, pop up a high fast ball in baseball, get suckered by a left hook in boxing, or can't finesse a drop shot in tennis; these are pretty much common knowledge in these sports. In short, they know why they did it wrong and they understand how to fix it (or, at least, they know who to see or where to go to find out). If they want to become more competitive, they know they need a lesson to get the "hitch out of their back hand," "the kinks out of their golf swing," etc. Their sport dictates that to do it professionally, or even competitively, you probably need to take a few lessons, unless you want to try to reinvent your own professional technique. Once in a great while, innovative or unorthodox forms do prevail. Consider high jumping in track and field. Today all jumpers use a technique that was considered "goofy" 35 years ago, until Dick Fosbury won the gold medal with his unorthodox, head first, backwards dive over the bar, now called the "Fosbury Flop."

Key Point #2

If you want to perform at a professional level or even competitively, you probably need to take a few lessons.

This is where archery, in my opinion, gets completely off track. It may be because archery hasn't had enough years of experience with equipment that has been technologically stable for a long time. In just 30 years, archery has gone from recurve bows to four-wheel compound bows to two-wheel compound bows to two-cam compound bows to one-cam compound bows — with arrow speeds increasing by over 100 feet per second

Tennis champion, Pete Sampras, probably took a lesson or two!

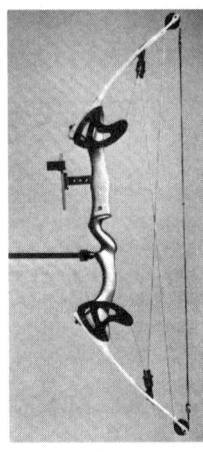
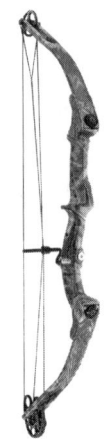

Four wheeler   One-cam   Two-cam

Bow technology has improved

in that time (see photos). Another possible reason for our problems is that some of the winners don't want to share their secrets with the losers or, more likely, most of the winners *can't tell you* why they really win because they do it subconsciously. This condemns professional archery to stay a small circle of shooters incapable of attracting a wide audience, creating a vast teaching network, or creating a viable living for many professional archers, as is the case with golf, tennis, and most other sports. My theory is that, unlike the other "sports" we mentioned, archery is a *discipline* that demands an *ordered mind*. A *naturally focused* archer (Type B personality) is usually the one who has the best chance at the very top level. Unfortunately, this top level is usually made up of less than 100 professionals at any given time. The majority of those that win (with any consistency), maybe twenty-five or so, are typically non-analytical. They are therefore *incapable of teaching* what they do so well, because they do it *innately* at the subconscious level and can't begin to tell you how they do it, even if they wanted to (more on this later in chapter 2). However, most shooters think that, if you don't have any national or world shooting titles, then you don't have enough credentials or credibility as a coach. I've even had a couple of jealous ex-national champion/coaches perpetuate that kind of BS about me.

In archery (as with any sport), a coach with *no credentials*, that turns hundreds of mediocre shooters into competitive archers, ends up with *great credentials* and *credibility*, with a reputation as a *great coach!* This happens because he or she has gathered the knowledge, skills, the passion, and a program that works . . . and are *naturally driven* to be great at coaching, regardless of the money or fame involved.

Key Point #3
At all but the very top level of archery, form is the biggest variable and becomes key; the mental programming necessary to win has less consequence.

Conversely, coaches that are driven by the *fame or the money* and *emotionally need to be perceived* as great coaches, have to go out and *recruit great shooters* (great credentials), to put on their resumés. But since they don't really have enough knowledge, or the skills to motivate and, most importantly, a *program that works on mediocre shooters* . . . they end up to be *mediocre coaches* . . . with *great credentials*.

Nevertheless, putting all the brand name and industry-generated hype, hero worship, professional jealousy, prejudice and bad-mouthing aside, we are really *repeating a discipline* (which usually pushes the non-analytical, introverted, and un-animated personalities to the top). Therefore, we will never have large numbers of top pro shooters coaching. As I said, great coaches have to be able to *analyze*, to *communicate*, and have enough *passion* to *motivate* their students. They don't have to be able to *beat* their students in their chosen sport. Butch Harmon is Tiger Wood's coach and Butch never could beat Tiger on the golf course. The late, great Vince Lombardi was one of the most celebrated football coaches ever and he never was a great football player. The world famous Olympic gymnastics coach, Bela Karoli, can't do a handstand, and Al Henderson, one of archery's most celebrated coaches, never shot scores close to his students'. In fact, most great coaches never started out with credentials or excelled to the professional or top levels of their chosen discipline.

So, if there aren't a lot of good coaches, what is the solution? For starters there is this book. I am going to show you *why some of the things you've been doing don't work*, and *what will work* and *why it will work*. I will show you that you *can shoot like a pro*, if you are willing to do the work that is necessary. You will see several of my students that *followed my program* and *did the work*, pictured throughout this book. These shooters are just a few of over 400 success stories that have been reported to us. But remember, it's not supposed to be easy to win in any sport. Mark McGwire didn't become the prodigious home run hitter he is by taking a few swings in the back yard now and again. How many times do you think he has swung a bat? Or Tiger Woods has swung a golf club? Or Pete Sampras has swung a tennis racquet? Or Shaquille O'Neal has shot a free throw . . . er . . . uh . . . bad example! While you are reading this book, you may notice some repetition of subject matter from chapter to chapter and also numerous **Key Points** throughout. This was done purposely because we have found that the concept that I am trying to get across is sometimes a *compound principle* that is multifaceted, like a chain reaction or, in some cases, *counter intuitive* (the opposite of your natural tendencies). Therefore, the repetition and the **Key Points** will help to tie things together, especially for people with short attention spans and low comprehension levels (like me and maybe you). It also helps people who don't read the book cover to cover and selectively scan the text for subject matter that fits their individual situation or shooting disorder. We learned the hard way that archers (in general) *don't like to read!* They won't even *read the directions* we pack in the **Can't Punch Releases** and **PanicMaster/Bow Simulator** *(See Appendix)* which we sell all over the world. But, I'm no different . . . I don't need to read no stinking directions! . . . So, what did I do . . . I wrote a book for *people who don't like to read!* Yeah, I'm a real bona fide MENSA member . . . that's me!

Anyway, I will show you what kinds of things will lead to the improvements you want and what will actually make you worse! There is also the NFAA Shooter's School, the Shooter School videos, private lessons, and other resources available to you.

But, if you don't want to "take the cure" for what ails your archery, you can still go out and just have fun **because** . . .
**After all, It Is JUST A GAME —
and if you are not HAVING FUN . . .
YOU'RE DOING IT WRONG !**

Key Point #4

If you don't want to "take the cure" for what ails your archery, you can still go out and just have fun!

If you are not HAVING FUN . . . YOU'RE DOING IT WRONG !

Here are a few of my students and their accomplishments! Look for more of them throughout the book.

Billy Myers of Indiana won the Pro Male Freestyle Division April 5-7, 2002 at the NFAA Indoor Nationals in Kansas City, MO. Billy had not shot his bow for over 2 years and he had never shot dots or leagues for score in his life. But, after watching the NFAA Shooter's School Videos series over and over again for a month, before ever picking up his bow, he borrowed some arrows and followed the shot sequence and aiming techniques that Bernie had on the videos. At the Indoor Nationals, he shot a perfect score of 600 with 120 Xs and ended up in a 4 way tie and shoot off for first place. Billy went on to win that shoot off! Altogether, he shot 156 Xs in a row for the weekend. He is one of the Robinhood Videos' new staff shooters.

Lee Ford of Wyoming, averaged 300 with 45Xs and wanted desperately to improve. Lee sold his backup bow so he could afford a "weekend at Bernie's." In less than six months, he turned professional and shot a 58 X 300 and 59 X 300 at the NFAA Indoor Nationals in the Pro Division. Not bad for his first tournament as a pro!

Butch Wright of Dayton, Ohio, was ready to quit archery because of target panic until he attended the shooter's school. He worked hard and mastered what Bernie taught him and went from 292 - 37 Xs to winning the Ohio State Indoor (over 50 class) the next year with a 300-57X score. He set a **new state record** with a perfect 300 - 60X, and the next year won again with 300-59Xs! Butch has also won two indoor state FITA championships and set a new FITA indoor state record. He set a new indoor national record when he won the 2002 NFAA Indoor Nationals 600-117Xs in the Senior Freestyle Division.

Vickie Wright of Dayton, OH, attended the shooter's school with her husband, Butch. She has since won the Ohio State Indoor Championship three times and has set five new indoor state FITA records. Vickie also won the 2002 NFAA Indoor Nationals. She now averages 300 and over 50 Xs.

For those who don't know how to keep score . . .

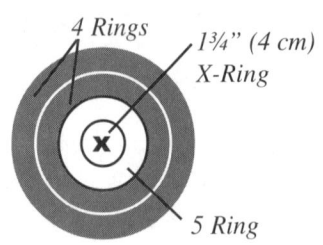

4 Rings
1¾" (4 cm) X-Ring
5 Ring

A perfect NFAA Indoor Round is 300 with 60 Xs at 20 yards . . . 60 arrows in or cutting the line on an 8 cm, $3^{1}/_{8}$", 5-ring will give you 300 (5 x 60=300). To break the ties you also count X-rings (4cm, 1¾") inside the 5-ring. These scoring rings are a part of a 5-spot target (see photo below and page 33).

Chapter 1

Equipment, Form, The Mental Game, and You!

The average participant in archery only stays in our game three to five years and then leaves in frustration. You may be one of those near quitting right now. It's not too hard to figure out that if the average archer does not know exactly why they miss and there's no professional or qualified coach available to correct them, they will eventually draw the conclusion that they are not "cut out for this" and go bowling or fishing. I've learned from owning a pro shop and teaching for years that everybody wants to shoot like Terry Ragsdale or Randy Ulmer (or whoever is hot that year), but nobody wants to do what Terry and Randy do. They want to buy what Terry and Randy *have* in the hope that this bow/release/arrow/whatever will cause them to shoot like Terry and Randy. And the archery industry has promoted just that notion — if you can't shoot a tight group, buy this bow! If you can't improve your score — buy this release! If you still can't win — buy these arrows! Sad, isn't it? Who are we really fooling? This is like telling a baseball shortstop that has made four errors in the last two games to buy a new glove! Or, if you shoot 115 on a par 72 golf course, buy these graphite clubs! When are we going to wake up and smell the bullsh-t they've been putting out? (Anyone want to buy a vowel?)

How to become a better archer? Buy some more stuff! Duh, I think not!

Bernie Pellerite

Wake up! Take a lesson! You wouldn't dream of becoming a state, national, or world competitor at any other sport without professional lessons. Realize this — it's hard to find a great archer with bad form and it's even harder to find a bad archer with great form! By teaching all over the U.S. and a couple of other countries, I have come to realize that archers are very hungry for knowledge. (If you have it . . . they will come!) Without proper instruction, how do we expect people to know that right-handed archers with draw lengths that are too long, tend to miss to the left? Or, if your draw elbow is out of line, you'll usually torque the bow. Or, if you roll your shoulder, or bend your bow arm, you'll probably never hold your sight very steady. Or, if you occasionally punch the trigger, you'll probably have full blown target panic in six months to a year, or less. Then, folks quit archery because they had no way of knowing any of this, or how to prevent or correct it. Currently, there are only about four shooting schools and probably fewer than a dozen qualified teaching pros and/or nationally recognized professional level coaches in the U.S. It's no wonder most people are lost. This is why I have strived to pass on this knowledge through the shooter's school, where we have certified over 900 instructors in the first four years, in the hope that several of them will, one day, become involved at a national level *(see photo next page)*.

Key Point #5

It's hard to find a great archer with bad form and it's even harder to find a bad archer with great form!

Since you aren't aware that bad form makes your sight shake and the response to that is to anticipate the sight crossing the X-ring . . . and then punch the trigger or pluck the string . . . and the anticipation of either of those leads to fear of missing or anxiety about possibly hitting . . . which develops into freezing off target, snapshooting, or flinching upon execution . . . which baffles, frustrates, and confuses us . . . which takes all the fun and fulfillment out of shooting . . . which causes us to play golf, etc.! Remember, there are supposedly three million people shooting bows in North America, and there are only four schools

Idiot Proof Archery

Advanced level instructors at Aspen Archery, Carson City, Nevada

and a dozen recognized coaches . . . what's wrong with this picture? If golf had twelve teaching pros instead of 11,000, do you think there would be 27 million golfers?

The title of this chapter is *Equipment, Form, The Mental Game, and You*. I am of the opinion that there is too much attention paid to equipment and not enough on form and mental preparation. To prove the first point, let's look at some of the myths about archery equipment.

Key Point #6

There is too much attention on equipment and not enough on form and mental preparation.

Magic Bows (This bow can't miss!)

Machined Riser bows . . . What a deal! Before there were machined riser bows, there were cast risers and only a handful or two of well-heeled manufacturers who made them. The machined riser was touted as being four or five times stronger than cast risers — "They will last you a lifetime!" So why do they try to sell you another one every year? The down side for the shooter was that machined risers were also two to three times more expensive than cast risers.

The real benefit was to the manufacturers! Instead of paying $10,000 to $15,000 a piece for molds to make the poured cast

Bernie Pellerite

The CNC machine has transformed the construction of bows.

risers (times ten for the different models in the line, then times two for right and left hand models, plus paint and R & D departments and lots of experience in the business — you do the math), all you need now is a CNC machine (sort of a computerized lathe/mill) and anyone can produce a machined riser for a fraction of the cost of a cast riser. And, since we don't "do" wooden limbs anymore, just order some fiberglass limbs for one fourth the cost of wooden ones. Then, add $5 to $15 for a set of cams, and a spool of "high tech" string and voilá, you have a bona fide speed demon bow for a fraction of what is used to cost. You can get into business with a little as $3,000 instead of $1,000,000 now.

But this is now backfiring on the manufacturers. A few years back I counted over forty bow manufacturers offering their version of just two or three different models of bows. Get real! And we wonder why two or three of these guys go bankrupt each year. Now, no one has enough market share to give anything back to archery clubs or organizations, support any outside educational programs or advertise like they used to, unless they have a new gimmick each year. All of the bow manufacturers are really feeling the pinch because the "pie" has to be split too many different ways.

Split Limb Bows were touted to be faster and lighter. Before this short-lived phenomenon died out, one shooter told me that when a limb cracked on his old bow, the manufacturer sent split limbs as replacements. The bow was set up exactly as before and he lost speed. A pro shop owner told me that he weighed a regular pair of limbs and also a pair of equivalent split limbs. They weighed exactly the same. (Think about it . . . if you remove fiberglass from a 60 pound limb and split it into two to make it lighter, it would no longer be a 60 pound limb, would it?) Now you can worry about four limbs being twisted or out of tiller instead of just two! I have found, however, one advantage

Idiot Proof Archery

of split limb bows. Sometimes, when you are really, really nervous, you have a tendency to drop your arm too soon, so you can see the arrow fly . . . and you usually will get low left arrows as a result. Well, with a split limb bow, you don't have to drop your arm ever again! You can just peek right through the limbs . . . cool! What will they think of next?

One Cam Bows are supposed to "never go out of time." When was the last time you lost a competition because your two cam bow suddenly "jumped out of time" in the middle of the tournament? I don't know of one *target record* that has been broken by one-cam bows . . . and if they ever manage to break one, it will be to the archer's credit, not to the bow's. A lot of amateur archers, who shoot better with them, like them for a different reason than they think. It is not because of the one cam . . . it is because they have a solid "wall" to shoot from, which makes their draw lengths consistent, thus producing better scores. Since top shooters don't have consistency problems, most pros shoot them because they are paid to shoot them . . . to make you think they're magic. Don't get me wrong — I see nothing wrong with one cam bows . . . but there is *nothing magic* about them, either. If there were, everyone on the planet would be shooting great by now! Don't you think?

Three Pound Ultra-Light Bows are wonderful for walking to and from your treestand or stalking a bighorn ram for 6 hours, but when it comes to accuracy . . . when was the last time you saw anybody win anything with a bow that has a total mass weight of 3½ pounds? Most of the pros have to add at least 3 to 8 pounds worth of stabilizers, V-bars, and back weights, just to hold one steady. That's why the competitive rifle shooters use

Split Limb Bow

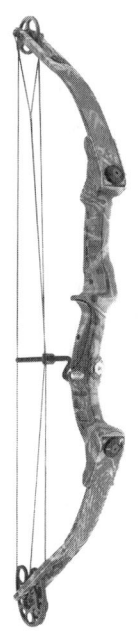
One Cam Bow

13

Bernie Pellerite

heavy "bull barrel" rifles (pistol shooters do the same) and why most successful target archers usually shoot heavier bows *(see chapter 6)*. The good news is, most stabilizer manufacturers say, "business has never been better!"

Short Axle-To-Axle / Short Brace Height Bows are the new speed demons. The bow manufacturers are all competing to have the fastest bow on the market. The only problem is that, with the exception of a few pros that shoot like machines with any bow, not many average archers can hit their hat with a bow that has a 32"- 36" axle-to-axle measurement and has a 5½" brace height.

There are many more "magic gadgets" produced daily (tunable carbon rod stabilizers, limb vibration dampeners, special twist bow strings, etc., etc.) that I simply won't take the time or space to "praise" here. But, where has all this progress gotten us, accuracy wise? For what it's worth, almost all the accuracy records ever set in compound archery (especially indoor records) were accomplished with heavy, two-wheel or four-wheel wooden limb, cast riser, long axle-to-axle, high brace height, slow target bows, shooting aluminum shafted arrows . . . and most all are still standing. That should be your wake-up call if you are mystified about the absence of "forgiveness" in your new, magic bow.

Don't get me wrong — I'm not against the manufacturers making money or inventing new technology — that's not the problem. It's the thousands of shooters like you who are in trouble because they aren't getting "what they need." Their "want to" is way ahead of their "can do."

As I said, we need to remember . . . this is not a sport . . . *it's a discipline.* It's a "let it happen" activity with a bunch of "make it happen" people. You need to have good shooting form which causes you to do it the same way every time. Just like a bad swing in baseball . . . a new bat won't help. (You can't hit a *thang* if you ain't got that *swang!*) In order for competitive archery to grow, it requires

 **Key Point #7**

We must come to understand that this is not a sport . . . it's a discipline!

Idiot Proof Archery

Korean archers dominate world FITA competitions because they understand that archery is a discipline.

lots of coaches, preferably coaching the same way (Duh!), which the U.S. does not have. That is why the Koreans are so good at it . . . they have lots of coaches, (about a thousand, I'm told) coaching the same way, and they *already* have a *disciplined culture*. We have just a few coaches who all teach differently. We are a very individualistic nation, full of very *undisciplined people* (especially in compound archery), trying to do one of the hardest disciplines on the planet . . . a little differently each shot. Lots of luck!

If you applied archery's rules and practices to any other business or sport, it would be a joke! That's why most archers are "fishermen under construction," which is where most archers go when they self-destruct from the insanity of it all. Fishing (at least at the amateur level) is the only "sport" I know that is based completely on luck and gadgets, takes no

BOWSTRINGS - - - - by William Calhoun

Most archers are just fishermen under construction!

Bernie Pellerite

*Bob Ragsdale
Archery Consultant
and Seminar Speaker*

🎯 **Key Point #8**

Ragsdale says, "The definition of insanity is doing the same thing over and over again, but expecting different results."

*Rick McKinney
Olympic Silver Medalist
and 3-time World Champion*

🎯 **Key Point #9**

McKinney says, "If you do what you've always done . . . you'll get what you always got."

brains, education, skill, practice, or coaching to achieve the end result . . . outsmarting a fish! "Gee, I can do that!" And, just in case you don't succeed, you have lots of built in excuses. Plus, you still get to drink beer and drive a power boat. Yee hah! What a sport! With 34,000,000 fishermen, no wonder it's one of the most popular "sports" in America!

For those of you who know me, I must apologize for trying to "sugarcoat" these problems. (Someone once told me that I need to break out of my cell . . . er shell!) I guess I should just come right out and tell you what I *really think*. For those of you who don't know me and think I go too far or that I should put a "happy face" on anything and everything that comes down the pike . . . well, in my opinion, I think *that is part of the problem*, not part of the solution. Besides, isn't that the same thing we've been doing for too long? To quote my friend, Bob Ragsdale, "The definition of insanity is doing the same thing over and over again, but expecting different results."

And, Olympic archer Rick McKinney often uses this quote from motivational speaker Anthony Robbins who says, "If you do what you've always done . . . you'll get what you always got."

Idiot Proof Archery

Chapter 2

Your Personality . . . Can You Handle the Truth?

No one wants to hear that they have a problem and the reason is . . . them! In this case, though, it is true — part of your problem *is based on your personality*, or rather that you haven't taken your personality into account. Not much has been written about the role that personality plays in top level archery performance. A few years ago, as I drove my friend and mentor Len Cardinale to the airport after shooting his two videos, the subject of personality came up. Len is a literal "encyclopedia of knowledge." He is an internationally respected coach, archery analyst, seminar speaker, contributing writer for **Bowhunter** magazine, and member of the Bowhunter Hall of Fame. His insightful and analytical view of archery is deeper and more diverse than anyone else I have ever met. We talked of many things on that ninety minute drive and Lenny, as always, was happy to share his knowledge. As he reeled off the

Len Cardinale
The "Einstein of archery"

highlights of his thirty-five-year archery history, I reeled it in. As he spoke of years, shooters and events gone by, many had a lasting impact on me; in particular the subject of this chapter.

The late 1960s and early 1970s were the heyday of the now defunct P.A.A. (Professional Archer's Association) when there were 450 members. Cardinale and others noticed a pattern in the occupations of the many archery champions of the period.

17

Bernie Pellerite

It was discovered, to the amazement of all, that there was a disproportionate number of champion archers with vocations involving electricity — electricians, electrical technicians, electrical contractors, installers, and the like. The conclusion drawn from this information was that there must be a parallel between the personality type it takes to handle lethal amounts of electricity for a living and the ability to perform well under the pressure of top level tournament archery. Actually, it is logical if you think about it. All top archers do everything the same, in a particular order, one step at a time, and do not skip any of the steps. Electricians do their jobs with the same ordered, step by step routine and do not skip any of the steps or they will probably come face to face with this "shocking" reality . . . "There are old electricians and there are bold electricians, but there are no old, bold electricians." The same could be said for any personality that is suited for coping with dangerous or stressful professions like airline pilots, deep sea divers, mountain climbers, doctors, pharmacists, or any profession that demands an ordered mind with an unalterable progression of steps toward a successful conclusion. The price of failure would be severe consequences, in most cases. The four champions pictured below and on the next page all have occupations that demand a "focused" or "ordered mind."

*Randy Ulmer,
World & National Champion
and veterinarian*

*Kirk Ethridge,
National Champion
and pharmacist*

Idiot Proof Archery

*Darryl Pace
Olympic Gold Medalist
and telecommunications
technician*

*Mike Leiter,
National Champion and
computer technician*

It seems that certain personality traits, whether learned or inherited, have a distinct advantage when applied to exact disciplines like tournament archery or rifle and pistol target competition, among others. The innate ability to subconsciously repeat and trust a complicated sequence time after time (under stress!) with machinelike duplication is not a common personality trait, especially in archers.

In archery, a *focused* or *ordered* mind has the ability to shut out all outside interferences, like noises and other similar distractions, temptations to do it faster, slower, push or pull more, etc. These do not seem to penetrate the inner sanctum of "confident, composed concentration" (organized thinking).

A few celebrated psychologists have divided us into four basic personality types, or profiles, as far as our social interactions are concerned. Different psychologists vary somewhat as to the type or profile names but they all describe the same behavior. For example, one divides us into passive, aggressive, intuitive, or analytical types. Another separates us into supporter, controller, promoter, or analyst as types. A third divides us into amiable, driver, expressive, or analytical. There are a few more, but as you can see, these three examples have very similar group names *(see chart pg. 20)*. I have coined my own profile names and phrases, called **Bernie-isms** . . . sort of a "naked truth

Bernie Pellerite

shorthand." This is probably because I never worried too much about kissing up or sounding "politically correct," I just wanted to make sure *nobody ever said* . . . "what the heck does that mean?" So, I sort of come right at you!

For another reason, the medical profession divides us into just two groups, Type A and Type B, for the purposes of evaluating the risk of heart attacks, strokes, high blood pressure, and the like. People with Type A personalities are usually impulsive, hard driving, in control, non-trusting, intense, always in a hurry, usually high stress and/or workaholics. People with Type B personalities usually have focused or ordered minds and are calm, patient, very trusting, deliberate, and even-tempered. It's easy to understand why Type A's are much more prone to stress-related heart disease than Type B's. Although you may have already tried to "pigeonhole" yourself into one of these categories, all personalities fall into *two or more groups with one dominant trait*. For example, I am a classic *dominant Type A/driver*, with analytical, and expressive traits. A *Bernie-ism* for this is . . . I am a Control Freak with tendencies to "over-

Group A	*aggressive, controller, driver*
	(Bernie-ism "control freak")
	Individuals tend to be intense, impatient, "in charge," and don't trust.
Group B	*passive, amiable, supportive*
	(Bernie-ism "focused")
	Similar in that they tend to be easygoing, patient, deliberate and very trusting.
Group C	*intuitive, promoter, expressive*
	(Bernie-ism "risk taker")
	Tend to be creative, spontaneous, emotional, and prone to gamble or take chances.
Group D	*analytical or analyst*
	(Bernie-ism "over thinker")
	People in this group tend to analyze everything and experiment a lot.

Idiot Proof Archery

think" everything and take risks. Not a pretty picture, is it! My wife however, is a *dominant Type B/amiable*, with expressive traits. It's a good thing, too, because without her focus, organizational skills and calming influence, I would have self-destructed years ago! As you can see, there are thousands of possibilities. For example, you could be 60% Type A/driver, 30% expressive, and 10% analytical, or 70% analytical, 15% expressive, and 15% driver, and so on.

So, what does all this have to do with archery? A lot, if you think about it. It may help you determine whether you are a natural candidate for high level archery competition, or if you should use a high or low power scope, or should focus on the sight or the target when aiming, or use a circle in your scope instead of a dot, to have a clear scope or a slightly blurry one, whether to use an index finger, thumb, or a back tension release.

You see, if your personality profile is like the medical Type B or Group B (amiable, passive, supportive), then you are more likely to be able to naturally duplicate a shot sequence with the machinelike precision of a top ranked professional archer. You will be able to *naturally trust* this "system" (your shot sequence) to work on its own without trying to improve, analyze, assist, or control any aspect of the system from shot to shot. This ability of your conscious mind *to trust* what you believe to be the best

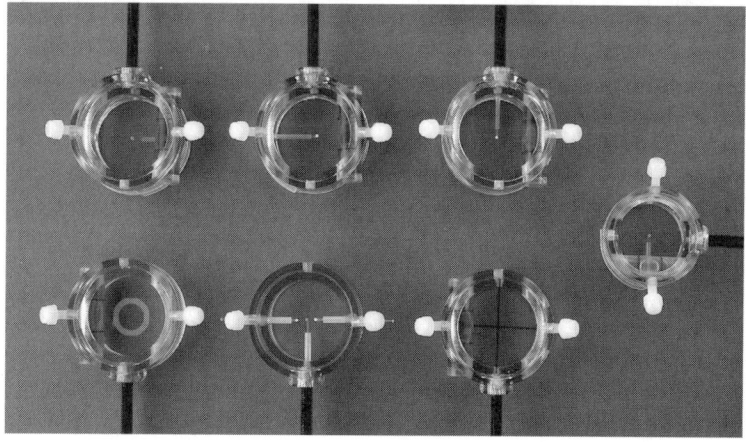

Based on your personality type, which should you use?

Bernie Pellerite

 **Key Point #10**

You must be able to trust your shot sequence to work on its own without trying to improve, analyze, assist, or control any aspect of it from shot to shot.

system for you, enables your subconscious mind to more quickly and completely absorb it. It follows that since the subconscious is now in control of the shot sequence, *your conscious mind does not have to be!* Your conscious mind can now focus entirely on aiming, trusting the subconscious mind to run the "release program" or "let-go" system, which is the only way truly excellent archery is ever achieved by most. Therefore, I will repeat this concept *many times* throughout the book because it is an integrated part of the whole philosophy and interweaves with different topics. It is the *real key* to understanding, and therefore unlocking, your potential.

On the other hand, if your personality corresponds to Type A or Group A profiles (controller, driver, aggressive) and/or possesses dominant or significant Group D (analytical) or Group C (intuitive, promoter, expressive) tendencies, then (theoretically) your chances of becoming a national or world champion archer decrease substantially — because top level shooting usually depends on trusting the duplication of form and execution, shot after shot, and the ability to concentrate and stay focused with a calm, confident, ordered mind.

However, the fact that you are not a Type B personality *does not mean* you cannot succeed at high level competitive target archery! It just means it will be *much more difficult* for your personality to overcome its natural tendency to consciously control the movement of the sight or the instant of the release. For example, in the case of "Control Freaks," if this is coupled with an overly analytical mind, you might tend to anticipate triggering your release, grab the bow, or over-analyze each shot and therefore pick apart, try to improve, or

 **Key Point #11**

Top level shooting depends on near–perfect form, shot after shot, and the ability to concentrate and focus for extended periods with a calm, confident, ordered mind.

Idiot Proof Archery

change one aspect or another from shot to shot, creating inconsistencies in shot execution. If substantial "Risk Taker" tendencies exist in your profile, you might tend to gamble and release a shot that does not feel right

Bernie working with a student.

instead of letting down and starting the shot sequence over. If you're analytical, your mind may wander from one thing to another, become easily distracted, and find it extremely difficult to concentrate all the way through the shot. Of course, all of the above can, and do, happen to Type B personalities, but not nearly with the same frequency or intensity, and it's usually much easier for them to handle those problems when they do occur. Why? Because truly "focused shooters" *trust their release* and are naturally focused *on the present.* (There are only about twelve of them nationwide. You know the ones . . . the ones who win most of the time!) They are not worried (like the rest of us) about the future or the past . . . where the arrow is going to go or where the last one went. These Type B shooters can use any release method, aim any number of ways, shoot any bow, use any form, and have less than perfect arrow flight, *and still manage to win!* They can focus on a B-B at 20 yards . . . for half an hour, and their minds never leave the B-B! They have no blood pressure, no pulse, and no nerves . . . you know the ones.

Personality traits may also affect the way you select or shoot different archery accessories. These traits do not always end up being compatible with the equipment or methods you have selected. For example, most Control Freaks prefer an index finger release so they can control the instant of the shot (possibly acquired from pistol or rifle shooting). Controlling the release

Key Point #12

Your personality traits may affect the way you select or shoot different archery accessories. These traits do not always end up being compatible with the equipment or methods you have selected.

Bernie Pellerite

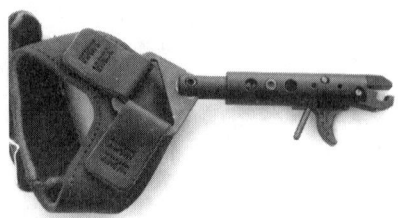

Bernie's Missing Link "safe draw" back tension release.

Bernie's Can't Punch Release "back tension" Wrist Strap Caliper

is exactly what we *do not want to happen*. These people and the Over Thinkers would do better if they shot thumb, or better yet, back tension releases, like the Stanisawski, Carter, Zenith, Tru-Ball, (or the ones that I invented) **Bernie's Missing Link**™, **E-Z Back**™, or **Can't Punch Release**™ (see page 162 & 168 and also the Appendix pages 324-329). The first two are **new** "safe draw," hand held back tension releases. **Bernie's Can't Punch** is a wrist-strap, caliper release, with two triggers that prevent trigger punching, but is still activated by your back muscles, like the other back tension releases. Generally, individuals with controlling personality traits also tend to have an overwhelming urge to "fight" the aiming dot in a scope, trying too hard to perfectly align the sight, leading to over-holding and eventually shaking. Often, these folks buy very clear, high powered scopes so they can see better to "aim more precisely," which compounds their problem because it also magnifies every movement. This practice often leads to frustration and punching or snapshooting. They would be better off with a pin sight or a slightly blurry scope lens or lower magnification that minimizes "perceived movement." Also, they might avoid the overcontrolling problem better with a circle in the scope or on the end of their pin so they can see the bullseye through the circle, even when the sight is moving around slightly. Sort of like having a ring the size of a quarter around a bullseye the size of a nickel — there is room to "let it float" and still see all of it. Another method is to use a low or no power scope with a larger dot or larger pin that covers the entire middle scoring ring on the tar-

Idiot Proof Archery

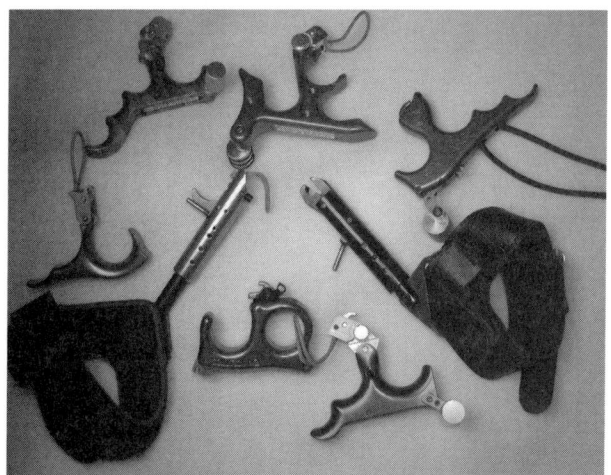

Based on your personality type, which release aid should you use?

get. For some personalities, this produces a calmer looking sight picture. People with controlling or excessively analytical personalities (really, most all the rest of us) should *focus on the X in the middle* of the target and let the sight become secondary and slightly blurry. This will help overcontrolling-type shooters who try to "muscle" the constantly moving sight into the "exact center" and then "snapshoot" or "punch" the trigger in an effort to release the arrow, before the sight moves out of the center of the target (more on this later).

You may be one of those people whose mind easily wanders (like me)! Scattered, jumbled, or flash thoughts are fairly common among several personality types. This makes aiming very inconsistent or fragmented. Fortunately, in addition to this book, there is help available as close as the local library or book store. There are many other books that can help improve concentration through a series of simple visual and mental exercises. By performing these mental drills, one can develop the stability and control necessary for focused and organized thinking, making it possible to more dependably and completely "immerse into aiming" shot after shot. People with concentration problems, like ADD — Attention Deficit Disorder, (or like me

Bernie Pellerite

Ed Eliason, National Champion and Classic Type A/controller personality. Archery's best example of an "I think I can" shooter.

with AD — double damn D) may need to mentally recite a *mantra* over and over to keep their mind in the center of the target until the shot occurs subconsciously, such as, ". . . find the center, find the center of the center . . . focus on the center . . . focus on the exact center!" . . . etc.

It is important to realize though, that personality is not the only thing that can determine your degree of success in archery. Things such as work ethic, attitude, determination, physical fitness, training, concentration, and preparation play big parts. A perfect example is my friend, Ed Eliason, 7 time NAA National Champion, who at age 57, won the Pan American Games. Ed is an ex-Green Beret with a classic Type A/controller personality. But, because he is as optimistic as an accordion player with a pager, as determined as a pit bull, as fit as a college athlete, trains like a boxer, concentrates like a Zen master, and is as prepared as a troop of Boy Scouts, he can overcome nearly anything. But Ed is the exception . . . not the rule! There aren't many that will put that much effort into this or any sport.

However, this goes to show that people like you and Ed, by being aware of your personality profile, can take steps to counteract or neutralize your undesirable tendencies and make full use of the desirable ones.

 **Key Point #13**

The important lesson here is to discover, counteract, or learn to live with your personalities' limitations so you can set realistic goals and continue to enjoy shooting archery for years to come!

The important lesson here is to discover, counteract, or learn to live with your limitations so you can set realistic goals and continue to enjoy shooting archery for years to come!

Chapter 3

The Importance of Bow Tuning, Shooting Form, and Draw Length

In the first chapter, I made the point that there are no "magic" bows that will somehow improve your shooting. So if the magic isn't in the bow itself, then it must be in the setup or tuning of the bow. *There* is where the magic is, right? Let's look at this.

Bow Tuning: How Important Is It?

Most bowhunters and target archers think bow tuning is the most important part of accuracy. In 1993, I surveyed several shooters at our archery range. The question was, "What percentage of *accuracy* is bow tuning responsible for?" The range of answers I got was from 50% to 95%.

This is no doubt attributable to the fact that in recent years there has been endless seminars, videos, books, and articles on the subject. And, from the time we first hit the practice range as novice archers, we are told by our fellow shooters that if your bow is not tuned properly, it is impossible to hit the target with any consistency. Therefore, in most archers' minds, bow tuning is the most important ingredient in the formula for accuracy.

Nothing could be further from the truth! In theory, bow tuning plays absolutely no role in accuracy. This is easily proven if you have access to a good shooting machine. Having experimented with shooting machines myself, I know that regardless of the tune of the bow, a shooting machine is capable of putting *every* arrow in the same hole, even when equipped with broadheads. This is assuming, of course, that all outside

Bernie Pellerite

influences such as fletch clearance, wind, nock and broadhead alignment, etc. remain exactly the same. To double check my results, I called a professional archer friend of mine, who was known for his candor, years of experience, and experimentation with various shooting equipment. He assured me that he had tested a bow in a shooting machine at long distances and found no difference in the groups of the arrows whether the bow was tuned or untuned, as long as all the arrows were identical. He got a 2" group at 60 yards with a perfectly tuned bow and then took off four turns on the bottom limb bolt and repeated the experiment. The arrows came out *wobbling* and *porpoising* but still impacted into a 2" group (at a different place on the target).

I know what some of you are thinking, that I must be *anti-tuning*. Not at all! I believe that bow tuning is an essential part of good archery and I'm for any book, tape, or article that shows us how. I'm no different than most diehard fanatics, afraid of not going far enough. We all have spent endless hours paper-testing, rest-adjusting, powder-testing, nock-aligning, group-testing, re-fletching, tiller-tuning, spin-testing, center-shotting, cable-shortening, string-twisting, bolt-cranking, arrow straightening, broadhead-aligning, point-weighing, front-of-center balancing, module-swapping, bare shaft testing, eye-balling, and rollover-adjusting until our fingers bled and we were reduced to a cross-eyed, stuttering lump of protoplasm with the I.Q. of a cooked turnip. If the shooting machine experiment proves that bow tuning has no effect on accuracy from shot to shot, why then did we waste our time making so many adjustments? The answer is simple . . . we are human beings, not machines, and only humans need to tune a bow. To determine how significant tuning is to us, first we must define exactly what "bow tuning" is and what it is not. And what, besides tuning, influences the result of a shot and to what extent.

What is Bow Tuning?

To me, tuning consists of different adjustments that we can make to one or more components of the bow and arrow combination in order to obtain the best possible result, given

Idiot Proof Archery

your individual shooting form. Tuning (mostly arrow and arrow rest tuning) simply tries to counteract the influence that a flaw in our execution has on the arrow's impact *(more on this later in chapter 4)*. It's important to note that the only reason for bow tuning is to improve our bad shots; our good shots all go where we aim anyway. And, as for our *really* bad shots . . . tuning won't help much at all.

What Bow Tuning Is Not

The key here is to understand that in theory, tuning is not related to accuracy. Tuning is related only to bow performance and forgiveness . . . accuracy is related to consistent execution of form. In simple terms, this means that tuning had no effect on accuracy in the shooting machine tests because all things remained constant, shot to shot. Therefore, the more consistent we are in our form, the more accurate we will be. For instance, if you gave an untuned bow to a professional archer, his accuracy would be much greater than an intermediate archer shooting a professionally tuned bow. A good example of this was in the late 80s when I attended the largest indoor tournament in the country in Las Vegas, Nevada . . . The Vegas Shoot. One of the fellows I was shooting with was Tom Crowe *(see photo pg. 30)*, a real nice guy from Oregon who has since become quite a successful professional target and 3-D archer. He was shooting a "new 75% let-off McPherson bow" with a draw weight of 65 pounds, holding 17 pounds, shooting 2413 arrows cut extremely short with a 5" overdraw that came well past the break in his wrist. Tom's shooting form was a bit unorthodox with his bow shoulder rolled forward and draw elbow well behind his head with what seemed to be a draw length that too long. He was using a wrist strap FletchHunter release. At that time, almost everybody was shooting round

Key Point #14

The key here is to understand that in theory, tuning is not related to accuracy. Tuning is related only to bow performance and forgiveness . . . and accuracy is related to consistent execution of form . . . a Bernie-ism!

Bernie Pellerite

Tom Crowe,
Professional archer and
Type B personality

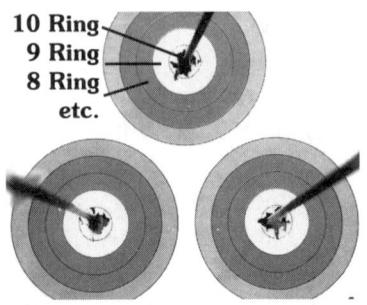

Tom Crowe shot a perfect 300 on the Vegas target face which is scored 10, 9, 8, 7, 6, and 0.

wheel 40-50 pound bows with 50-60% let-off, no overdraw, regular length arrows and back tension release aids. However, at the end of the tournament Tom had broken the Vegas record with the *only perfect 300 ever shot* in the Bowhunter Freestyle division (compound, pins and release). The other amazing thing was Tom's arrow flight and number of holes in the target. However, I noticed that Tom's arrows were fishtailing 6-8 inches as they left his bow. But, as we walked to the target to pull our arrows I noticed that Tom's arrows, on each of the three targets, were going *in the same hole!* When he finished his perfect round of 300, there was one hole, a little larger than a nickel, in each of the three targets made up of twelve arrows each . . . two practice ends and ten scoring ends. When I looked at my target, shot with a very forgiving Hoyt Medalist with no overdraw, 9" brace height, round wheels at 45 pounds holding 21 pounds, I noticed that I had about 25 holes in three targets. But I had a perfectly tuned bow with perfect arrow flight and a very mediocre score of 289 . . . go figure!

Another good example of this phenomenon was Terry Ragsdale of Tucson, Arizona, in 1978. (Terry and his wife, Michelle, are arguably the best target archers to ever shoot a compound bow.) Terry shot the only perfect 1200 ever recorded in Vegas and it has never been duplicated since. He was using a four-wheel model PSE Citation. By the end of the

Idiot Proof Archery

tournament he discovered that the bow string had five broken strands directly under the nock. When Terry returned home, he had heard rumors of a *new tuning method* called "paper tuning." Curious to see how his winning bow setup fared with this "new" process, he shot the same arrows used in the tournament through the paper. To his amazement he had definitely flunked the new test with a 10 o'clock, high-left 5 inch rip in the paper which would have probably prevented him (and most people) from leaving the house if he had done it before the tournament.

Barely a month later, Terry duplicated that feat at Cobo Hall in Detroit, Michigan, at the North American Indoor tournament. What's even more remarkable about these two consecutive feats is that the bow he used at this shoot was a *"new" two-wheel* model with the top wheel leaning so severely,

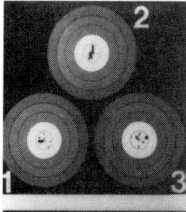
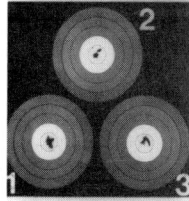
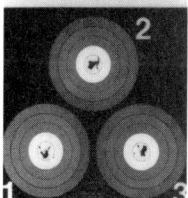

Terry Ragsdale's
Perfect
Vegas Targets

Terry Ragsdale's consistent form and focus was responsible for his perfect 1200 . . . the only one ever shot at the Las Vegas Tournament (45 arrows on Friday and Saturday, then 30 on Sunday)!

Bernie Pellerite

that it looked like the cables would jump out of the track at full draw. Out of Terry's 138 arrows, shot in three days, *only 5 even touched the 10-ring line.* All the rest were completely inside the 1¾" 10-ring.

This leads us into the fundamental principle of competitive archery and that is, "you don't have to do it right, you just have to do it the same way each time." If you do it the same way each time, like a shooting machine, whether the bow is tuned or not, the arrows will go in the same hole (as long as the arrows are all exactly the same). Unless something is damaged, the bow can't change from one shot to another, *without operator assistance.* If you can't shoot 30 arrows with exactly the same form and execution, then the perfectly tuned bow can't save you. Therefore, *The Paradox of Tuning — Tuning can only be relevant if you have consistent form . . . and if you have consistent form, tuning then . . . becomes irrelevant! . . . a Bernie-ism!* The secret is, if you duplicate each shot, *so will the bow* . . . tuned or untuned. Now, the only variable becomes the arrows and your mental program.

● **Key Point #15**

The Paradox of Tuning — Tuning can only be relevant if you have consistent form . . . and if you have consistent form, tuning then becomes irrelevant . . . a Bernie-ism! The secret is that, if you duplicate each shot, so will the bow . . . tuned or untuned. Now, the only variable becomes the arrows and your mental program.

Importance of Tuning At Different Levels

A friend of mine and well-known pro archer compares bow tuning to a professional car race. According to him, in an auto race, it's 50% car and 50% driver. Likewise, he says, archery is 50% tune of the bow and the other 50% is the shooter. His theory is that if you put Mario Andretti in a car that goes 220 m.p.h. and a less experienced professional driver in a car that goes 225 m.p.h., sometimes the best car wins and sometimes the best driver wins. I disagree with this example, at least when it applies to *nonprofessional* archers. My argument is this; my friend is a professional archer and has reached what most would

Idiot Proof Archery

consider the peak of human capability in execution and form. Therefore, he and other pros can repeat the execution of the shot with extreme consistency time and time again . . . similar to the shooting machine. The only physical thing left is tuning — to try and counteract the relatively few, slightly bad executions they do make. Therefore, bow tuning can mean the difference between a score of 300 with 58 Xs and 300 with 59 Xs. Pros also release fewer bad shots than we do. (They do let down a lot, don't they!) The few shots that "cut the line" *(see below)* may have been out by $1/64$" if they hadn't tuned the bow until it "forgave" those one or two, ever so slight, poor executions. Tuning could then be responsible for a victory on any given day. This could also make the difference between a wound or a clean kill while bowhunting, especially when it comes to reducing wind planing.

However, his theory about racing and archery *assumes* that the driver or the shooter can drive the car or shoot the bow to its maximum capacity. I think there is a flaw in this logic because very few people can do either one. Put Mario Andretti in the same 220 m.p.h. car and put an average driver (like you or me) in the faster 225 m.p.h. car. The average driver could not drive well enough to get anywhere near peak performance out of the car and would probably crash and burn on the first turn at 160 m.p.h. and Mario would win every time. Perfect

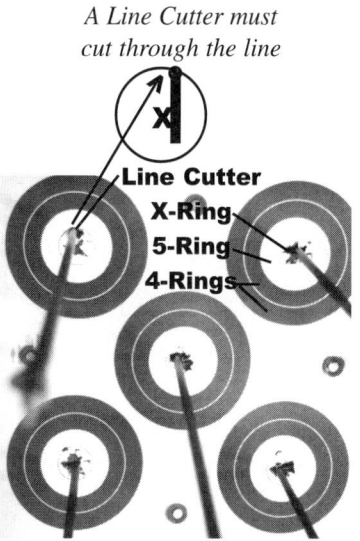

A Line Cutter must cut through the line

A perfect round is 300 with 60 Xs . . . 60 arrows in or cutting the line on an 8 cm, $3^{1}/_{8}$", 5-ring will give you 300 (5 x 60=300). To break the ties you also count up to 60 X-rings inside or cutting the line (4cm, $1^{3}/_{4}$"), at 20 yards. Outside the 4-ring scores zero.

Bernie Pellerite

 **Key Point #16**

Perfect tuning is wasted if the ability to use it is not there—Bernie-ism!

tuning *is wasted* if the ability to use it is not there. Here's another example: imagine playing golf with Tiger Woods. (Yeah, *imagine that!*) He uses a set of K-Mart clubs and you use Tiger Woods' personal clubs. A simplified conclusion can be drawn that the quality of the clubs doesn't make much difference if you can't play golf . . . and the tune of the bow doesn't make much difference if you can't shoot.

Tuning and Its Effect On The Average Shooter

My point here is not that tuning is worthless, but that it's not nearly as important as most of us think. Tuning is important only to the extent that we can push the equipment to its limits and that we can repeat the shot execution consistently. Remember what we said: You don't have to do it correctly . . . you just have to do it the same way every time. A few types of tuning can compensate somewhat for *slight flaws* in shooting form. For example, if an archer has a tendency to torque the bow sometimes because of improper bow hand placement in the grip, bow tuning for him might be accomplished by changing the rest from a stiff side-pressure plate to maybe a springy rest or a lighter button-type rest. An arrow that would have been off-center by two inches at 20 yards would maybe now only be thrown off-center 1½", thus "cutting the line" and tightening groups. However, being human and not a machine, he will not torque the bow the same every time. Another archer may, for example, "heel the bow" (at the moment of release he pushes up on the bow handle with the heel of his bow hand to "help" a low shot). The result is usually high arrows. There again, the type of rest he uses could be critical. He might need to reduce the up and down spring pressure of his rest to soften the effect of the rest on the arrow, or raise the nocking point slightly to help those heeled shots clear the rest. This can help reduce the distance the arrow

 **Key Point #17**

You don't have to do it correctly . . . you just have to do it the same every time.

Idiot Proof Archery

is thrown out of the group or off target by ½" or so at 20 yards. As you can see by these examples, the bow (actually, the arrow rest) can be tuned to "forgive" these slight flaws and therefore correct the impact point to some extent. However, at this level, most bad shots are much more complicated and erratic, moving the impact point sometimes 4 to 12 inches off target at 20 to 30 yards. This happens because the average shooter is much more likely to make random and/or multiple mistakes of different severity. For instance, plucking the string and dropping the bow arm at the same time, or punching the trigger on the release, grabbing the bow handle, and popping his head up to see where the arrow is going. It's easy to understand that you can't tune out these "6 inch boo-boos," because they are too severe, too random, and have too many possible combinations.

"This flier" is way out of center . . . "How do I tune that out?"

What Else Influences The Shot and To What Extent?

By now, it should be obvious that *consistency in execution* is much more important than tuning. This is not to say we shouldn't set up our arrows/rest/nock/centershot combinations so everything is "in line," especially in a hunting situation because of broadhead wind planing. We should continue to strive to achieve the best possible arrow flight and check to see that the wheels or cams roll over at about the same time. If you have confidence in your equipment, then you can better concentrate on your execution, especially for those of us who are easily distracted or who worry a lot (anal retentive analyticals).

Key Point #18

If you have confidence in your equipment, then you can better concentrate on your execution.

Bernie Pellerite

It is my opinion that in most cases, execution or form is probably 80% to 90% responsible for whatever accuracy we experience at the *beginning* and *intermediate* levels. Bow tuning or matching our equipment and mental programming play relatively minor roles. At these levels, lack of "muscle memory" and target panic are mostly responsible for our hits and misses. Compare this to driving a car. We drive home from work through traffic, and somehow end up safely in our driveway without even remembering most of the trip, because we were daydreaming about one thing or another or engrossed in the song on the radio. Can you imagine what would happen if you daydreamed when you were learning to drive? Back then, every thought process was directed at keeping the car on the road and getting home safely. Similarly, a beginning or even an intermediate archer still has to consciously think about and control each step of the shot process from nocking the arrow to followthrough. We are too busy mentally controlling each step to handle anything else. Because we have to think about and therefore try to control all of the different elements of the shot, we have a tendency to do a lot of them a little differently, in a different order, or in a different amount of time. It's therefore my opinion, that very little subconscious mental programming is involved at the beginning and intermediate level. At this stage, when you miss, it's almost always caused by a glitch in conscious execution or our inability to hold steadily and/or aim consistently.

The Real Secrets of Accuracy

By the time you progress into advanced or professional levels of 3-D, target archery, or bowhunting, your form has become more and more refined and subconscious. At the advanced stage, most of us will be able to shoot subconsciously (like driving a car) a lot of the time, and at the professional or expert level, most all of the time. This ability greatly changes the value of tuning. At the advanced level, we are subconsciously "programmed" so to speak, and our mistakes become much less frequent and much less severe. Most bad shots are only off by ¼" to 1" at 20 to 30 yards, making them much more

Idiot Proof Archery

correctable by tuning. At the professional level, nearly everyone is mechanically capable of shooting a perfect score which is 60 arrows in a $3^{1}/_{8}$" (8 cm) circle and 55-60 inside or touching the $1^{3}/_{4}$" (4 cm) X-ring at 20 yards (see target pg. 33). Therefore, raising the performance level of the bow by tuning can also make *a little more* of a difference because the archer at this level is capable of utilizing more performance.

By this point, most have discovered and mastered the ability to hold steadier on target. The pros have discovered that by adjusting their draw lengths, eliminating most muscular involvement and maintaining good muscle tone with proper body and elbow alignment, their sight picture has four to five times less movement and, in some cases, it almost stops moving all together (at least for a few seconds in practice).

Most importantly, at the top level of archery, there are very few secrets left concerning form or tuning. So, it almost always depends on mental programming. As we are able to subconsciously execute the steps to the shot, our conscious mind is free to concentrate on aiming only. My good friend, Len Cardinale, taught me that, " . . . at the moment of the release, we must be immersed in aiming," to get predictable accuracy which, I believe, is the most important secret of the world's best archers. Just like many other professional sports, whoever has their mental act together on a given tournament day, or at the moment of truth in the woods, will usually succeed (more on this later).

So, if tuning isn't as important as you thought, what aspects of setting up a bow *are* critically important? (I'm glad you asked!) Obviously, when you get a new bow you need to set a number of things on the bow: draw weight, draw length, nocking point, and center shot are the four most obvious. But I think improper draw

Key Point #19

"At the moment of the release, we must be immersed in aiming," to get predictable accuracy."

Key Point #20

Whoever has their mental act together on a given tournament day, or at the moment of truth in the woods, will usually succeed.

Bernie Pellerite

 **Key Point #21**

Improper draw length causes the most problems with shooter's form and ends up causing the ultimate "mental programming virus" to take hold.

 **Key Point #22**

Many archers have draw weights that are way too high for them.

weight and, in particular, improper draw length (too long usually) cause the most serious problems with the average shooter's form and end up causing the ultimate "mental programming virus" to take hold. Therefore, the draw weight and draw length are tied to shooting form and ultimately . . . *"panic."* There are also several other aspects of bow setup and arrow setup that I will address in the next chapter. Some are more applicable to finger shooters, some are for more advanced shooters, and some are, in my opinion, simply myths that need to be exposed. As for draw weight . . . excessive draw weight causes the shooter to recruit *way too many* muscles instead of relaxed, bone-to-bone form with the back muscles operating the "let-go" system. In short, if you can't draw your bow without pointing it to the ceiling and pulling the string into your chest before you come to anchor, or you have to change the expression on your face when you draw . . . then this "sucker" might be cranked up a little too high!

Draw Length

In my opinion, this is where most of the archers first start down the road to disaster. Unfortunately, not much has been written about the methods and importance of finding the correct draw length and its relationship to accuracy. It remains one of the unspoken mysteries of correct archery form. At least we now have a standard definition. It is defined by the Archery Manufacturers and Merchants Organization (AMO), as — *the distance, at full draw, from the nocking point to the pivot point (or most forward point) of the grip plus $1^{3}/_{4}$ inches.*

Idiot Proof Archery

Methods of Measuring Draw Length

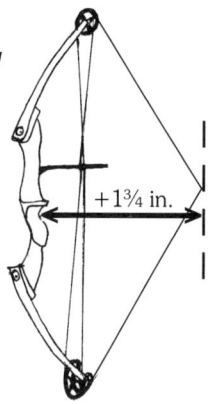

In the past, there have been many methods designed to determine proper draw length. Pro shops have "draw arrows" attached to ten pound fiberglass recurve bows. The customer draws it back and, without formal instruction on where to draw it to, their draw length is determined. This frequently results in a draw length that is much too long, because the customer can and will push the bow arm out as far as possible, lean back, and draw the string almost back to their ear. Another method is to stand straight up, put your fist on the wall and measure from the wall to the corner of your mouth. Unfortunately, this is not accurate either because there are numerous variations on how much the shoulder is rolled, whether the head is upright, whether you are leaning back or forward, or whether you are standing with a straight stance, or an open stance. Draw lengths measured these ways can vary by as much as six inches.

Without instruction on proper posture, you will probably end up with the wrong draw length. A third method (passed down through the years by recurve shooters) is to put a yardstick end in the middle of your chest and stretch your arms up both sides of the stick as far as possible. Where the fingertips meet on the stick, is supposed to be your proper draw. There again, depending on exactly where you place the yardstick on your chest, the measurement could vary by several inches.

In the first 6 ½ years of teaching NFAA Shooter's Schools we have had plenty of experience in determining draw length. Of 1600 students, I would guess that only 150 students had correct draw length. Maybe 40-50 had too short of a draw, which leaves a whopping 1400 students whose draws were too long. This is a critical observation because, in my opinion, draw length is tied directly to form and execution. The following is a formula I created that will determine correct draw length for about 95% of the archery population.

Bernie Pellerite

All elements of good form can be seen in this photograph — the archer is erect with his body slightly open to the target because of an open stance. His bow shoulder is low, locked, but relaxed. His grip is low and relaxed and his draw forearm is above the line of the arrow.

All of the elements of bad form can be seen in this photograph— the archer is leaning back. His bow shoulder is high, rolled and tense. His grip is high and tense and his draw forearm is below the line of the arrow. Notice how "stretched out" he is. This kind of bad form is generated by a draw length that is too long (and vice versa).

Idiot Proof Archery

Defining Proper Form

First of all, the correct draw length will only be valid for archers using proper form, so what is proper form?

- The archer should be standing straight up, not leaning back, with his aiming eye directly over his belt buckle or navel (for you analyticals . . . yes, that holds true regardless whether your navel is an in-y or an out-y!).
- The stance should be preferably slightly open (slightly facing the target 15 or 30 degrees or so) or square (toeing a line that points to the target) and the feet should be should-width apart.
- The bow shoulder should be low, locked, but relaxed in the shoulder joint, as opposed to extended, tense, and/or rolled.
- The grip on the bow should be in "the low wrist position," (in most cases) with the pressure of the bow handle on the base of the thumb and on the thumb side of the lifeline of the hand (lifeline should be vertical 12 o'clock - 6 o'clock).
- The string should touch the tip of the nose at full draw (shooters who wear glasses will probably find it necessary to put the string on the side of their nose).
- The tip of the draw elbow should be *at least* as high as the nose and the crease of the elbow is on the same level with, or above, the line of the arrow at full draw.

This is what I call "bone-to-bone" form *(see photo on pg. 40)*. It furnishes a solid base of support and eliminates as many muscles as possible, thus minimizing sight movement at full draw. This creates the most stable shooting platform for most compound archers (and the majority of recurve shooters, too), regardless of their muscularity.

The Draw Length Formula

Understanding that this is the form that we are looking for, we can now use the following formula to calculate draw length.

The archer should stand with his or her back to a wall, with arms stretched out as far as possible at shoulder height

Bernie Pellerite

with his palms facing out *(as in photo)*. We are measuring "wingspan." Measure from tip of the middle finger of one hand to the tip of the middle finger of the other. (No long fingernails!) Here is a partial chart that you can use to determine correct draw length. I developed this system in 1996 and use it in the shooter's school. You can complete your own chart based on the following measurements:

69 inches	=	27 inches AMO draw
70 inches	=	27½ inches AMO draw
71 inches	=	**28 inches AMO draw**
72 inches	=	28½ inches AMO draw
73 inches	=	29 inches AMO draw . . . **and so on.**

For every inch of "wingspan" over or under 71" add or subtract a ½" from 28" of AMO draw, respectively.

This formula works for about 95% of all archers. However, there are exceptions to this, such as people with shoulder or elbow problems, or people with abnormally long or short fingers or hands.

When using my formula, the important thing you need to be aware of is, if the fingers or hands are not normal length,

Stretching across a tape measure against a wall will measure your "wingspan." (See insert . . . "wingspan" measures 77." By the way this handsome fellow is the Editor's husband who is 6'4" or 76" tall. Normally your height is very close to your wingspan.)

Idiot Proof Archery

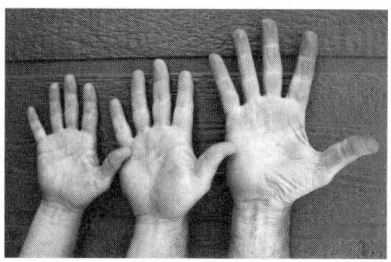

Normal hand (center) — no correction. Short fingers add ½"-1" (per hand) until it looks normal and deduct ½"-1" for long fingers.

you will have to add or subtract a half inch or so *on each hand* to make up the difference. For example, if you have short stubby fingers, you might have to add approximately ½" to each hand to get a more correct draw length measurement. People with extra long hands and fingers do the opposite.

This formula should get you within ¼" to ½" of your correct draw length. Most of the time though, no compensation for long or short fingers will have to be made. However, if you shoot with a high wrist grip, you will probably have to add up to 1" to the final AMO draw length.

Side Effects of a Draw Length That is Too Long

Since hardly anyone has too short of a draw length (1% maybe), let's look at the consequences of having it too long.

If your draw length is too long, your draw elbow will drop down, and instead of maintaining control of the shot with your back muscles, the control will end up in the top of your shoulder and you can't contract those muscles and get your elbow to move *(see X, middle photo, next page)*. I'll tell you why that's critical to back tension later. Also, as a result of your elbow being down, frequently, your draw wrist will be bent which causes excessive string oscillation and causes left and right misses.

The correct draw length will get your elbow in a position high enough to allow your back muscles to be able to move the tip of the elbow when you contract them on the draw side *(see top photo on next page)*. These muscles are called the *rhomboid* muscles which located between the shoulder blades and under the *trapezius*.

Excessive draw length usually causes you to fully extend your bow arm, which in turn causes right handed archers to

Bernie Pellerite

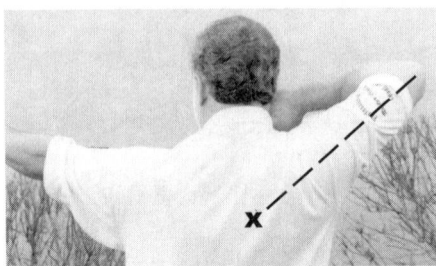

A high elbow will help you use the rhomboids as the pivot point.

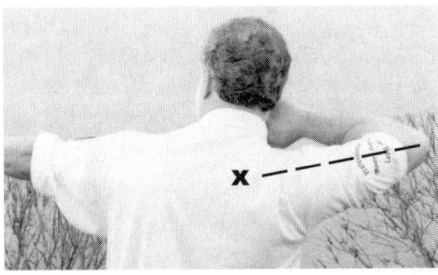

A low elbow will cause you to have your pivot point too high above the rhomboids.

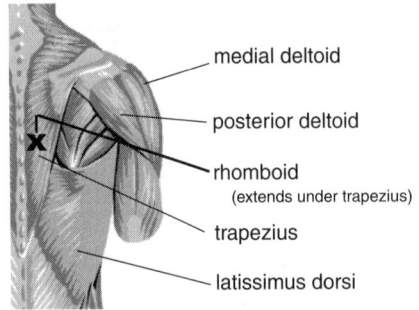

pre-load and/or push the bow to the left, causing left arrows. Since the shoulder is a "ball joint" and the arm is already fully extended, there is no "slack" in the shoulder unit. Now, the bow has nowhere else to go but to the left upon release. Also, most archers will have a very difficult time keeping the sight from shaking with a fully extended arm. The deltoid muscles surrounding the top of the shoulder will be tense while holding the arm in this position, and tension causes movement. Correct draw length will help you place your bow shoulder in a low and relaxed position in the shoulder joint (bone to bone).

Excessive draw length will sometimes cause you to throw your front hip toward the target and lean back with the upper body (especially if you shoot with your feet close together — see *44 Form Flaws* in chapter 11) and sometimes tuck your head into the string. It is nearly impossible to duplicate these angles each and every time, especially if you are shooting up and down hills. This can make your shooting form very inconsistent. Correct draw length will keep you from

Idiot Proof Archery

leaning back. Feet should be shoulder width apart and the feet, hips, and shoulders should line up, one above the other. As I said on pg. 41, your aiming eye should be over the belt buckle and the buttons on your shirt should run straight down when looking at the side profile.

The worst "chain reaction" result of too long of a draw length can be very debilitating. The deltoid muscle in your bow shoulder becomes the "pivot point" and the primary muscle holding the weight and controlling the direction of the bow. If you engage the deltoid muscle, this causes tension in your bow arm, thus causing movement of the sight. Because your sight moves, you will try to stop it . . . by using more muscles and/or holding longer. The longer you hold, the more the sight picture deteriorates and more muscle tension and anxiety builds. In an effort to control the exact millisecond of release to coincide with the sight picture "being perfect," your mind signals your release finger to punch the trigger (or your fingers to release the string), thereby causing you to anticipate "the explosion." However, if the draw length is correct, the shoulder will be relaxed and the sight picture will be much steadier. Also, the mind is much calmer because the anxiety to get rid of the arrow before the sight picture deteriorates is greatly reduced, or sometimes disappears altogether. If the shoulder is down and relaxed into the shoulder socket, the bow is being held mainly with bone against bone, instead of relying on muscle tone *(see photo)*.

If you build your form around the skeletal system instead of muscles, you will find that even on tournament day, your sight will be much steadier. This is because, when you become nervous (afraid you'll miss), that shaky feeling and the "butterflies" (anxiety) in your stomach causes the release of adrenaline into your blood-

*If you **had** to lean against a wall for thirty minutes, you'd figure out how to find this relaxed shoulder position!*

45

Bernie Pellerite

 Key Point #23

If you build your form around the skeletal system instead of muscles, you will find that even on tournament day, your sight will be much steadier.

stream. Adrenaline has no effect on bone, but it sure does on muscles! When adrenaline enters the system of a muscle-based shooter, their sight picture will deteriorate a lot faster than a bone-to-bone based archer, who will have less extremes in "peaks and valleys" in their shooting performance. Therefore, they will have less of a difference in scores on a "good day" versus a "bad day." Don't be afraid to shorten your draw length because you may lose six or eight feet per second of arrow speed. You will *lose* ten times as many points because you can't relax and hold steady than you will *gain* with a "speed burner" setup that you can't control (more on all of this later).

Warning! It is not easy for some people to find the "down, back but relaxed" shoulder position *(see photo)* without proper instruction (although it should be), especially if you have been shooting with a high shoulder for a long time. (I'm told the Korean Olympic archers spend up to three months perfecting the shoulder position and other elements of good shooting form, before even picking up a bow!) The trick is to raise the bow arm *without raising the bow shoulder.* If you have problems mastering this shoulder position, you should find a qualified NFAA Certified Instructor, attend the NFAA Shooter's School, watch the Shooter's School video series, or the **44 Form Flaws** video (*Robinhood Video Productions — see Appendix).*

Give this a try and you will find, like our students have, that you will be able to hold (verified with a laser) *at least twice as steady* at full draw, because your muscles will be relaxed.

Correct shoulder position is down, back and relaxed into the shoulder socket.

Idiot Proof Archery

When there is fewer muscles involved in the shot, your sight picture will be less shaky, which in turn, will cause less anxiety. You'll be amazed at how all of this fits together! Read what the following students accomplished with it.

83 year old Hollis Lankford used to shoot 260 out of 300 until he got Bernie's PanicMaster and Bow Simulator and the NFAA Shooter's School Video Series and began reprogramming his shot sequence. The techniques he learned evidently paid off. Hollis shot a 296 with 37 Xs on the first day of the 2002 Indoor Nationals in Kansas City, MO. Most people his age are more concerned with finishing all their prune juice! Great shooting, Hollis!!!

Idiot Proof Archery works for both young & old!

*At age 15, **Chris Glass** of Oxford, MI, started taking private lessons from Bernie. In less then one year he set two new world records, one of which was at the 2001 FITA Indoor World Championship in Florence, Italy. As a Junior Division competitor (18 and under), Chris shot the highest score recorded in any class, including the adult divisions. Chris and his two teammates won the Junior Team Gold medal and established two new junior world records (258 Semifinal round and 257 Gold Medal Match). Bernie said, "Since Chris came for private lessons, he has greatly improved and routinely shoots 300 with 57-59 Xs. He has the work ethic, maturity and focus that it takes to make him one of the best shooters in the sport."*

Bernie Pellerite

Glenn Campbell (not the singer!) of Lincoln Park, MI. Since attending the shooter's school and shortening his draw 3 inches, Glenn placed 4th in Las Vegas BHFS, 1st MI State FITA Indoor, 2nd NFAA MI State Indoor and set 2 Michigan Archery Association state records. He has turned pro and is now routinely shooting 300s with 57-59 Xs.

In Feb., 2001, Glenn's 5-man team set a new national record of 3,000 total points and won a Gold Medal at the Canadian Indoor Nationals.

At Lansing, MI, for the NAA Indoor Nationals, Glenn placed second behind top pro, Dee Wilde. He has since become a Certified NFAA Master Coach and is eager to share his knowledge with any shooter.

Glenn writes, "I never could have come this far if it wasn't for Bernie and Jan's school and all of the tapes Robinhood Videos offers. I'm living proof that, with the right schooling and a lot of work, you can be a winner, too!"

Glenn Campbell, Mathews Pro Staff Shooter

Rob Spencer, Dayton, NV, had target panic so bad he could not shoot a 5-spot target. His average was 225. After attending the shooter's school, he now averages 300 with 57X's. He recently shot a perfect 300 with 60 X's! Now, he regularly dominates most of the tournaments in his area!!

Idiot Proof Archery

Chapter 4

The Magic and Myths
Of Bow & Arrow Setup and Tuning

Introduction

It's my opinion that too many archers spend hours and hours "tuning" their bows and reading about tuning . . . and talking about tuning . . . and worrying about tuning! Some of it is helpful . . . but most isn't. As I pointed out in chapter 3, the purpose of tuning is to make adjustments in your bow/arrow setup to make your setup more *forgiving* of less-than-perfect shots. So, here is a basic guide to what I consider the facts and fiction of compound bow and arrow setup and tuning. For the purposes of this book, I think that it is necessary for me to explain how some of these methods of tuning and setup are done and why people *think* they do them. Several of these are commonly used even though they can't technically change where your arrow hits if you have *consistent form* and a *perfect* set of arrows. Because, in my opinion, 90% of tuning has nothing to do with the bow. It's simply producing a *perfect set* of matched arrows and then trying to improve their relationship with your arrow rest. However, as you will find out, if you read further, everything that affects your head, can and will affect your arrow impact in one way or another. So, for some (especially the anal retentive knit-picker who sleeps with his calipers and weighs his breakfast food), a lot of these methods actually won't change your arrow impact but might "help your head," and therefore

Key Point #24

"90% of tuning has nothing to do with the bow. It's simply producing a perfect set of matched arrows and then trying to improve their relationship with your arrow rest" . . . a Bernie-ism!

Bernie Pellerite

improve your score. So you might as well try all of them . . . besides, what else did you have to do this year? No wonder so many gun shooters are switching to bows . . . there's just not enough *stuff* to screw around with and adjust on a gun!

Bow Fitting

If your bow doesn't fit you, no amount of tuning will do a darn bit of good. It's important to get your draw weight and draw length set correctly first; otherwise you're just wasting your time. Part of bow fit and feel is the bow's "grip." The "bow grip" is really a *misnomer*, because you are *really* not supposed to grip it . . . are you? Anyway, many of the standard grips are too fat or curved to fit your hand properly . . . so, grind it down! Many of the pros take the grip off and shoot with their bow hand directly against the riser. Remember, that grinding or removing the grip lengthens your *draw length* (because the pivot point moves forward). The last thing you touch during a shot is the "grip." If it isn't right, you will torque the bow resulting in erratic arrow flight. I will discuss this further in chapter 7.

 Key Point #25

If your bow doesn't fit you, no amount of tuning will help!

Basic Bow Setup

Now, assuming your bow fits you correctly (draw weight, length, and bow grip), there are basic settings you need to make before you can even begin tuning. I believe these need to be set in approximately the following order because changing one can affect the others.

Setting Tiller Most modern compound bows are made to be shot at even tiller. However, because a compound is a *closed system*, due to the cables attaching to each cam and each axle, everything is tied together. So technically, they *don't have to be* even. This is not to be confused with a recurve that shouldn't be set up with even tiller because the handle is below center and the system is not tied together with cables and wheels. Therefore, an even tiller would cause the bottom limb to flex more at full draw. The only reason to change tiller on a

Idiot Proof Archery

compound is to change the feel of the bow in your hand. All such changes involve *only* a simple turn of the limb bolts.

The "Magic" of Tiller Tuning

In past years, much has been written and videotaped about a magical method of fine tuning bows called "tiller tuning." What is "tiller tuning"? Supposedly, it is a method of adjusting the tiller on the bow to the way you set your hand in the bow in order to make the limbs balance equally at full draw, thereby causing the bow to hold much steadier. The tiller is the measurement from the string to the point where the limb meets the riser *(see diagram)*.

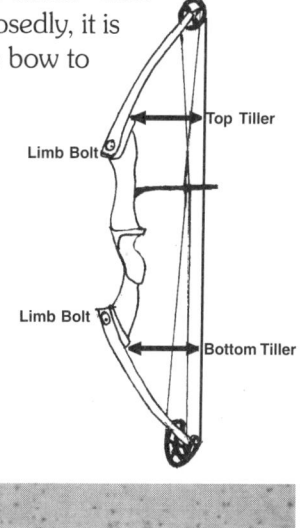

How to Tiller Tune

You start by taking nine paper plates and mark each one as follows: "0 tiller," "¼ top," "½ top," "¾ top," "full turn top," "¼ bottom," "½ bottom," "¾ bottom," and "full turn bottom." Shoot each one from 60 yards (or as far away as you can keep six arrows in a paper plate). Start at zero tiller; this is when the tiller measurements are exactly the same at the top and bottom of the riser/limb intersection (measuring from the string). Shoot six arrows at the "0 tiller" plate. Now, put ¼ turn on the top limb bolt and shoot six arrows at the paper plate marked "¼ top" and repeat this process on the rest of the plates. Be sure to reset the nocking point and peep sight back to normal

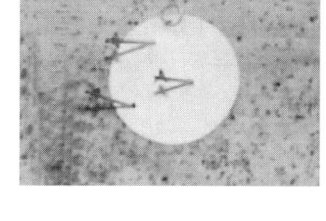

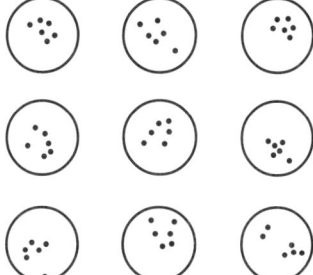

Nine paper plates

Bernie Pellerite

before shooting at the plates at each of the next four ¼ turn positions on the top limb. Then, return to even or zero tiller. Put ¼ turn on the bottom limb bolt and shoot four more groups, starting with "¼ bottom" and repeat the process on the four bottom plates. Supposedly, after each paper plate is shot and you examine all nine, one or two of them will have much tighter groups than the other. That is the tiller adjustment at which you should shoot that bow.

Who Can Tiller Tune?

The first problem I see is, in order for this method to have any scientific credibility, the archer would have to release *every arrow perfectly* (six arrows at nine paper plates = 54 shots) while the sight is *exactly in the center* of the target and without any variation in bow hand torque or wind, etc. After seeing over 1600 laser sight pictures in the school at just 20 yards, I can safely "bet the farm," there *ain't no way that's gonna happen!* The average shooter that comes to the school shoots 290 to 300 with 45-55 Xs indoors at 20 yards and over 30% are state, sectional, or national champions. Ten to twenty percent admit that they have tiller tuned their bows already. Ninety-five percent of these same shooters can't keep the laser in a three inch circle at 20 yards for four seconds when they arrive at the school. In short, I haven't met an archer (including the ten or so national or world champions I've done on video) that can execute 54 perfect shots and hold exactly on the center 54 times at long yardage, which is what is required to get a *true tiller tune reading*. It's just like bench firing a rifle . . . you can't shoot off hand and get correct results.

Adjusting the limb bolts *will make* a very slight difference in the way the bow sits in your hand. The same could be accomplished with a rubber band or tape under the top or bottom part of the bow grip to change the angle a degree or so.

Watching The Fights

Advocates of tiller tuning *correctly* point out that no two limbs on a bow are exactly the same. For example, the bottom

Idiot Proof Archery

limb on a *theoretical bow* is 41 pounds and the top limb is 40 pounds. If the tiller is equal in this example, according to these advocates, the imbalance between the top and bottom limbs will cause the limbs to "fight" each other up and down, causing the sight to move up and down.

A lot has also been written about "fights" between cams on two-cam bows. If the cams are out of synch, they will "fight" each other, making aiming difficult. (This particular theory has been perpetuated mainly, by the manufacturers of one-cam bows.) I guess that as long as you have two cams on a bow, one will always pick a fight with the other! (Sounds like a personal problem to me!)

Back when I first read the argument that no two limbs are the same and therefore they fight each other, it sounded logical . . . if you didn't think about it too long. But, as I started to analyze it later, it became clear to me that it was *selective logic*. Here is an example of well meaning, but misguided, *selective logic*. A scientist put a grasshopper on a table and clapped his hands. The grasshopper jumped off the table. Again, the scientist put the grasshopper on the table and clapped his hands. The grasshopper jumped off the table, again. Next, the scientist cut off the back legs of the grasshopper and clapped his hands. The grasshopper just sat there. The scientist then concluded that, "if you cut off a grasshopper's back legs, then . . . *it can't hear!*"

If you're still undecided about this theory that two limbs on a compound bow can fight each other, analyze again the example of the bow with 40 and 41 pound limbs. If the stronger 41 pound limb on the bottom pulls the bow sight down . . . what pulls it back up? The 40 pound limb? How exactly does 40 pounds *pull up* 41 pounds? An answer I get frequently is . . . the muscles in the bow arm pull it back up! Okay, just for argument's sake, let's buy that answer for a moment. What then, pulls the bow back down again? Duh! (There's a grasshopper in this logic somewhere!) The compound bow with its wheels and cables is a closed system and everything is equalled out at full draw, like I said before. Consider a set of balance scales. Put a 40 pound weight on one side and put a 41 pound weight on

Bernie Pellerite

 **Key Point #26**

The compound bow with its wheels and cables is a closed system and everything is equaled out at full draw.

the other. The 41 pound side will tip down and stop. The 41 pound side cannot be lifted by 40 pounds on the other side. (I'm almost nearly positive that I'm sure, about that!)

Zero Gravity Grasshopper Logic

Still think that mismatched limbs fight each other? Let's take this "grasshopper" one step further. We'll take this same theoretical bow right out of the box from the factory. It's mass weight is four pounds and it has a 41 pound limb on the bottom and a 40 pound limb on the top. According to this theory, when you try to hold up this bow at full draw, your arm would have to exert one extra pound of lift to compensate for the 41 pound limb pulling down, one pound more on the bottom (so it feels like you are shooting a five pound mass weight bow). Let's assume that one full turn on a limb bolt is equal to two pounds draw weight. According to the theory of tiller tuning, a half turn on the top limb would equal out the one pound difference in the limbs, making this bow feel like a four pound mass weight bow again. If this logic is correct, then if we put another two turns on the top limb, that would exert four pounds of extra

upward lift and the bow would now weigh . . . *zero pounds*, right? We should then be able to just walk away from the bow and . . . *it would hang there in mid air!* Cool! What a concept, grasshopper! (Someone has definitely been inhaling!) Do you still believe in tiller tuning? If so, read on.

The Mad Scientist

In Volume 6 of the **NFAA Shooter's School Videos**, *(see Appendix)* we did an experiment to prove or disprove tiller tuning once and for all. We took a *perfectly tuned bow* that was set at zero tiller and placed it in a contraption that would hold it

Idiot Proof Archery

at full draw. A piece of foam rubber was placed on the bracket that held the grip to represent the consistency of the human hand. The only other place the bow made contact with this contraption was at the nocking point on the string, simulating being held with a release aid. The bow was free to move up and down or side to side if it was capable of doing so (or if it felt like it!). Next, we attached a laser to the bow sight and pointed it at a target on the wall. If the bow, cams, or limbs decided to move, we would see the laser dot move! As I expected, the laser revealed no movement. Then, four full turns were taken off the bottom limb bolt to simulate a bow severely out of tiller tune. (You can just imagine the fighting going on between those two limbs!) Guess what! The laser revealed no movement again. All present were shocked and amazed! We even attached the laser to the top cam to see if there were any fisticuffs going on there, but alas . . . still no movement. We attached the laser to the limb. Again, no movement. I knew that some people would say that this was a static test and did not involve the human element, so I bravely put my hand between the grip and the bracket and watched the laser dot on the wall again. But, other than a slight side to side pulse-induced twitch of the laser dot, there was still no up and down movement. Go figure!

    I was so frustrated by my inability to watch the fight, that I went the final mile. I talked about this matter with my friend, Norb Mulaney, a well known engineer and writer. He said he has tested lots of bows in his shooting machine with lasers attached to the bow sights and pulled the string back from different points on the string, several inches above or below the nocking point. This would also severely effect the tiller and the balance of the bow. But, he also failed to find the elusive "fighting" that takes place before tiller tuning. Who would have thunk it! Maybe the cams that are out of synch or the limbs that are out of balance on a given bow don't really fight each other . . . maybe they are just really mad at each other and don't talk to each other! Who knows!

Bernie Pellerite
Show Me The Money

For any diehards, blow-hards, or gamblers left standing, consider this; if tiller tuning really works, then you should be able to get the same results over and over again. Right? I challenge anyone to prove that tiller tuning works on video and I'm willing to make the following wager. I will put up $10,000 to their $5,000 and we will do a double-blind experiment. We'll use a bow that the shooter is not familiar with. The archer will shoot it from 60 yards at the nine different tiller settings and paper plates, but not in any particular order. He will not know which tiller setting the bow is on, nor will he be allowed to use binoculars. To win, all he has to do is go through the tiller tuning procedure five times and hold the tightest group on the *same* tiller setting three out of the five times. If he does, he wins $10,000 and we'll put it on video. If he doesn't, he loses, and forfeits the $5,000. Any volunteers? Thought not!

It's All In Your Head

After all these experiments, I've concluded that tiller tuning (and all the levity I've levelled at it . . . ha, ha . . . that's not funny!) is *just for your head*. If you think it makes a difference, then do it! If your head feels better, then you will probably shoot better! However, mechanically or scientifically, it has no foundation. Think about this: if you were going to bore sight a rifle or set your scope, would you try to shoot at a target 200 yards away free hand, or would you put it on a bench rest? Obviously, a bow is much more critical than a rifle. The only way to duplicate 54 perfect shots is with a shooting machine that ensures the sight was exactly on target every time. As you can probably see by now, mismatched cam settings or limb pressures are not capable of *perpetual motion*, or pulling up and down without your help (if they were, they would be in the Smithsonian!). You see, the only thing that really effects how steady you hold your sight is . . . *you!* Any questions?

 Key Point #27

After all these experiments, I've concluded that tiller tuning is for your head. If you think it makes a difference, then do it!

Idiot Proof Archery

Setting Wheel/Cam Rollover (Applies only to two-wheel or two-cam bows) If you have a two-wheel/cam bow, conventional thinking dictates that it is important that the wheels be synchronized. With the bow at full draw, have someone check to see if the bow string comes off of the wheels at the same point on both wheels. It doesn't have to be perfect, $^1/_{16}$" of an inch difference won't matter, unless you are an engineer, machinist, or math teacher. (Then the only difference will be that *you* can't sleep until you get it perfect so . . . you need to get them *exactly* the same.) With this done, mark the wheels so you can tell later if they somehow got out of synchronization. This can be done with correction fluid or by making a mark in indelible ink where the wheel aligns to some point on the limb (at rest) or anywhere where you can tell if the marks have moved *(see photo below)*.

If the wheels are out of synch, follow the bow manufacturer's procedure for synching them (usually this requires shortening or lengthening one of the cables by twisting or untwisting one of them until the wheels roll over the same). You need to check this by drawing the bow to anchor and having a friend check the marks on the wheels to make sure that they roll over together. To show you how important wheel rollover is, I'll tell you the story of *"Jane Doe"* (her real name was deleted because she's afraid of the political fallout). She attended one of my shooter's schools and as we were adjusting draw lengths on the students' bows, we finally came to hers (by the way she shoots a left-handed, round wheel bow). *Jane* had recently won the state indoor championship with this same bow. After carefully analyzing her shooting form and measuring her "wingspan" (see chapter 3), she needed to shorten the draw length by approximately 1½" from 28" to 26½." Before beginning this process the bow tech, who is also left-handed, drew the bow back. To his amazement, he was able to draw

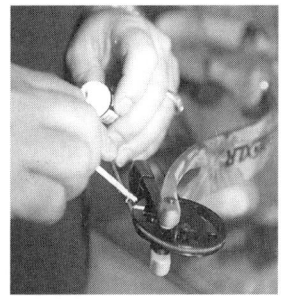

Bernie Pellerite

it to 31". As he called me over to try and solve this puzzle, I took the bow and drew it back left-handed to the middle of the valley at about 28" (which is my draw length). Being completely stumped, we then called in more help; three more students came to our aid. Now we had five people trying to figure this out. After some time measuring and re-measuring we discovered that one of the cables was over 3" longer than the other . . . Jane had a rare, but legitimate . . . "two-humper" . . . this bow had *two valleys*, several inches apart. Apparently, *Jane* didn't know about the longer one (the back hump) when she won the state championship a month before. Maybe she was shooting all the arrows the *same way* from the *same spot* on the bow . . . do you think? Oh well! So much for cam synchronization. Maybe we could sell this "two-humper concept" as a "dual draw length," indoor target/3-D speed burner!

Setting Centershot (Basic) This procedure subscribes to the theory that, if the arrow rest is set too far out from the line of centershot, you will get erratic arrow flight. If it is set too close to the bow's riser, you will also get erratic arrow flight and may have severe problems with the arrow clearing the rest and/or bow. To determine where this line is on your bow, place a business card across the width of the limb up next to the wheel. Mark the edges of the limb and the inner and outer edges of the cam/wheel on the card. Move the card down near the limb pocket (where the limb fits into the riser or handle). Using the outer marks to center the card (the limb is wider here than at the tip) transfer the position of the wheel/cam onto the limb with light pencil marks (or use tape so as to not mar the limb). Do this for both limbs, or Beiter makes a pair of clips that fit onto bow limbs to simplify this process *(see photo).*

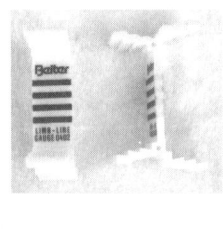

A. *The Beiter Limb Line Gauge clips on the limbs to help set the centershot.*

Hold the bow out away from you and sight along the

Idiot Proof Archery

bowstring while aligning the string to those marks you just made on the limbs. *If you shoot a release*, your arrow should then be directly behind the string from this view *(see photo B)*. Since your arrows nock to the string, the rear end of the arrow is always okay. If the tip of the arrow sticks out away from the bow, your rest needs to be moved closer into the bow. If the tip sticks inward toward the bow, you need to move the rest out. *If you shoot with your fingers*, your arrow tip

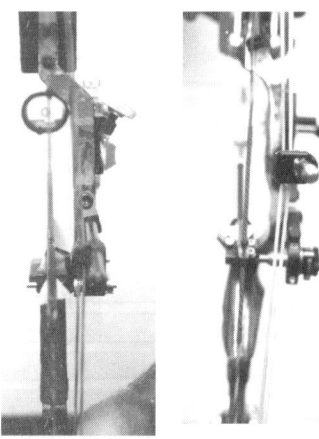

B. Centershot for release shooter

C. Centershot for finger shooter

should be just visible, sticking out away from the bow, from a behind the string view *(see photo C)*. If it is not, adjust the rest inward or outward accordingly. Measure the distance from the inside surface of the riser to the center of the arrow and record this number in your log book. But remember, most all indoor Vegas target records (perfect 900) were set with old style non-centershot riser bows (including the two 1200s shot by Terry Ragsdale, *see pg. 31)*. Tuning is spooky . . . huh!

Setting Centershot for Finger Shooters (Fine Tuning) These two methods are usually done by finger shooters with recurve or compounds. Once your bow is tuned fairly well, you can fine tune your centershot setting. One method is to put a 1" wide piece of tape vertically on a piece of cardboard as a target *(see diagram)*. Shoot six arrows at this tape from 15-20 yards. Don't worry about where the arrows go up and down, just space them out so you don't bang them up. Record the width of the group in your log book (disregard any obvious bad shots). Move your rest a small (tiny!) increment in or out from the starting position and shoot another group.

1" Vertical line

Bernie Pellerite

Measure the width of the group. If it is better (not as wide), this may be a better centershot setting. Keep making small adjustments in the same direction until the group gets wider. The setting that gives you the narrowest group is the best setting for you. If you started moving the rest away from the riser, go back to your original setting and try closer or *vice-versa*. Obviously, if you can't hold a small group at any setting, your form may not yet be up to this method of fine-tuning your centershot or you may just be shooting from too far away. Use your own judgment here or, even better yet, work with a coach.

Another method of fine-tuning centershot is the *French* or *"walk back"* method. Find a tall target butt and place a small target near the top of it. Set your sight for 15 yards. Do not change your sight setting for any of the following shots. Stand about five yards from the butt and shoot one arrow (or a group of three if you are a fussbudget) at the center of your target. Move back five yards, and *without resetting your sight,* shoot another arrow (or set) at the same target. Keep moving back in five yard (or regular) increments, shooting arrows at each distance *without resetting your sight!* Stop when your arrows are hitting near the bottom of the bale.

Your centershot is perfect if the arrows march down the target butt in a straight line. If the arrows form a straight line but angled to either side, there is a left-right pressure problem with the rest. (If a plunger-type rest is being used, the spring is too weak if the arrows trail off to the right, for a right-handed archer; the reverse is true if you are left-handed.) If the arrow line curves out to the right and comes back toward the center, the rest is too far to the right. If the arrow line curves out to the left and comes back toward the center, the rest is too far to the left. Make very small adjustments to the left-right position of the rest and reshoot.

Centershot Tuning for Release Shooters This method is usually for release shooters with launcher type rests without plunger buttons but is almost the same as for finger shooters. Often times, especially if you are shooting pin sights, you may notice that your 20, 30, 40, 50 and 60 yard pins don't line up vertically . . . they have what we call a "Christmas Tree" configuration *(see illustration)*, and they come down on a slight diagonal (60 yard pin is farther to the left than the 50 yard pin, the 50 yard pin is farther to the left that the 40 yard pin, etc. for a right-handed shooter). If you shoot a movable sight like a drop pin or scope, you may notice that as you move back to the longer yardages, you have to make windage adjustments either in or out and these windage adjustments increase as the yardage gets longer. This may be due to three common problems . . . *pre-loaded torque, bow cant,* or *incorrect centershot.* If a person has too long of a draw they will normally (for a right-handed archer) "pre-load" the shot to the left. This is evidenced by the 20 yard pin being to the left of centershot (when viewed from the string side of the bow). If the archer always pre-loads the shot, sometimes when they move back to longer yardages, the arrow moves farther and farther to the left because of the distance. Then, to be able to hit in the middle, they chase this left arrow with the pin to move it back to the center of the target. Therefore, the pins keep moving farther and farther to the left (or vice versa) giving them this "Christmas Tree" effect. The second problem can be that most right-handed archers naturally cant the top limb to the right. If the bow cant is *severe* enough and if they don't shoot with a bubble level, they will throw the arrow to the right *very slightly* at short yardage and *increasingly more* as they move back, creating the same "Christmas Tree." The third problem is incorrect centershot. You can check this two different ways. The first is similar to the "French or Walk-Back Method." Start by shooting at a vertical tape, paying no attention to high and low hits; just try to hit the tape from 20 yards back to 60 yards in 5 or 10 yard increments. Another method is similar, except you put a target at the top of the bale. Go back to 30 yards and set your sight for 20. Shoot one to three arrows at the target with your 20 yard sight setting and, of course, they will drop low into

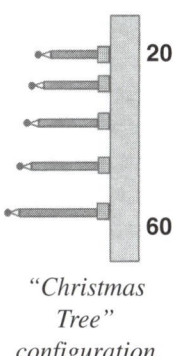

"Christmas Tree" configuration

Bernie Pellerite

the top section of the bale. Walk back in five yard increments with the *same sight setting* until your last arrow or group of arrows are at the bottom of the bale. Now observe the vertical line of arrows you've shot. If they walk out to the left, for a right-handed archer, move your centershot to the right very slightly and retest (and vice versa), until the line of arrows is directly below the bullseye set at the top of the bale.

Setting Nocking Point (Preliminary) First of all, you have to decide what kind of nocking point to use. There are three basic types. First is the brass nock set, that everybody is familiar with, that clamps on the serving. The second is a "tied-in nocking point" made with No. 4 nylon or Fast Flight that can be screwed up and down a monofilament serving *(see photo A)*. The third is a string loop *(see photo B)*. There are advantages and disadvantages to all of them. If you shoot old-style nocks without the "nock grooves" in them, the brass nock set will eventually cut a small groove out of the top of the nock from pulling to full draw over and over. If you shoot long yardage (60 to 80 yards), this can cause a problem if all of your arrows have grooves in them but one (the one you just broke and replaced with a brand new nock). This arrow, of course, will shoot in a different spot than the rest at long yardage. The "tied-in nocking point" is used by a lot of field shooters and prevents nock wear and, if it's not tied in too tight, can be screwed or twisted up and down the monofilament string serving when tuning your nocking point. Once you have discovered your final nocking point, then you can tie it in permanently. Finally, there is the string loop, which is popular with a lot of caliper release shooters. This prevents serving wear from the jaws of a caliper release, keeps your arrow on the string when you let down and re-draw, and rolls your peep over the same all the time. However, this nocking point requires

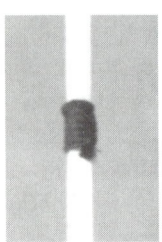

A. *Tied-in nocking point*

B. *String Loop*

Idiot Proof Archery

some maintenance, as it may stretch out or even come loose if not carefully tied in *(see Appendix for the Burley Hall video **Winning at 3-D**).*

The *initial placement* of your nocking point may be different, depending on whether you use fingers or a release. The best starting point for a release shooter is with the arrow right at, or slightly above, 90 degrees to the bowstring. Using a bow square, set the nocking point a small distance (approximately the thickness of your nock . . . $^3/_{16}$" to $^5/_{16}$") above "square." If you shoot with fingers, you'll probably want a slightly higher setting, about $^3/_8$" above square to start with.

Setting Nocking Point (Fine Tuning) If you shoot a release, your best bet might be to use the paper test (see next section) and you can fine tune your nocking point by turning the limb bolts. For example, one quarter turn (clockwise) on the top limb bolt will pull the nocking point up slightly to produce the desired tear, and vice versa.

If you want to have a second option, try this. Get out the 1" tape, again, and put a stripe *horizontally* on a piece of cardboard (or you could also try the "Homer Simpson method" and use that other cardboard on pg. 60, that had the vertical line on it . . . and turn it sideways! D'oh!). Anyway, shoot six arrows at this tape from 15-20 yards (space them out and don't worry about where the arrows go left and right). Record the height of the group in your log book. (Disregard any obvious bad shots.) Move your nocking point a small (tiny!) increment up or down from the starting position and shoot another group. Measure the height of this group (vertical spread). If it is better (less high), this may be a better nocking point setting. Keep making small adjustments in the same direction until the group gets taller. The setting that gives you the narrowest vertical group is the best setting. If you started moving the nocking point up, go back to your original setting (You did write down the original setting, didn't you?), and try moving it down. Obviously, if you can't hold a small group . . .

1" Horizontal Line

Bernie Pellerite

again, your form may not yet be up to this method of fine-tuning your nocking point, or you may just be shooting from too far away.

Another way for fingers shooters to fine-tune their nocking point setting is with *bare-shaft testing* that I will go over later *(see pg. 67)*. After completing that test, be sure to record the best setting in your log book. Also, changing arrow size changes all of this and requires you to reset your nocking point. Keep in mind that if you put a bow in a shooting machine with all the arrows made exactly the same and they all came out porpoising because of a bad nocking point setting . . . they all would *porpoise into the same hole!* Does that sound *fishy* to you? So, to tell the difference between the *real* and the *imagined* benefits my rule of thumb is — if a method of tuning makes no difference using a shooting machine and a perfect set of arrows . . . then, that method usually only helps the believer's head. Therefore, it may *actually help* his score, but not for *very long*, and not for the *reasons* he thought. The only possible exception I can think of is, using a slightly higher nocking point for release shooters so you get a $3/8$" high-left tear (for right-handed archers) while paper testing. This makes the setup more forgiving (this is verified by powder testing), mostly because the arrow leaves the rest sooner, and therefore can be influenced less by dynamic hand torque from the shooter.

Powder Testing One of the prime causes of erratic arrow flight can be the arrow hitting the rest (or the riser!) as it leaves the bow. To check for *good arrow clearance*, spray the back of an arrow with foot powder or any aerosol spray powder, then shoot the arrow. Check the arrow for tracks left by the arrow rest in the powder. At most, there should be tracks where the arrow shaft slid along the rest. If the vanes are contacting the rest, rotate the nock a small amount, clean the arrow, re-spray it and retest until you get good clearance. Then, align all of the nocks on the other arrows exactly the same as the arrow that shows good clearance *(see Aligning Your Nocks later in this chapter)*.

Idiot Proof Archery

Paper Testing / Paper Tuning Many pro shops have "frames" that can be used for *paper testing*. **NOTE:** *Be sure to powder test your arrow before paper testing to eliminate any bad paper tears that may have been caused by fletch contact with the rest.* The idea is that a thin sheet of paper (like newspaper) is stretched on the frame and taped or clamped there. The frame is put several yards in front of a target butt. You stand 4-5 yards (release) or 8-10 yards (fingers) in front of the paper and shoot an arrow through the paper. The hole the arrow makes tells you whether the tail of the arrow is following the tip or not *(see illustrations below)*.

The problem with paper tuning is that it can only tell you what is happening to the arrow at *that particular distance*. If you stand a different distance from the paper, it may tell you something quite different. Basically, *paper testing tells you what the back end of the arrow is doing.* It is a form of testing that will tell you whether your nocking point or centershot is way off (that is, if you don't create excessive tears with hand torque). Archers who spend hours adjusting their bows to get a perfect "bullet hole" tear may be wasting their time unless they are doing it for the purpose of bowhunting with exposed blade broadheads. (Then, you definitely want a perfect hole.) Most top target shooters find that a ¼" to ⅜" high left tear (for right-

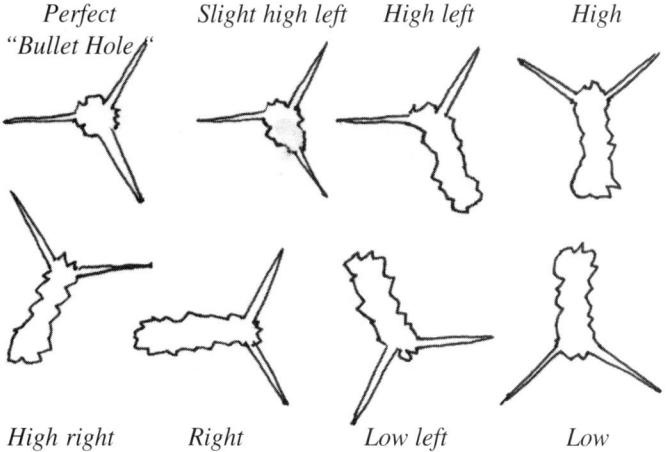

Bernie Pellerite

handed shooters) is the most forgiving, because the arrow gets off the rest much quicker and therefore insures fletch clearance of the rest and the riser and will forgive "more mistakes." Any slight porpoising or fishtailing caused by this angle of launch dissipates in five or six yards. The arrow will be flying straight long before impacting even the shortest field target (which you should check with another paper test at the shortest distance you normally shoot in a tournament . . . you should get a perfect bullet hole at that distance). When trying to correct a "bad paper tear," the rule of thumb is to move the nocking point up if you get a low tear . . . and vice versa. Move the centershot to the left if you get a right tear and vice versa. If you get a diagonal tear, move the nocking point first, until you get a left or right tear . . . then move the centershot in or out until you correct the horizontal tear. Sometimes arrow cycling or paradox can *reverse* the results, and you may find that you need to do the exact *opposite* of what is recommended. But remember, on page 31, when Terry Ragsdale had a 5" ten o'clock tear after he a shot a perfect 1200 ? *What's up with that?*

Setting Rest Pressure If you use a *launcher rest* (which means you are probably shooting a release), the rest only needs as much tension as will keep the rest from sagging at full draw with your arrow on it. Too much pressure can be detrimental to good arrow flight. As the arrow moves forward after release, it depresses the launcher because a release-shot arrow primarily cycles (flexes) up and down. The fletched end should clear the launcher completely, but if the rest pressure is excessive, the launcher will not stay depressed long enough and will spring back up and contact the rear end of the arrow. This can cause porpoising and/or a high tear during paper testing. If you use a *plunger style rest*, start in the middle of the stiffness range and use the French or Walk Back fine tuning method or bare shaft testing (finger shooters), covered earlier in this chapter.

Idiot Proof Archery
Arrow Tuning —
(stuff that actually affects where your arrow hits)

Bare Shaft Planing Test (for right-handed finger shooters, reverse for left-handed). This test will approximate what happens if you shot fletched arrows with exposed blade broadheads. In bare shaft testing, you need to have two arrows with no fletches. If you've already fletched them all, you'll need to strip two of them. (Ideally, the bare shafts should weigh exactly the same as the fletched ones. You can try adding a weight equivalent to the difference of the fletched and stripped shafts to the back of the bare shafts like shrink tubing or masking tape until the arrow weighs the same.) If you don't add the weight to compensate for the removed fletch, the arrow will probably test too weak. This test is less effective at 300 f.p.s. than at 180 f.p.s.

From about 15 yards, set your sight so you can shoot a good group of three fletched arrows in the center of a target. Then shoot the two bare shafts. (You shoot two to tell if you shot a good shot with the first bare shaft; they should group!)

- If the bare shafts impact *above* the fletched group, your *nocking point is too low*.
- If the bare shafts impact *below* the fletched group, your *nocking point is too high*.
- If the bare shafts impact to the *left* of the fletched group, your *rest is too far to the left* or the *draw weight* is too low.
- If the bare shafts hit to the *right* of the fletched group, your *rest is too far to the right* or the *draw weight* is too high.
- If the bare shafts impact anywhere else relative to the fletched group, you have a combination of adjustments to make.

Many top finger shooters actually prefer a low-left impact point for the bare shafts (for right-handed archers; it is reversed for left-handers). The feeling is that the arrow coming out of the bow with the nock slightly high and away from the bow should be more forgiving of a "less-than-perfect" release.

If you find that you cannot tune out a left or right bare shaft impact point with a left-right adjustment of your rest, try

Bernie Pellerite

changing the pressure on the plunger button or changing the bow weight. If you do not have such a setting, or if that doesn't change the impact of the bare shafts, check your arrow spine. You may have to change the point weight to stiffen or weaken the "effective spine" or even change arrow size. The spine (stiffness) of the arrow is critical for finger shooters. If the arrow is too stiff, it will cause bare shafts to hit left of a fletched group. If the arrow is too weak, it will cause bare shafts to hit right of a fletched group. It is also true that underspined fletched arrows will shoot to the right of the target and overspined arrows will shoot to the left of the target. A poor spine match to your bow will also result in bigger groups and poorer performance at short distances (the fletches have less time to correct the arrow flight).

Because finger shooters experience fairly severe side to side arrow bending or cycling (archer's paradox), spine becomes much more important than for a release shooter who normally gets very little arrow cycling. And, nearly *all of that* cycling is up and down, because the string is moving straight forward after leaving the release in most cases. However, when using a rope-type release, a very slight deflection of the bow string *does* occurs. A finger-shot arrow, however, has ten to twenty times more string deflection, which is why spine is much more important for finger shooters.

Tuning for Groups After *you think* you have your bow and arrow setup tuned about as well as you can using the above methods, (the key here is that *you must believe* that everything is as good as you can get it!) then you must get a *perfect* set of sight marks. I recommend setting all your pins or your sight tape with a ½" horizontal line, not a round bullseye . . . it is much more precise. Now, pick the longest distance from which you can shoot reasonable groups . . . for example 40 to 60 yards. Shoot a large number of arrows (35-50) in groups of no more than 5 or 6 at a time at the same kind of ½" horizontal line (yes, you *could* use Homer's target . . . if you want — see pg. 63), paying no attention to left's or right's . . . just up's and down's. Then, if necessary, micro-adjust your front sight setting to correct arrows up or down. Now using the same

Idiot Proof Archery

procedure to adjust windage, shoot at a vertical line (that's right, turn Homer's target one quarter turn counterclockwise . . . or clockwise! D'oh!) and adjust your windage in or out until the arrows hit the line. Now you are ready to group tune. Most people shoot a round bullseye. But as my friend, Bob Ragsdale (ex-marine rifle instructor), points out ". . . groups are seldom round, they are usually square, with a rifle or with a bow. So, I recommend you shoot at a crosshair-type target" *(see diagram,* you better make this target yourself . . . this one's probably over Homer's head!).

Crosshair-type target

Now, shoot several groups of six *numbered* arrows; log the results on a spare target or diagram and then adjust your centershot (or nocking point height) by small increments. Shoot another group of arrows, recording all shots. Keep adjusting and shooting until you find the setting that gives you the best groups. These should be the most forgiving settings. **NOTE:** When numbering your arrows, don't put the number where you can see it, while it's on the string! For example, if #4 arrow is suspect because it hit low left twice in a row, and you see that you are about to shoot #4 . . . *that* will distract you and cause you to *predispose* where #4 *is probably going to go.*

Obviously, *you have to be able* to shoot good groups at that distance. Remember if you have, for example, a #4 arrow that consistently drops out of the group, you may have one of five problems. You may find that it doesn't weigh the same, is cracked, is bent, the nock is on crooked, or that it is fletched slightly different than the rest. The first four problems are easy to determine and to fix. Once you

Keep a record of your results in your logbook

Bernie Pellerite

have eliminated them, here's how you fix the latter: You need to rotate the nock *one full position* and align the next fletch as if it were the cock vane or cock feather, and reshoot the arrow. Half the time the arrow will go back into the group with the rest of the arrows. If not, rotate the nock again to the last vane position and retest. Most of the time, this arrow will group with the others. If not, discard it. If you are a finger shooter, you might have a spine problem with that arrow. See section on importance of arrow spine in this chapter.

WARNING: This is really a lot of work! Don't expect to get it done in one day. Fatigue will change your group size as much as anything! Also, don't try this unless you think you have a "perfect set" of matched arrows and your bow is set up and "tuned" to *your standards!* Because if something is way off, this is a lot of work to flush down the drain.

Weighing Your Arrows Do you weigh your arrows? You should! Even small differences in weight can cause significant differences in arrow impact at longer distances. Weigh the fletched shafts and points of your arrows separately, on a powder scale *(see photo below)*. You'll need to number or label your arrows and the points with an indelible marker to tell them apart. Match up the arrow and point pairs from heaviest to lightest. *For Aluminum Arrows* — add hot melt glue to the tip of the lighter ones until those tip-arrow combinations weigh as much as the heaviest combination. Tiny slivers of hot melt glue work best. Now, hold the tip with pliers and heat it until the glue melts inside the tip. Once they cool, glue in the tips. *For Carbon Arrows* — you do just the opposite. Find the *lightest* tip and arrow combination. Grind down the end of the rod that inserts into the arrow on all the other heavier tip and arrow combinations until they all weigh the same as the lightest combination. Now glue in the tips.

Weigh your arrows, especially if you're shooting long distances.

Idiot Proof Archery

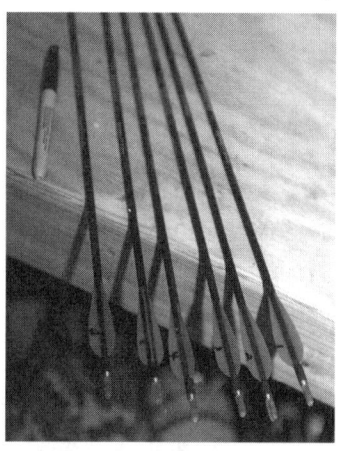

Most professional archers that shoot field rounds (up to 80 yards) match their arrow weights to within *one-tenth of a grain!* To show you how much difference weight makes when shooting at long yardage, we did a test on my first series of videos in 1990. We tested seven arrows, that were otherwise identical, that weighed 340, 341, 342, 343, 344, 345, and 346 grains. These arrows were shot repeatedly at a target 60 yards away at approximately 210 f.p.s. We discovered, to our amazement, an 8 inch drop between the lightest and heaviest arrows. There was approximately 1¼ inch per arrow difference in impact height for each arrow *(see diagram).* If your arrow speed is much higher and/or your arrows are heavier, then your results could be quite different, so perform your own test.

Number your arrows, but not where you can see it while it's on the string.

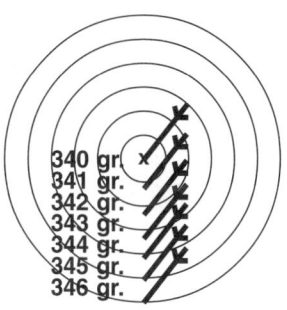

You will find that past 50 yards, in most cases, you'd better weigh your arrows . . . if you want to win. A few top pros might say that they don't weigh their arrows . . . but, that's not *exactly* so! These pros usually get their sight marks with a ½" horizontal line. For example, they shoot two dozen arrows at the line at 60 yards. Guess what? . . . the only arrows that get to go to the *dance* (tournament) are the eight or so that consistently hit the line! Hmmm . . . why do you suppose those eight hit the line? Maybe . . . they all weighed the same! Duh! Of course, these top pros *are actually capable* of hitting the ½" line with some consistency, therefore the arrows they take to the tournament probably all *do weigh*

Bernie Pellerite

the same. But, if you can't hit a trash can lid at 60 yards (D'oh!), *this test* won't be valid for you!

Aligning Your Nocks Typically, in the school, students will seldom have two out of six arrows with their nocks aligned exactly the same! Therefore, how could each arrow fletch clear the rest in the same manner? A $20 nock alignment gauge or "nock jig" will align them all *to the test arrow* that gave you a *good powder test.* But my wife, Jan, invented the best and cheapest "nock jig" I've ever seen. Simply find an Allen wrench that fits snugly in the throat of the nock of your "best arrow" example. Set the arrow on a counter top and insert the long part of the Allen wrench into the throat of the nock *(see photos A & B)* so it's at a right angle to the arrow. Push the arrow nock and Allen wrench against the wall and trace the Allen wrench. (You might want to tape a piece of paper to the wall first, unless you have a kid to blame for the mark, when your wife comes home and screams, "Who the hell put that *mark* on my wall??") Anyway, put the Allen wrench in the nock of the next arrow and slide the arrow up against the outline of the first Allen wrench. They should match perfectly, but I bet they don't. Rotate the nock one way or the other until they match. Repeat this process with all your arrows. This will ensure that the rest of your arrows will have the same clearance as the first one you powder tested, assuming that you used the same fletching jig when making all of your arrows. If not, you have two chances of getting them to group *tightly together* at 50 plus yards . . . *slim* and *none!* . . . even if you shot them from a shooting machine!

Nock alignment gauge

A. Trace Allen wrench in the nock of your "best arrow" against the wall.

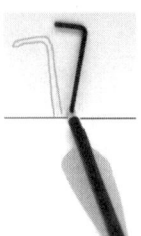

B. Adjust all the nocks using this outline as a template.

Idiot Proof Archery

Spin Testing Arrow spin testers generally cost less than $40 or you can use an arrow straightener like this one *(see photo)*. The best ones allow the arrow to spin quite a few seconds. While the arrow is spinning, you can watch to see whether the nocks are symmetrical (they can be deformed or be knocked out of alignment when struck by an arrow). Similarly, the arrow points should be inspected. Arrows can be bent right behind the point which may not show up during a casual inspection of the arrow. And, if the arrow is bent, it will bounce up and down on the spinner. A spin tester is well worth the money, especially when you need to check broadhead-tipped arrows for alignment. You can also make one like this with four nails and a piece of wood *(see photo above)*.

Arrow straightener

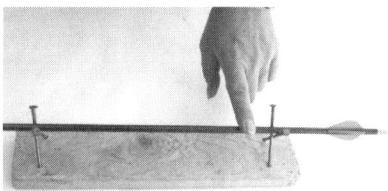
Spin tester made with wood and nails

Significance of Archer's Paradox and Arrow Spine As you know by now, arrow spine is much more critical for finger shooters than for release shooters. The best test of whether your arrows are spined correctly for finger shooters (after you bare shaft test) is *group testing*. Over- or under- spined arrows will cause poor arrow flight and cause poor groups to be shot. Basically here's why . . . when a shot is loosed, the arrow's mass can't move forward as fast as the string, and because of the sudden load on the nock end it flexes or cycles. The weaker the arrow, the more it flexes. As I said before, for release shooters, this flexing is mostly up and down. For finger shooters, because the string comes off and around the fingers sideways, the flexing is mostly side to side.

Back when archers shot only wooden (non-centershot) bows, someone noticed that the string is directly behind the

Bernie Pellerite

limbs and therefore so was the arrow's nock. The arrow's tip, then, necessarily pointed off to the left for right-hand archers. But the arrows did not fly off to the left when shot. So why didn't the arrow shoot off to the left if pointed that way? This is called, "The Archer's Paradox." This term "Paradox" in plain English means "this phenomenon happens but we don't know why." The solution to the paradox came with high speed photography (in the 1920s) which showed the arrow bending around the bow! The bending of even the stiffest arrows is noticeable to the high speed movie camera. If the arrow flexes back too much it will impact to the right (the fletched end of it may also hit the bow and/or rest). If it doesn't flex back far enough, the arrow will hit to the left.

When choosing arrows, use a good spine chart such as the Easton arrow chart *(see Appendix for address)* to make a selection; then find a buddy or pro shop that will let you use some arrows to test. A lot of top recurve finger shooters, use a method that may seem a little extreme and probably is if you are shooting high speed arrows at short yardages with a release. However, spine to a finger shooter can make a huge difference when you are shooting a relatively slow recurve bow at a 90 meter (99 yards) bullseye. Before they fletch their arrows or glue the points in, they use a nock to plug up the front of the arrow and float their arrows in a bathtub full of soapy water in order to tell where the "high spine point" is on those particular arrows. Here's the theory . . . since no mass-produced arrow will have the exact same wall thickness 360 degrees around the shaft, there has to be (for lack of a better word) a "heavier side" and a "lighter side." If, for example, you had #2 arrow with the heavy side on the left of the cock vane and #3 arrow had the heavy side on the right, then it would be theoretically impossible at long yardage

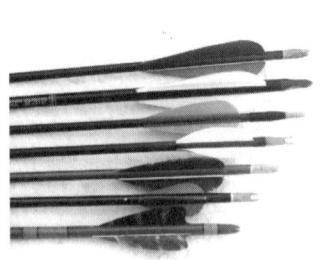

When choosing arrows, use a good spine chart.

Idiot Proof Archery

to get these arrows to group. Having said that, they mark the mark the top side of the arrow (that's above the water) which would obviously be the light side. The heavy side would roll toward the bottom! — by the way . . . did I tell you I am a MENSA member? Anyway, when they remove the arrows and install the points, they fletch all their arrows with the light spine side that has the mark on it *in the same place* in the fletching jig, either on the top or the bottom. It doesn't matter, as long as they are consistent.

Adjusting the Bow to the Arrows or the Arrows to the Bow If the arrows are *close* to the correct spine, there are adjustments you can make. If the arrows are a little too stiff, add draw weight to match them (heavier draws require stiffer arrows) and vice-versa. You may also have to adjust rest pressures (if plunger type). If the bow is right where you want it and you don't want to change anything — you can make the arrows weaker by not cutting them as short (if they are already cut, it's a little too late to tell you that now! . . . I knew that!), or stiffer by cutting them shorter (if they will still stay on the rest at full draw).

You can also make arrows weaker by using heavier points or lighter fletches. You can make arrows stiffer by using lighter points or heavier fletches.

Feathers vs. Vanes Some people shoot with feather fletching, others with vanes. Which should you use? This is somewhat a matter of personal choice, but consider what happens if you were to switch from vanes to feathers of the same size. Your arrows would now be lighter and hence you would gain arrow speed and cast (out to about 30 to 40 yards). The feathers are more fragile and they won't perform as well when they get wet, so you have to take better care of them and/or replace them more often. Also, since the feathers weigh less (a 3" feather weighs about 1½ to 2 grains and a 3" vane weighs about 6 to 9 grains) and they are on the back of the arrow . . . the arrow will behave as if it had a weaker spine! (Adding weight to the *front* of an arrow *weakens* them and, contrary to popular belief, adding weight to the *rear stiffens them*). This is because of a phenomenon called "column

Bernie Pellerite

loading." (It's a physics thing . . . trust me, you don't want to know!) Aren't you glad you bought this book!?!

For general recommendations, *most field archers* (shooting targets from 60 yards to 80 yards with release aids), normally shoot about 2" or 3" inch plastic fletch. Hunters usually prefer about 4" to 5" fletch (big broadheads require a lot more *steerage* from the back of the arrow, to fly well). Finger shooters tend to be somewhere in between. *Most* prefer feathers (3½" to 5"), largely because the feathers will correct side-to-side oscillations faster (about 1½ times quicker than the same size plastic fletch). Target archers with releases *generally* prefer plastic vanes because their arrows don't need as much steerage, and feathers don't hold up as well.

Most pros fletch arrows at a slight (1 to 2 degree) offset angle. Don't fletch them straight (aligned to the shaft). Whether you fletch with a straight clamp or a helical one is pretty much immaterial, as long as you angle them so you can get rest clearance. This should give your arrow about one revolution per yard (rule of thumb). Finger shooters with larger broadheads with a recurve or longbow sometimes have to use 5" or 6" feathers with a fairly severe helical angle to make their arrows fly properly. A lot of pro release shooters will shoot full-length (32"- 34") large diameter arrows (2512 or 2613, for example) with extra heavy points (200-225 grains) which helps break down the overspined shaft, and 5" or 6" feathers with 2 to 6 degree offset for indoor target shoots (18 meters or 20 yards). They generally use fairly low poundage bows (45 to 55 pounds). This slows the arrow velocity way down to 165 to 200 f.p.s. and gives their *bad* or *mediocre* shots a little extra time to straighten up before hitting the target. However, the *main reason* they use these large shafts, called "line cutters," is to get two or three more "X-rings" because of the large diameter.

Setting Peep Height/Kisser Button The height of your peep sight determines your anchor position to some extent, so the easiest way to set this is to install the peep in the string, but don't tie it in yet. Now, with your eyes closed, draw your bow and settle in to your most comfortable anchor. Then open your

Idiot Proof Archery

sighting eye. If the peep isn't exactly in front of your eye, move it up or down until it is. Then, set your sight for the distance you want your most comfortable anchor. Some field archers set this at the midpoint of the range of distances they will be shooting (usually 7 to 80 yards). A lot of top pro field archers set their peep sight, comfortably, at 60 yards. They think that a less than perfect anchor at 20 yards won't keep them out of the center of the target, and tournaments are often won on the longer shots, so why not have everything perfect for those harder ones. Obviously, this would be way too far for a 3-D shoot, so they might try 30 or 40 yards.

After setting your sight for the distance you choose, repeat the drawing with your eyes closed, anchor, and open your sighting eye procedure, moving the peep each time, until it is perfectly in front of your sighting eye when you open it. Then tie it in place so it doesn't move. Finally, measure the distance from your nocking point to the hole in the peep and *write it in your log book.*

Draw your bow with your eyes closed. Then open them to see which way to adjust your peep sight.

The same procedure works for setting a kisser button (but put the kisser button against an upper tooth . . . preferably *your tooth*, because moving your lips to touch it, isn't really consistent). **NOTE:** You do not need to use both a peep sight and kisser button. Two references on the string is *redundant!*

Setting Peep Roll Over Nothing is more irritating than a peep sight that doesn't roll over in front of your eye correctly. There are some bow strings that don't twist when the bow is drawn, but they are rare. Most strings do twist somewhat when drawn and the peep must be aligned so you can see through it when at full draw. The best way to do this is to move one or two strands of the string from one side of the peep to the other until it rolls over correctly. Some would rather use a peep that

Bernie Pellerite

incorporates a piece of rubber tubing that attaches to your bow limb, or elsewhere, that pulls the peep into alignment each and every time. These seem to work well when newly set up. But invariably the tubing gets old and breaks off near the end. Plus, slow-motion film shows that the tubing *pulls the nocking point upward* upon release. This can become more erratic when the tubing gets old, stretches more when it gets hot, and stretches less when it's cold. It also pulls harder on the string (and therefore the nocking point) when it breaks off and you shorten it. This can cause the arrow to go low when the tube is shortened or the rubber is much colder than normal.

Set your peep up right (it may take two or three tries) and it will roll over correctly for you for the life of the string. If it doesn't, try using a string loop *(see page 62)*, which will align your peep consistently.

The size of the hole in the peep sight is determined by your own vision and the amount of light available. For bowhunting, shooting in the woods or for indoor tournaments where the amount of light is low, you may want to use a larger peep. Outside in bright sunlight, or at a well-lit indoor tournament, you will want to use a smaller one. Target shooters always want a large enough peep so, at anchor, they can *see* the body of their scope to make sure it is exactly centered in the peep each time.

Stabilizers The type and style of stabilizer you use can affect how steady you hold, how *quick* you *get steady*, and how much shock your bow arm and elbow will receive. Whatever size or type of stabilizer you use, you want the bow to be balanced in your hand and you want the top limb to roll forward *slowly*, after release. If it drops quickly, you will end up grabbing the bow eventually. Longer stabilizers will make the bow "stabilize" easier than a short one of the same weight. If you need a long stabilizer or one with a fair amount of weight at its tip, try using a *back* weight below the grip on the *"back* side" of the riser to balance this out. **NOTE:** In "official bow language," the *back weight* really goes on the *front* of the bow. Actually, the *back* of the bow faces the target because it's looked at it

Idiot Proof Archery

from the archer's perspective . . . yeah, they *were* inhaling! Stabilizers are supposed to absorb shock and noise, steady your sight picture by making the bow harder to move, balance the bow in your hand (front to back), **and** counterbalance the sight and cable guard so your bow sets in your hand relatively level (left to right). This keeps you from overholding and fighting the sight picture to get the bow level (a major cause of misses). The more mass weight that is added, the more the bow resists moving. If the bow jumps sideways or torques in your hand due to improperly balanced stabilizers, you may drop points you shouldn't. Have someone watch you or video tape you and see what happens to your bow as the shot goes off. The stabilizer (and everything attached to it) should jump straight toward the target. If the bow "kicks" in any other direction, first check your bow hand position (and release hand for plucking, punching, etc.), for possible bow hand torque and then check your bow's stabilizers for balance.

Make sure your stabilizer is also a good *shock absorber*. It can diminish accumulated shock that causes wear and tear on your bow arm, elbow, and/or shoulder that cause aching and shaking later in the day. It also keeps things from vibrating loose on your bow. I've recently invented a new patent-pending, "shooter controlled" stabilizer/dampening system called **Bernie's "Control Freak™" Custom Stabilizer**. It has joinable 1" diameter aluminum sections of different weights and lengths (4", 5 ½", 10" and 22") with **screw-off caps** so, for the first time ever, the shooter can add, subtract or move around

"Jel-lubber"™ Modules and Patties

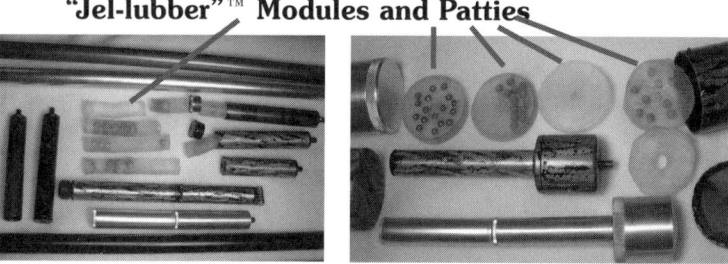

Bernie's ShockBlockin-NoiseTrappin-Flubberized-HoldinSteadylizers . Weighted "Jel-lubber" modules/patties absorb vibration (see Appendix).

Bernie Pellerite

the internal contents for a truly *customized system*. Inside the 1" tubing are "molded Jello®-like-rubber" modules (some with weights inside and some without), made from a secret processed elastomer I call "Jel-lubber™" that is extremely soft like Jello®, that can be moved around . . . front to back, back to middle, etc., for that *custom feel*. These anodized tubes can be joined to make any length stabilizer up to 36", and from 4 ounces to 30 ounces in weight. Also available is a variety of "shock blocking" canister-type stabilizer/back weights (see photo on pg. 79). These 2 ¼" to 2 ¾" diameter *"cans"* have screw-off tops and will accept a 1" diameter *"Control Freak™" Stabilizer* (or any stabilizer for that matter). They also have weighted "Jel-lubber™" patties that can be adjusted for custom weight distribution. The entire *Control Freak*™ line comes in various colors including camo. We also have available quick disconnects (both straight and with a 10 degree drop), offset brackets, and stackable stainless steel end weights. (See Appendix.)

Bow sling can help you shoot consistently!

Bow Slings Many people set them too loose or too tight. Too tight will cause the bow to torque . . . too loose and you may not trust them to do their job and you will end up grabbing the bow after each shot. You know the pattern, you *shoot-grab, shoot-grab, shoot-grab* . . . then *grab-shoot!* "D'oh! I *missed!* You should have a maximum of ¾" of slack (looser for hunting).

Armguards If the string slaps your wrist, even on the "rebound" after the arrow's gone, your mind will cause you to do all kinds of weird things "subconsciously" to avoid the pain. You don't need another distraction! Several top pros wear an armguard . . . if you need one, wear one — don't be macho!

I could go on for 150 more pages about tuning, bow setup, and what's possible to do or try with different setups, strings, arrows, bows, rests, etc., but that's not what this book is about. For more on the subject, there are several books and videos on tuning and setup, especially from Larry Wise *(see Appendix)*.

Idiot Proof Archery

Chapter 5

How the Pros Do It
Part One — Aiming

⋯e that in reading the previous chapters I have ⋯ you that the reason you miss is *probably not your bow* and *probably not your tuning* or any other aspect of your equipment. Much of what you could have learned about archery by reading and talking to other archers has had to do with tuning and setup. Correct those equipment problems (real or imagined) and you will be ready to move on.

I have made a fairly comprehensive study of professional and champion archers and how they shoot. We can learn a lot from what they do. Out of all of the categories in archery, the majority of bowhunters, 3-D, and target archers are beginner, intermediate and semi-advanced shooters (nearly 90%). A second group, probably less than 10% of the total, would be classified as advanced and less than 1% (no more than 100 in any category) are registered professionals. If you surveyed a lot of the first group (which I have) about how much sight movement they see through their peep, you might be amazed. Most will tell you that, ". . . my sight moves around fairly rapidly, in and out of the bullseye or kill zone." Some will say, ". . . it shakes violently," and still others say, ". . . it hops up and down, staying on the target about 50% of the time." Some try to make it form a "figure eight" and shoot when it crosses the middle. There are a lot of variations, but they all have a few things in common. First, they move fairly rapidly and continuously in, out, and around the spot where they are aiming. Second, in general, the longer they hold the worse the picture gets. Third,

Bernie Pellerite

the amount of movement can change from week to week, day to day, or shot to shot. This usually depends on how often they practice per week, how long per session they practice, and/or how much importance they place on this or that arrow. For example, "This shot is at a 10 point buck," or "This is the last arrow in a money tournament." Fourth, most think it's perfectly natural to consciously trigger the release or let go with the fingers at the instant the pin or dot intersects the X on the paper or the kill zone on the animal. Below the advanced level, it is sort of a "timing thing" or "drive-by shooting" for most of them.

This is not the case for the pros. So what's the secret that allows them to hold steady, aim and release consistently unlike the rest of us? In the next few chapters, we'll analyze their key attributes, techniques, and practice regimens like: personality, discipline, shot sequence, shooting form, focus, trust, programming, concentration, anticipation, release/let-go systems, target panic, aiming, the conscious and subconscious mind, and how they all relate to top level archery competition. I will *repeat* critical components that affect certain fundamental principles *several times*. Not only in the hope that *the repetition will ultimately help you understand and absorb them, but also because a lot of these subjects are multilevel and intertwined with other subjects!*

Personality

As I've already mentioned in chapter 2, personality type can dictate much of a shooter's success or failure, and most great shooters are not very analytical and tend not to be "Type A" (control-type) personalities, nor are they risk takers. To refresh your memory, the four main personalities we discuss are: 1) The Type A *(control freak);* 2) Type B *(focused);* 3) Intuitive/ creative *(risk-taker);* and 4) The analytical *(over-thinker).* All of us are a composite of two or more of these, one of which is our dominant trait. The first and last two personality types are *naturally disinclined to repetitiveness* and to the *disciplined sports* like archery. In short, doing it exactly the same way all the time . . . *is against their nature (counter-intuitive)!*

Idiot Proof Archery

Over the years, I've found that the majority of archers (that are not national champions) fall into the same three categories . . . 1, 3, or 4 . . . very few fall into the 2nd (Type B's). Most of us are unable to focus at full draw on one thing for more than a split second and, of course, *that ability is required* in top level archery. Our minds wander back and forth from keeping the sight on target, to parts of our shooting form (usually the finger on the trigger, etc.), both of which we are trying to control simultaneously. If you are this type of shooter, it doesn't mean you can't succeed . . . you just have to work harder! On the other hand, the champions are able to narrow that focus to just one thing . . . aiming, and their minds naturally don't tend to wander. They *trust* their form, their bow, and their release method. They don't analyze or control. These great shooters are in the smallest minority.

Role Models

Most of us cannot do easily what the champions can do. They have focused, *ordered minds*, and are calm cool and collected, usually introverted, and are not terribly interested in, or concerned about what happened on the *last shot*, or even in what might happen on any *future shots*. They are only concerned about the *process* of the *present shot, not the end result*. Therefore, they have no problem doing multiple tasks subconsciously without trying to control any one of them thereby, *changing them*. On the other hand, most of us are "goal-oriented" people, who are *naturally preoccupied* with controlling where, when, and how the arrow *is about to go*.

Defining Archery

Once we've come to grips with the influence our personality has, then we can start to tackle the rest of the obstacles. First of all, it's very important to remember, as I said, that archery is not a sport . . . *it is a discipline.* Disciplines require single-mindedness

Key Point #28

It's very important to understand that archery is not a sport . . . it is a discipline.

Bernie Pellerite

and complete concentration and focus. In baseball, football, or basketball, you can always modify your behavior slightly (running, tackling, dribbling, throwing, catching) and still have a successful outcome. In a discipline like archery, however, even a slight modification works against you. For instance, most archers try to "make this shot a little better than the last," or "put a little more hand in it," or "use a little more back tension this time," or "push or pull a little harder," etc. To quote Larry Wise, "Tournament archery is a two-step process. Step #1: Shoot it in the middle. Step #2: Repeat step #1." Whatever kind of form you have, be it conventional or nonconformist, it should be *duplicated exactly* from shot to shot. Most top professional coaches agree that the hardest thing to do in any "sport" is to duplicate something exactly, over and over again. Some archery forms are more easily repeatable than others (that's what **Idiot Proof Archery** really is . . . the *easiest to repeat!).* But basically, an archer with terrible (but consistent) form and an untuned bow who aims with 100% concentration will always prevail over the archer that has perfect form and perfectly tuned equipment, but can *only concentrate 50% of the time while trying* to aim. The ultimate scenario, of course, is the archer that has perfect form, matched equipment, and is immersed in, and focused on, aiming 100%!

Aiming — What It Is and What It Is Not

What is aiming? Most archers have false impressions of what aiming is and the things they need to understand to be able to aim. So, to clarify this, here are three basic fundamental principles:

Principle #1: Aiming is not physical . . . it is mental! *It's what your mind sees!* . . . not what your eyes see!
Principle #2: Anything that is repetitively done consciously carries a penalty . . . *anticipation!* Anticipation causes us to change the discipline (our shot sequence) from shot to shot. In short, as we start anticipating the release, we judge . . . analyze . . . change . . . lose trust . . . fear missing

Idiot Proof Archery

. . . start freezing . . . or punching, etc. . . . then buy this book . . . or buy a fishing pole!

Principle #3: Anything that is done *subconsciously* carries no penalty and cannot be anticipated. However, if we have "bad" form, like a rolled shoulder or an unorthodox grip and it is done subconsciously, then it will *usually* be done the same way each time. For example, they say we all blink our eyes about 20,000 times a day. We do it the same way because we do it subconsciously. We don't have to think about blinking and if we do . . . we start doing it differently every time . . . try it *now* and see!

Key Point #29

Aiming is not physical . . . it it mental! It's what your mind sees . . . not what your eyes see!

Things that are repeatedly done consciously are judged, then analyzed and then usually changed by the controlling or analytical-type shooter. Physically, we are trying to hold the bow sight in the *exact center* of the bullseye and, *at the same time*, operate the "let-go" system . . . both *directly controlled* by the conscious mind (that can only think about one thing at a time). However, we won't accept *any help* from the subconscious mind that can do a thousand things *simultaneously* . . . but now, we *don't trust it!*

In general, the way we go about archery is *contrary* to any other sport. For instance, in pitching a baseball, when we throw a ball to the catcher, we don't focus on the ball, we focus on the catcher's mitt. We don't pay attention (consciously) to how we let go of the ball or how the fingers come off the ball. Once we have consciously gripped the ball, we trust that the grip is okay and our concentration is then focused on where the ball is going, not on the ball itself, or how the fingers come off of it or how the wrist snaps, i.e. the "let-go" system. The same goes for the basketball free throw. Once we're ready to shoot, we don't alter or analyze the grip or "let-go" system. We simply focus on where we want the ball to go, and shoot it . . . subconsciously.

Bernie Pellerite

In archery, however, we do it differently. I've asked many archers, "What do you do at full draw?" The reply is usually, "I aim, and then I increase the pressure on the trigger." Believe it or not . . . *this is the problem.* We shouldn't aim and then put more pressure on the trigger. What we *should do* sounds complicated and confusing at first, but I will cover it many more times by the end of the book so you can understand it. At full draw, after we align our *eye* and front sight in the middle of the peep, we *calibrate* the bow sight *physically*, in the *approximate center* of the target. It doesn't have to be *exactly* in the middle of the X, just close. *Calibration is not aiming!* At this point, there should be no concern for where the arrow is going. Aiming is *complete concentration* and *mental concern* for where the arrow is going. Therefore, we are not yet aiming. Aiming is done without any flashing thoughts or interruptions of focus, on how the finger is on the trigger, or where the shoulder is or where the elbow is. These thoughts should have already taken place previously. (Two possible exceptions to this are Type B personalities, which seem to be able to do it any way they choose. The other is shooters who have shot pistols or rifles *extensively* and who have become acclimated or who naturally prefer focusing on the sight instead of the target.) Once at anchor (with both the aperture on target, centered in the peep, and the finger on the trigger, etc.), we must then *commit to the conclusion* of the shot . . . or let down. Committing will trigger you to *start* your individual method that *eventually causes* "let-go" (for example, back tension) that *begins activating* your release mechanism or starts relaxing your fingers off the string . . . with the *anticipation* of *going past followthrough . . . to conclusion!* An example of conclusion would be touching your draw shoulder with your release hand.

Your particular release method (or "let-go" system) is what we call *the motor.* Once you have (consciously) *started* your "motor" and the process of the release system *has begun*, it

Key Point #30

Aiming is complete concentration and mental concern for where the arrow is going!

Idiot Proof Archery

should normally take between three to five seconds for the release to happen (if you have a properly trained, *subconscious* motor). The instant the motor has started, you now *must trust* that it will cause release in three to five seconds and then focus your concentration completely and totally on the *center-of-the-center* of the target. Mentally, pick out a molecule in the *middle of the X* to concentrate on and your pin/sight ring/dot *will go there automatically. (Don't try to keep it there.)* It's called a *self-centering subconscious* (more about this later)! This is the real secret of aiming (for all but Type B's). Don't worry if your aperture moves around a little . . . that's normal. At this point, you cannot think or *"look back" mentally* to see if the motor is still running, try to assist it, speed it up, or analyze how or when it will cause release. If you do, you'll lose the sight picture, i.e. pin or aperture on target! Your *mind* is the only thing that *keeps* it on target . . . not your eyes! This is where most archer's troubles begin. You must learn to trust that the release will happen (not consciously *cause* it

*Can you see the molecules in the middle of this X . . . look hard . . . you're not looking hard enough . . . can you see it . . . can you see it in your mind? No, . . . you're looking at the one next to the one in the middle . . . that's right . . . that one right **there!** Now, that's how **hard** you aim!*

to happen). You must get the motor to run on the subconscious or automatic level. This is achieved by practicing it *off target* extensively (usually 2,000 - 3,000 shots) on an empty bale, or with one of the two patented, laser-equipped training devices that I developed **Bernie's PanicMaster and Bow Simulator** *or* **Bernie's Laz-Air Shot Trainer** *(see illustration pg. 88 and in the Appendix).* The first can be set to simulate your bow's mass weight, holding weight, and draw length. The **Laz-Air** is a pneumatic tube with an arrow/piston that attaches to your bow, without removing your arrow rest, enabling you to dry fire your bow without damage. Both simulate arrow impact with the laser dot and help deprogram target panic and help program back tension, aiming, and other critical areas of your shot.

Bernie Pellerite

Bernie's Laz-Air Shot Trainer attaches to your bow without removing your arrow rest. A switch in front of the tube turns on the laser which projects a dot on the intended target. As the arrow/piston is drawn and fired inside the tube, the air pressure turns off the laser dot which shows the archer the simulated arrow impact had he been shooting an actual arrow. (See Appendix.)

Bernie's PanicMaster BowSimulator has adjustable draw lengths and an internal spring that simulates the holding weight of the bow. It has an adjustable draw length from 24"-32", a mass weight container, and is drilled and tapped for stabilizers and your sight bar. Adapter for finger shooters is optional. As the archer reaches anchor, the built-in laser comes on and projects a red dot on the intended target. Upon release, the laser light goes off which again shows the simulated arrow impact.

Trust Your Program

In the Shooter's School, I demonstrate how "motor programming" works. I tell a student to walk over and open the door. As he reaches for the door knob, I yell "stop" and I say, "How did you get there?" The reply is always, "I walked." I then ask him, "Did you think about putting one foot in front of the other?" The answer is always no. I then ask him what he was thinking about when he was walking. He usually says, "The door knob." Your conscious mind says, "walk," and your subconscious program, or motor, for walking takes over in a millisecond. Then, all your conscious mind has to do is think

Idiot Proof Archery

about where it's going . . . in this case, to the door handle on the door, which is the "target." We therefore must trust that our subconscious program for walking will take us across the room without guidance, outside assistance, or influence of the conscious mind. The archery shot is no different. The conscious mind says, "start the motor" (i.e. start squeezing or pulling), and the subconscious program for releasing the bow string takes over (just like walking). Then, all the conscious mind has to do is think about where it wants the arrow to go . . . *aiming!* You must

Dave Hryn of West Seneca, NY. Since he went to the shooter's school he won the Atlantic City Archery Classic and the NFAA Outdoor Nationals twice. In IFAA, Dave has won 5 times and set a world record for the Field Round (FSL), co-holds the Hunter Round record and has the Animal Round record, a perfect 560. Dave says, "Bernie's shooters school and personal instruction helped me put together the pieces of my physical and mental shot sequence." Dave also credits the video tapes from Robinhood Videos and Bernie's PanicMaster and Bow Simulator which he used to reprogram that information.

trust that the motor will carry out its assigned task without consciously thinking about it, just like not having to think about walking.

Pressure and Consequences

When there's no penalty involved or no price to pay if the shot is missed, such as in practice, we may be able to successfully aim consciously and run the rest of the shot subconsciously. However, as the shot becomes worth more, or there are consequences if we miss, such as shooting in a competition or breaking a personal scoring record, we normally find it hard to trust the program to run on its own. We have an *overwhelming impulse* to monitor what's going on (analyticals) and to make sure everything gets done exactly right (controllers) because there

Bernie Pellerite

is so much at stake. Consequently, the following mental scenario usually takes place: "OK. Get the sight pin on the target. Now, jump back (mentally) and start to squeeze the trigger. Oops! I've lost the pin . . . so wrestle the pin back to the center. Hey . . . I stopped squeezing. I better get that started again . . . uh-oh, the pin drifted off again. Oh hell, the next time it gets close to the X, just punch it!" Recognize this? It is typical, because we don't understand the process.

Eyes Versus The Mind

The process is simple — *calibrate* first, then *start the motor. Immediately immerse into aiming until the arrow has cleared the bow.* Sounds simple . . . and it is, to most Type B's that don't have an analytical, risk-taker, or controlling bone in their body! But, for the rest of us, it's a lot harder. Our biggest mistake is not taking into account our personality traits, and the order or sequence of the process to this discipline we call archery. Most of us think that *visually aligning the sight* on the target is aiming. Again, the real secret is . . . the eyes can put the pin in the center of the target (calibration), but *they can't keep it there!* The conscious mind is the *only thing that can keep it there (aiming)!* What the mind sees and is concerned with will always override the "cameras in our heads" that we call eyes. For instance, if you hear or read the words "hot dog" or "play baseball," what you see in your mind is a *hot dog* or *someone playing baseball* for that split second. Even though your eyes are looking at this page, you see those pictures or images. The same thing happens at full draw . . . your eyes see the sight on the target, but when you want to shoot, your *mind overrides the eyes* and you see your finger on the trigger (in your mind's eye). That's why when your conscious mind finally gets back to the target, it discovers that you've *lost the pin*, because you were not concerned for that short moment with . . . the middle of the

Key Point #31

The process is simple — calibrate first, then start the motor. Immediately immerse into aiming until the arrow has cleared the bow.

Idiot Proof Archery

Key Point #32

middle. Instead, you were thinking about and were concerned with the *"let-go" system*. The eyes are only cameras and *cannot feel concern or desire!* Only the mind can do that. What a concept! Yeah, I know, it was difficult at first for me to wrap my hard Sicilian/Irish head around this notion, too. But, try as I might . . . I couldn't punch any holes in it! Trust me . . . it's absolutely *bulletproof!* Read on . . . it gets better!

The eyes can put the pin in the center of the target, but can't keep it there . . . the mind is the only thing that can keep it there!

Want a Perfect Sight Picture?

With the help of dozens of my students, that achieved "predictable accuracy," I have proven that Type A's and analyticals (like me) don't have to *be consumed* or *even concerned* with keeping a perfect sight picture, with a still pin in the middle . . . like a bench rest rifle sight picture. It's okay for it to move around a bit. This is called "natural arc of movement." This movement is perfectly natural and shouldn't concern us because we all have a *center-seeking mechanism* in our subconscious that runs the *hand to eye coordination program*. This system will continually move the bow arm, and therefore the sight, back toward the center (if we *concentrate consciously* on the center).

You can test this now, by making a circle with your index finger and thumb to simulate a sight. "Aim" at the clock or something (a target) . . . look at your hand (sight) . . . notice how much your "sight" is moving while you are *trying to keep* the target *in the exact center* of the circle you formed, for about five seconds. Now rest your arm for about twenty seconds and try it again. Except this time, after you have encircled the target, don't pay *any attention* to your sight . . . just focus on the *exact center* of the target and *talk to yourself while you do it* . . . find the center . . . focus on the center of the target . . . focus harder, etc., etc., for four seconds! Then, notice where the target is . . . *it's in the center of the circle you made!* It

Bernie Pellerite

happened without you having to consciously move your arm or hand to center it. The human brain prefers symmetry! Dozens of perfect scores (indoor 300/60X) have been reported to me by my students! I put some of them in this book. Unfortunately, I didn't have room for most of them. However, hundreds of them have reported winning 3-D or target tournaments and some have set national and world records using their *natural self-centering subconscious* to guide the sight! All they have to do is *stay "hooked up" mentally* to the *exact center* . . . and *trust* that the sight will always go *where you think* . . . not where you look! Therefore, if you *focus* and think about the *middle* . . . the arrow will go there! But, if you focus and think about the sight or pin . . . the arrow will go where the pin **is** when the shot goes off. So, for 95% of the personalities, it is *a lot easier* to focus on the exact center *(because **it doesn't move!!**)* than to focus on the pin, that dances all over the place! This movement causes us to *mentally chase the pin* and *forces* us to over-hold, overcontrol the sight and therefore, mentally melt down! That's why a lot of pretty good shooters don't do well in tournaments or *any time* when they say to themselves, . . . "I don't want to *miss* this one! I'd better be *careful!*" The fear of missing and the resulting anxiety causes their muscles to be charged with adrenaline and makes their sight move three times faster than it did in practice. This rapid movement is outside their *visual (and mental) comfort zone!* So, they fight the scope four to six seconds *longer than usual* (which violates their physical comfort zone), trying to get the pin to stop in the middle. Because they held too long, they start to lose back tension and consequently, try to compensate and then push harder with the bow arm to keep from collapsing. When the shot finally goes off (because the left shoulder was pre-loaded, at that point) . . . they miss to the left (for right-handers)! Another common scenario is when the pin drops down below the center and they mentally follow it down to 6 o'clock low, below the spot. Because they are thinking and focusing *on the pin* at 6 o'clock low . . . they *freeze there!* Ask yourself this question, "Why would the sight move back up into the

Idiot Proof Archery

center, on its own, if you're thinking about *the pin*, at 6 o'clock low?" Your *hand-eye coordination* is tied directly to your conscious mind! Wherever you concentrate and focus on mentally . . . is where the bow arm and sight will point . . . and the arrow will go! It works the same with a baseball pitch, a skeet shot, a dart throw, a football pass, a boxing punch, a basketball shot,

Think of the money I could make selling Type B Pills!

etc. Thus, for the great majority of shooters, focusing on where you want the projectile to go will give you the best results! This method works best in nearly all sports for most all personality types. However, I found that Type B's can use most any system. In archery for example, they seem to be able to focus on the pin or the target, or go back and forth without analyzing, mistrusting or overcontrolling the sight picture. I wish I could bottle that! Hmmm . . . Type B pills or maybe Ragsdale Pills or Ulmer Pills! Hmmm!

So, unless we finally realize there's really no other way for us to succeed (except to subconsciously execute while we consciously aim), most of us "focally challenged" shooters will continue to bounce mentally back and forth from aperture or pin to the motor system, until we *cause* the explosion of the shot. Then, anticipation and fear of missing will (eventually) take hold of us and we all know where that ends . . . buying a fishing license! Understanding the *complete process* is usually very challenging but also enlightening for most. It has changed hundreds of Type A's and analyticals' perspectives, and they have gone on to improve by leaps and bounds, winning or at least posing a threat to win many of their tournaments! In the **Shooter's School Master Series** videos, you can find more in-depth discussion on this subject in **Mental Keys That Unlock Target Panic, Part 1 and 2**, by Len Cardinale, and **Target Panic and a Discipline Called Archery** by yours truly *(see Appendix)*.

Bernie Pellerite

The Surprise Release

Because the subconscious mind is handling the release of the arrow while you are consciously aiming, the release comes as a "surprise" to your conscious mind. Many of my students are so surprised when they finally achieve a subconscious release that they almost drop their bows. Here are several methods that we use to make sure that the conscious mind is totally plugged up to aiming, while the shot is happening subconsciously and "takes the conscious mind by surprise." This is the *only way for most* to achieve greatness or even competitiveness in upper level tournament archery.

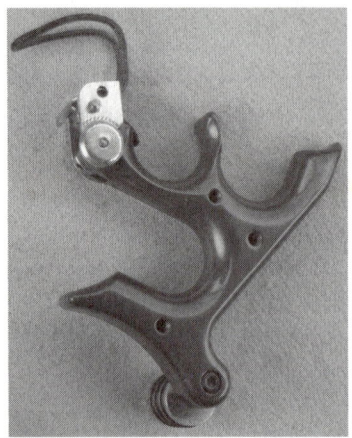

Bernie's E-Z Back Release™

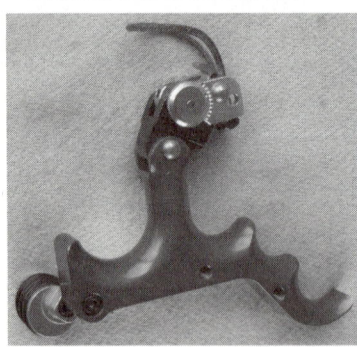

Bernie's Missing Link Release™

Any back tension triggerless release, like the Stanislawski, Zenith, or Carter, was designed for you to rotate the handle with back tension. I have come out with two new and improved versions of this type release. They are much easier and safer to pull back because you can use all of your fingers on the handle to reach full draw instead of pulling with just the index finger and thumb like the others *(see Appendix)*. But, like the rest, the handle is rotated by using back tension while the mind (not knowing or anticipating when the release will happen), consciously aims until the release fires (more later).

The **Bernie's Can't Punch**™ by Scott is an index finger, wrist strap, caliper release that has two triggers *(see Appendix)*. One stationary trigger keeps you from punching, while the other

Idiot Proof Archery

trigger is set off by aiming and pulling, using your back muscles, until the release happens (more on this later).

Shooting a Clicker

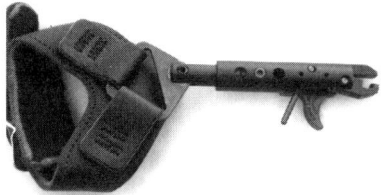

Bernie's Can't Punch Release™

As a last resort, a clicker attached to the bow (for finger shooters) can, with enough practice, subconsciously trigger the "let-go." A clicker is a thin piece of spring steel (4" - 6" long) attached to the riser several inches above the rest. The arrow is loaded underneath the strip of steel. As the archer comes to full draw, the arrow tip is slowly pulled out from under the clicker. It then snaps back against the riser making an audible click, hence, the word "clicker." There is some controversy as to whether or not the clicker was invented as a draw check for recurve archers or whether it was invented as a cure for freezing and snapshooting which were the most common symptoms of target panic at the time. In any case, the clicker (if used properly) will cause the shooter to be aiming when the clicker goes off. It will teach you to continuously pull and aim until the subconscious is signaled to "let-go" by the "click."

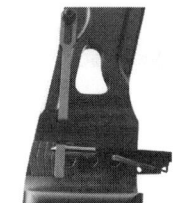

A clicker attached to the bow for finger shooters, subconsciously triggers the "let go."

*Riley Cox of Mt. Sidney, VA, is a 14 year old 3-D shooter who had target panic. His dad purchased a **Bernie's Can't Punch Release** for him. He placed 2nd at the 2nd Leg of the IBO Triple Crown at Erie, PA, and by the way, cleaned the course the first day with a perfect 200!*

Bernie Pellerite

The Bottom Line

Nearly all top shooters aim *consciously* and release the shot *subconsciously*. The "let-go" system is *only* started once the archer is ready and aligned on the target. Then aiming begins and continues through the explosion of the shot to a predetermined conclusion (*more on this later*).

Paul Cybart, Dunkirk, NY writes:

Dear Bernie,

My form of target panic was freezing. It surfaced when I changed from using pins to a scope for 3-D. This led me to get a back tension release. It's amazing how my affliction with freezing totally disappears when using it. However, at first I failed to have confidence in using it outdoors for 3-D, so I would go back to using a regular caliper release . . . and the freezing would resurface. The first time I used the back tension release, I liked it! The second time I used it . . . I shot my best score ever! Then I used it for the first time on a 3-D course at the North Coast Challenge Triple Crown in Conneaut, NY. My son shot the first arrow on target number one. It was a good one; binocular confirmation looked like it was an X (in the middle of the ten). So, I held on his arrow and released. It was a good one, too! When it hit, we heard what we thought was an arrow slap. When we got closer, it was more than that . . . it was a robinhood! Anyway, I used that new back tension release again at a local 3-D event and finished with a 288 out of 300.

The new release I bought was one of your **Bernie's Can't Punch** wrist strap caliper models. Be assured that I will be promoting and recommending this release.

Thanks, again,
Paul Cybart

Idiot Proof Archery

Chapter 6

How the Pros Do It
Part Two — Holding Steady

So, you have now heard that these pros aim consciously and release their shots subconsciously. Does that automatically equate to being steady? No, it doesn't; the pros have more to teach us. A veteran professional archer told me, ". . . you can only shoot as good as you can hold." That's not always true (I'll explain later) . . . but it does help!

Key Point #33

You can only shoot as good as you can hold . . . not always true . . . but it helps!

The Steps To Becoming Steady

Most advanced and pro shooters see a sight picture that is entirely different and is three to five times calmer than yours . . . they see a very slowly floating pin or dot that seldom leaves the aiming area (1¾" x-ring at 20 yards) or kill zone and, in some cases, nearly stops for two to three seconds. Ideally, most can hold it there for four to seven seconds without getting much worse, and in the best examples, it usually stays fairly steady day to day in practice or in tournaments. By now, you are probably asking yourself two questions . . . "What's the secret, and how come we haven't heard more about this?" The answer to the second question, I think, is threefold. First, as I have said before, most pros (with a few notable exceptions) are better shooters than teachers and the rest of them see no advantage

Bernie Pellerite

in educating the competition. Second, good coaches and teaching pro shops are not easy to find. Third, most sports writers are usually much better writers than coaches or shooters and don't know the answers themselves. To answer the first question, we need to look a little deeper into the cause of the problem. In my opinion, the primary reason that most people shake or can't hold their sight still is they are using *muscles* to try and hold it steady. To me, the words "using muscles" and "holding steady" in the same sentence is a contradiction in terms. As illustrated in one of our videos, **Winning Form** *(see Appendix)*, Randy Ulmer points out ". . . any time we recruit muscle fiber, there is tension, and tension causes movement." The more muscular involvement we have, the more movement we get. At this point, it is important to note that this muscular involvement, so prevalent in beginner through semi-advanced levels, can be traced to four primary problems not present at the top shooting levels:

 **Key Point #34**

"Any time we recruit muscle fiber, there is tension, and tension causes movement."

1. Incorrect draw length
2. Bad form
3. Too much draw weight
4. Not enough bow mass weight

Incorrect Draw Length

When we first tried to pull back a bow, most of us grabbed the riser or bow handle, pushed it out as far as our shoulder would allow and pulled with the other hand as hard as we could. We held it back somewhere around the corner of our mouth, or jaw, or in some cases, our ear. In most cases the ability level and qualifications of whoever helped us pick out and fit our first bow determined what kind of chance we had of learning correctly. If you had an advanced or professional archer or qualified coach with you, then you were extremely lucky. (Most of us

Idiot Proof Archery

had a buddy named, "Bubba.") If you were like me, you were fortunate enough to be advised by a burr-headed 17 year old who resembled the kid who played "Dueling Banjos" in the movie, **Deliverance**. He was recently promoted from stock clerk to manager of the sporting goods department at the local K-Mart. Unfortunately, most bows at K-Mart, Wal-Mart, mail order catalogs, and

A draw length that's too long will cause your sight to shake.

most so-called "pro shops" were (and sometimes still are) ordered in at 30 inches of draw, or more. Maybe it's because when you don't know what you are doing, it is easier to sell too long of a draw length than too short. This is sort of like the "one size fits all" concept. For example, if you *should* shoot a 28" or 29" draw like most people between 5'10" and 6' tall with normal proportions, and you are handed a 30" or 31" draw bow, there are several things you can do to make it "fit" . . . anchor farther back or use a high wrist grip or lean farther back or, easiest of all, extend the bow shoulder as far as you can. What does all of this do for us? It teaches us to extend or flex our muscles to pull and hold the bow (bad form!) and . . . you guessed it . . . causes our sight to shake!

It also promotes punching the trigger or plucking the string, in a futile attempt to control the instant, and thereby the impact point of the shot of the arrow. Because we flex or recruit muscles in the shoulder and arm (and in the case of high wrist grip, the back and front of the hand) when we draw a bow that's too long, all of these muscles are in a state of tension. This is the biggest reason for movement. The obvious solution is "if you want to stop shaking . . . stop flexing!"

Key Point #35

If you want to stop shaking ... stop flexing!

Bernie Pellerite

If you don't have your draw length close to being right yet, go back to chapter 3, find the "draw length formula," follow the directions and get your bow adjusted. There's not much else you can do until you get your draw length right.

Shooting Form

To improve your form, and therefore your chances to achieve predictable accuracy, shorten your draw until you have a relaxed bow hand, with the pressure on the heel of the hand or more precisely, at the base of the thumb directly in front of the wrist bones (see chapter 3). This eliminates any possible muscular involvement from the elbow forward and *puts the bow against bone*. Continuing with this guideline, relax the bow shoulder and keep a straight, but relaxed, elbow joint. As for the shoulder itself, it needs to be in the "down, back and relaxed" position. The level or height of the bow shoulder should be about the same as the other shoulder; not rolled forward and not held higher than the other shoulder. It should be relaxed and seated (locked) in the shoulder socket with the bow weight held by the bones of the skeletal system, not with tendons and muscles. This bone to bone form will eliminate most muscular involvement. Obviously, if the elbow is bent, not only do you have to recruit muscle to hold it in that position, but it is inconsistent also. Theoretically, if you could remove your arm at the shoulder joint and replace it with a 2" x 4" or solid wooden arm . . . now, how steady would your sight be? . . . As *steady as a rock* with *no bow hand torque (see Fig. A)!* If you have trouble finding the low-locked shoulder position, try opening your stance a little. Turn slightly toward the target, 15 to 30 degrees. The shoulder socket is *not* at the end of your shoulder. It faces slightly forward, otherwise you could swing your bow arm across your back as far as you could across your chest. As you can see in *Fig. B*, the front of the skeletal shoulder . . . is a ball joint and also notice the rear view *(Fig. C)* shows the scapula (shoulder blade) and the angle that the shoulder socket sets on the skeleton. Therefore, when you open your stance, that will also cause your arm to point slightly forward *(Fig. D)*, thus al-

Idiot Proof Archery

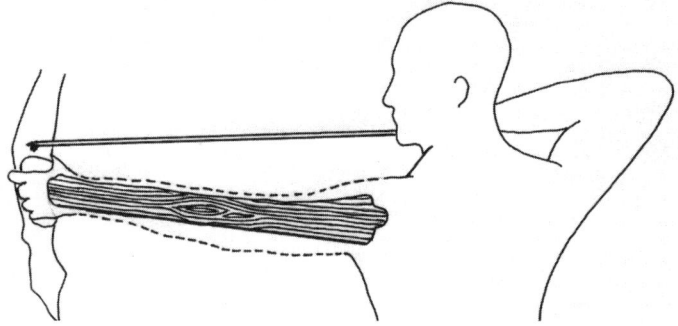

Figure A — Imagine how steady your sight would be if you could replace your bow arm with a 2" x 4"!

lowing the ball on the end of the humerus bone (upper arm bone) to relax down into the shoulder socket. Remember, your head should be centered over an erect but relaxed torso with your feet at shoulder width. Your aiming eye should be directly over your belt buckle. The tip of your draw elbow should be at least as high as your nose with the forearm above the line of the arrow *(see photo E, pg. 102)*.

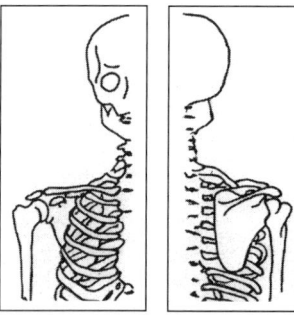

Fig. B - Front   Fig. C - Rear

If you are in doubt as to why you should adopt this shoulder position and an open stance as opposed to shooting with a closed stance (the feet on a line to the target and the shoulder

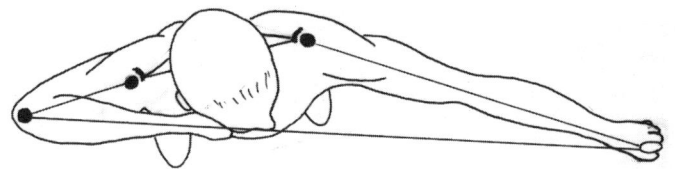

Fig. D — With a slightly open stance, the arm joint lines up naturally with the shoulder socket and the string is clear of the bow arm.

Bernie Pellerite

and bow arm on the same line) look at *Fig. F* with the arms angled to align with and drop into the shoulder sockets. Then look at *Fig. G* with both arms straight out to the side which are not in the middle of the shoulder ball socket. You can feel for yourself which one is the most relaxed with the least muscular involvement. Start out by imitating *Fig. F*. Simply raise your arms (not your shoulders) parallel with the ground to the position shown in *Fig. F*. Slowly rotate both arms out to your sides as in *Fig. G*. Notice that before you reach the position shown in *Fig. G*, you will feel a pulling sensation and tension in the top front of both shoulder muscles (deltoids) as the arms swing out of, and away from, *the natural shoulder socket.*

Fig. E

To achieve correct form, relax the bow shoulder and keep a straight, but relaxed, elbow joint. The shoulder itself needs to be in the "down, back but relaxed" position. The level or height of the bow shoulder should be about the same as the other shoulder; not rolled forward and not higher than the other shoulder. Your head should be centered over a relaxed torso with your feet separated about shoulder width. Your aiming eye should be directly over your belt buckle. The tip of your draw elbow should be at least as high as your nose with the forearm above the line of the arrow.

With this body position, the anchor is the only other factor that will vary. The anchor can be almost anywhere as long as it is solid, touches bone, involves multiple points of reference, and does not "float." For example, the string hand should be touching and locked into, under, or behind the jaw bone. Then, the eye centered in the peep sight and the string touching the nose (or the chin for recurve tournament archers who shoot long distances) can be two other points of reference. Some shooters add a kisser button to the string as a reference point (not necessary if you use

Idiot Proof Archery

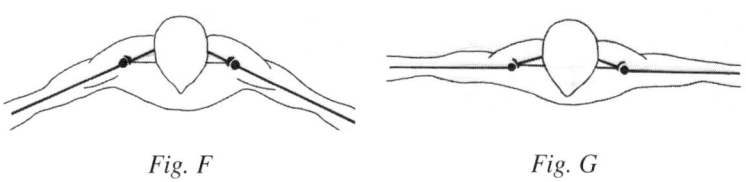

Fig. F   Fig. G

a peep sight). These should give you a good, solid anchor. With a straight, relaxed forearm, wrist, and elbow directly in line with the arrow, the only muscles we want to feel flexed are the rhomboids, between the shoulder blades, *on the draw side only (see pg. 44, diagram of muscles).* This relaxed form with "passive physical aiming," dictates that, "we move the trunk of the body up or down to change our point of aim," instead of recruiting muscle fibers in the arms and shoulders. If your draw length is too long, you will never be able to relax and stop shaking in such a stretched-out position. This is because of all those muscles you used to pull and hold the bow at full draw. Conversely, if the draw length is correct you *won't be able to stretch out,* and you can relax at full draw.

Draw Weight

The average shooter shoots ten to thirty pounds too much draw weight at full draw, "helping" them to have a shaky sight picture. In recent years, bows with high let-offs have claimed to change that somewhat, but because of their huge cam(s) and the fact that they stay at peak weight much longer through the draw cycle, they have *actually made it worse* for most archers. After muscling past the peak weight, they have all the wrong muscles completely flexed by the time they've gotten to full draw. They do not, and cannot, effectively relax those muscles at this point, thus causing their sight pictures to be extremely shaky.

Now that you understand about muscular involvement, it should be easy to grasp why most people don't have much of a chance trying to hold a 60 to 90 pound bow steady. Give yourself a chance to win! Crank it down to a reasonable poundage, something that your body can handle comfortably, *all day!* If,

Bernie Pellerite

 **Key Point #36**

The average shooter shoots ten to thirty pounds too much draw weight.

"Skying" the bow and drawing across the chest to get to full draw is a sign that the archer is pulling too much weight.

when you draw your bow, you have to hold your bow anywhere but on the target (pulling into your chest, *see photo*), grunt, or change the expression on your face, you are pulling too much weight.

Mass Weight of the Bow This brings us to another weight problem — mass weight of the bow. Most of the top shooters have discovered that adding heavier stabilizers, front and/or rear, helps a great deal in holding the bow steady. I've picked up several of their bows at major shoots and while doing their videos. Most weigh twice to three times as much as the standard 3-4 lb. factory bow. When I was shooting competitively, I shot a nine to ten pound bow for target and 3-D, and about an eight pound hunting bow. It helped steady my sight picture by at least 25%, especially when shooting in the wind. That's why I developed the first shooter-controlled variable internal weight modular stabilizer system *(see Appendix)*. Experts have known for years that target pistols and rifles with heavy frames and bull barrels hold much steadier than standard-issue weapons.

A word of **Caution** here. You can't change from a four pound bow to an eight pound bow overnight (yes, you do need to use *some muscles* . . . even with bone-to-bone form). You must build up your muscles, your endurance, and increase the amount of mass weight slowly, *or you will make things worse* and find your bow shoulder aching, your elbow quivering, and your sight

 **Key Point #37**

Adding mass to your bow helps a great deal in holding the bow steady.

Idiot Proof Archery

wanting to "drop out the bottom." Go slow! An inexpensive way to build your muscles is to use a milk jug *(see photo)*. One gallon of water weighs approximately eight pounds, so calculate how much water to add to make the jug weigh what your bow does . . . then add one cup (½ pound). Practice lifting and holding it 30-50 times per day. Add one cup once or twice a week until you have arrived at the total bow weight you want.

Practice lifting a jug of water to build up your muscles gradually.

The Mental Side of Holding Steady All of the above changes along with good muscle tone will add up to a much steadier sight picture, but it evolves into something even more important. This will calm your mind and give you confidence that you do not have to rush the execution or have to hold perfectly steady or wrestle the sight into the exact center of the target, for the arrow to go in the center (more on this later). There is no problem then, with concentrating on the center of the target and squeezing the back muscles until the release happens. At this level, your good days and your bad days are also much closer to being the same. When you haven't shot for some time, or are extremely tired, nervous, or anxious about a shot or series of shots, your sight picture *always gets worse*, regardless of which aiming method you use. The difference is that if your holding or aiming ability depends *entirely* on muscular involvement, underdeveloped, tired, nervous, or adrenaline-charged muscles will always cause a *shakier* sight picture. This more rapid movement of the sight increases anxiety, frustration, and panic in the shooter's mind. This moves the shooter's concentration from the target (where it should be) . . . to the pin or dot, then back to the trigger or fingers . . . then back to the target . . . and then the conscious mind tells you, . . . "Hurry up! I can't hold it much longer! I'm going to miss! Hit the trigger. SHOOT! . . . SHOOT! NOW!" Sound familiar?

Bernie Pellerite

Eye Dominance and Sight Picture Before trying to achieve your ideal sight picture you may want to determine your eye dominance. To check to see which eye is dominant, here's an easy way: have your buddy face you. Make a small circle with your hands. Extend your arms and put the circle around his face with both eyes open. Whichever one of your eyes he sees, is your dominant eye (see photo). There are several other ways, but this is the simplest.

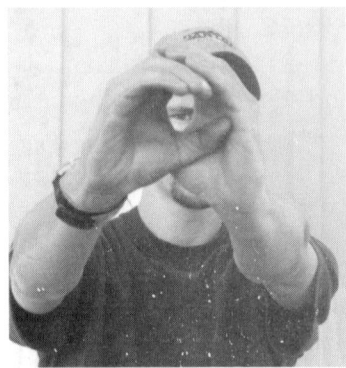

He is right-eye dominant.

Jan is left-eye dominant but shoots right-handed.

A lot of people think that they must shoot left or right-handed based on which eye dominance they have. I believe you should shoot a bow (left or right handed) based on whichever way feels *natural* for you! Here's an example; my wife Jan is a left-hander . . . writing, eating, playing other sports, etc. The first time I had her shoot a bow, we discovered she was more comfortable shooting a right-handed bow. (I thanked the Archery Gods right on the spot that I didn't have to buy left-handed equipment for her!) Think it might be due to eye dominance? Nope! She's left-eye dominant, so that's not it. And, because she is aiming with her non-dominant eye, she has to close her left (dominant) eye. Shooting with only one eye open is not a disadvantage. Some of the best shooters of our time shoot with one eye closed. Some people will tell you that you need to shoot with both eyes open. You can only do that *if your dominant eye is also the strongest*. As you begin to concentrate

Idiot Proof Archery

on the target, initially you will see two images . . . soon they will come together as one. This is called convergence. However, if you can't get convergence because, for example, you are right eye dominant, but your left eye is stronger (this is MY problem!), then close your left eye! The proponents of shooting with both eyes open will say that you get more light with both eyes open, therefore you can see the target better. This may be technically true, but I think it's very minimal, and sometimes that can be a disadvantage for analyticals and controllers because of *greater perceived movement*. You'll also hear that you can judge yardage better with both eyes open. Well, duh! How many people do you know walk up to the shooting stake and guess the yardage with one eye closed? (I estimate the yardage, *then draw the bow,* and *then* close my eye!) Bottom line: shoot whichever way is natural for you, close one eye if you have to, and don't worry about eye dominance.

Pursuing the Perfect Sight Picture Because many of us have shot a pistol or rifle, we assume that we should get the same, or nearly the same sight picture with a bow and arrow. However, *the pursuit of the perfectly steady "rifle-like" sight picture* is actually the *basis of most of our problems in archery!*

After many years of coaching and seeing over 1,600 laser sight pictures of my students, I have come to the inescapable conclusion that *nobody normal* can achieve a perfectly steady "rifle sight picture" using a "legal technique" for holding a bow.

Most shooters start out on the wrong foot by buying a 4X, 6X, or 8X scope so they can see much better . . . the spot . . . *that they can't stay in the middle of already!* Go figure! You see the "head games" we play with ourselves are a never ending, vicious circle. We buy a highly magnified scope so it magnifies our shaky sight picture, so we can freak out more . . . because we can't hold it perfectly still! Makes sense to me! I wasn't any smarter . . . I once invented a 14 power scope with a 3½" lens . . . that *really* calmed me down! If you're not into big scopes, chances are you've got the smallest pin or fiber optic known to man . . . so you can obsess over trying to keep it in the exact center! You see, *the smaller the pin or the higher the*

Bernie Pellerite

A scope with a circle will help some archers eliminate most "perceived movement."

magnification, the more **perceived movement** you will have. We just never learn, do we? That's why I finally figured out and now advocate that most personality types will do much better if they understand the stupid things that they are *predisposed to do*. Then, they can go buy a scope with a *circle in it*, a lower power scope or a big fat pin (less perceived movement) and improve immediately *(see photo)*. **Caution**: If you use a circle, make sure it doesn't line up *tight* around the bullseye. If so, you'll overcontrol and obsess about lining them up, too! Make sure there is plenty of room around the bullseye so the circle can float or bounce around *outside* the bullseye. For example, on the 20 yard, five-spot target, the circle should be about in the middle of the four ring. If you want to take it one step further, you might try a slightly blurry scope . . . this also *cuts down on perceived movement* and makes certain personality types calmer, because they are less aware of exactly what the sight is doing. For pin shooters of the same mentality, try "fatter pins," or set your pins up with the target *between* the first and second pins. This makes you less aware that the pin isn't in the exact center all the time and is less likely to cause a mental meltdown!

A shaky sight picture, caused by the above mistakes, creates the "head problem" that we must, above all things, have the sight in the *exact center* of the bullseye when the shot goes off (which is *absolutely not true* as I said in chapter 5) before we can get the arrow to go in the exact center. Consequently, since our sight picture is extremely unsteady and deteriorating rapidly, we figure we only have one or two more seconds at full draw before the sight picture gets completely out of control. Now we are trying to snapshoot or execute a "drive-by-shooting." We accomplish this by having the sight and the finger on the trigger or fingers coming off the string, timed in such a manner that, as the sight crosses the bullseye, we immediately send a conscious signal to the trigger finger that it's "hammer time" at that

Idiot Proof Archery

milisecond. This pitiful attempt at consciously aiming and consciously causing "let-go" (*two thoughts at one time*), takes form and fashion in four primary, but different symptoms — *flinching, freezing, snapshooting,* and *punching.* Some people can develop two or more symptoms and there are some variations. The punching scenario translates into *plucking* the string for finger shooters. Freezing can be subdivided into freezing outside of the center (and snapshooting while jerking it through the center), or freezing in the center (but being unable to shoot). Also, *tournament nerves* for competitive shooters and *buck fever* for hunters are opposite sides of the same "coin."

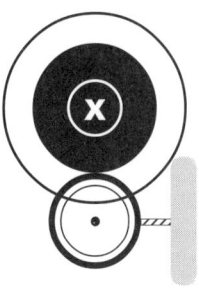

Freezing below the target

All of these have one thing in common; we will not allow our subconscious programming to take over and cause an automatic (or surprise) release . . . like sometimes happens in practice. Remember sometimes in practice, when you were really aiming hard with all of your conscious mind . . . it sometimes just went off by itself (so to speak) without conscious thought? This happened because the shot wasn't *all that important,* and/or there was *no pressure* to hit the middle and you were totally immersed in aiming, *which is the real formula for predictable accuracy.* Unfortunately, most of us won't allow this surprise release to happen too often, except when the value of the shot is not very high. When we start trying to do it "really well" for whatever reason, such as first or last arrow, or to beat "Bubba," or break our personal best, or to shoot five Xs in a row, or hundreds of other scenarios . . . we turn off the "auto-pilot" and go back to manual control. If we *really want this one*, we all of a sudden *don't trust* the "auto-pilot" to release the arrow. We think it might go off when the sight is *not in the exact center,* so we try and do the aiming and the release . . . at the same time! Hence, our self-destructive obsession with the perfect sight picture. That's when it all turns to crap and that's the beginning of the "fear of missing" programming scenario that we feed

Bernie Pellerite

ourselves until we are full blown panic patients looking for a way out!

Putting It All Together

In the next two chapters I am going to show you how you can put everything together and end up two to three times steadier (mentally and physically) than you were before. Then you can start being competitive, and often times, winning those shoots you used to go to . . . just "for fun!"

George Kong of Honolulu, HI, was one of Bernie's first students. He later organized and attended an NFAA Shooter's School. George has since won many state championships and regularly shoots 300 with 56-58 Xs. He is also a Certified NFAA Master Coach, operates his own pro shop and frequently coaches shooters in Hawaii.

Lonnie Collins of Westland, MI After attending the shooter's school, he has since won the NFAA State Outdoor, the Metropolitan Archery Assn. Male Freestyle Shooter of the Year, the Mid-States Marked 3-D in the freestyle class and finished 4th in the Canadian Indoor Nationals.

"Keep telling the truth in your own direct style. Good luck, may God bless you both and thanks for the support!"

Chapter 7

The Shot Sequence
A 12 Step Program, Part One— The Defense

A lot of us have discovered, and to some extent mastered, the physical side of the archery shot. But most of us haven't got a clue about how or why the subconscious, or "hidden side" is supposed to work. As with any profound discovery process, it usually involves endless hours of exploration, experimentation and analysis. And, because of the way we teach archery (or conversely *don't* teach archery in this country), most of the search for this "hidden side" has been made in the dark, without a light, a map, or a guide. So, in this chapter, that's precisely what I'll try to provide for you . . . a map of the shot sequence . . . a guide and a training method that will help you to understand and absorb the what and why of it, and a light to bring it out of the darkness.

In the Beginning . . .

After we've shot for a month or so, most of us have developed somewhat of a "shot sequence." Although these individual sequences vary in length, having usually from three to fifteen steps, they all have the same theme. At first we practice loading, gripping, drawing, anchoring, "aiming," and shooting the bow, all the *while evaluating our equipment and our performance based on hitting or missing the target.* Because we are humans and must always think, our training methods allow and even encourage us to anticipate the end of our effort which is, unfortunately for most, the millisecond of arrow release. We then *judge* what we've done and then *analyze* it, based on where

Bernie Pellerite

 **Key Point #38**

If we hit where we "aimed," we judge that we did it right. If we missed, we judge that we did it wrong. And, if we did it wrong, then we must analyze it and . . . change something.

 **Key Point #39**

Because we will never "always hit and never miss, . . . we are doomed to change something every time we miss."

the arrow landed; if we hit where we "aimed," we *judge* that we did it right. If we missed, we *judge* that we did it wrong. And, if we did it wrong, then we must *analyze it* and *change something* . . . hand placement, anchor, push more, pull more, adjust the arrow rest, try a different release, or even a new bow. This system of finding what's wrong and *trying to fix it* is never ending. In short, it's *shoot until we miss* . . . *then change something!* This "negative training" can only lead to total frustration, because we will never . . . "always hit and *never* miss," so *we are doomed to change something every time we miss!*

Because we dwell on discovering what's wrong while shooting at a target, instead of practicing what's right without a target, and because we "train" ourselves to anticipate the instant of "let-go," we frequently set up a self-destructive combination. This promotes a fear of missing, anxiety about winning, or *trying to think about two things at once ("on target" and "let-go").* Our problem lies with our target-based practice methods and shortsighted shot sequences. My friend, Len Cardinale, "turned on the lights" for me in this regard years ago when my wife and I produced his first videos, **Secrets of the Shot** and **Target Panic; Its Causes and Cures** (*see Appendix for Len's new videos*). All you need to do to succeed is fully understand and *modify your existing shot sequence,* and then change your practice methods.

The Basic Elements

As far as the shot sequence goes, here's the "blueprint" that Len Cardinale teaches for you to follow. Later I will give you my "blueprint" which is a "12-Step Program" (based on these 7 Steps) that I teach in the shooter's school, but for now it

Idiot Proof Archery

is important to see what those steps are trying to accomplish. Remember, you don't have to do it *my way or Joe Blow's way or do it right;* you just have to do it *the same way each time.* Your shot sequence may be shorter, longer, or more complicated, but basically it needs to contain these same *seven principles.* In the following example, the real differences between mediocre and excellent shooters should be apparent, especially in #4, #5, and #7. As usual, *I will repeat these principles many times throughout the book because a few of these concepts may be completely foreign or even counter intuitive (against your natural logic) and confusing to the uninitiated.*

1. *Stance or Posture* — weight distribution and total posture (body parts relative to other body parts)
2. *Finger Placement* — or release mechanism placement on the string
3. *Grip* — placement of the hand on the bow grip
4. *Anchors . . . At Least Two* — *Front and Rear* After full draw is reached, the rear anchor is on the face, just as you would expect, but there is a second or front anchor, which is the pin or dot placement on target (for sight shooters) . . . for instinctive shooters, it's "sight picture arranged." Remember, the front anchor (sight on target or picture arranged) *should not induce us to let go or shoot and it is not really aiming;* it is merely a front location piece of form. It is a second anchor and allows calibration or sight acquisition to occur, which is only a physical reference, like stance or finger placement. Aiming happens later.
5. *Position Attainment* — is the sum total of principles #1, 2, 3, and 4, organizing these to a "maintainable and stable state." As soon as we feel we can athletically *maintain* and *control* these principles through to #7 which is "conclusion" and our effort (the end of #6 Followthrough), *only then* do we "commit" to go ahead. After commit, we *consciously* start a "motor system" (our release technique) that *eventually* releases the arrow subconsciously. Aiming occurs *immediately after* the motor is started and eventually *"let-go"* happens, then followthrough, and finally *conclusion.*

Bernie Pellerite

We will analyze some of these concepts more in depth later. At the point of commit, if we don't feel everything is okay and controllable through #7, we should "let down" and start over. "Letting down" is another big difference between pretty good and exceptional shooters.

6. *Followthrough* — This is simply the action part of #5 through #7. This is the involuntary dynamic reaction of the body to the release of tension at the moment of execution. Most movement should be confined to the bow arm (straight forward) and/or the string hand/arm (straight back).
7. *Conclusion* — This is where we *end our followthrough* and *end our mental and physical effort*. There are three basic types of conclusions: *sight, sound,* and *touch*. There are many variations on each of them, *but they all must take longer to do than it takes for the nock end of the arrow to clear the front of the bow,* i.e., *touching* the draw shoulder after release, *seeing* the arrow hit the target, or *hear* the arrow hit the target. All of these happen after the arrow is gone and *we can no longer affect its flight*. Whichever you choose, it should be the one *you trust the most* and should be consistent shot to shot.

Touching the shoulder is one of the most popular types of conclusion.

Committing to the Conclusion of the Shot

Some of the concepts I mentioned earlier in #5 need further explanation. After #5 (Position Attainment) is accomplished, which means we have our anchors in place, sight on target, finger pressure on trigger, and think we can keep this position through the end of conclusion; *it should cause us to* **"commit to"** or **anticipate going to** the **conclusion** of the shot . . . **not** *to trigger the release or "let-go."* This is where it's easiest to separate the champions from the also-rans. The "commit" stage is where we decide to go ahead with the shot to

Idiot Proof Archery

its conclusion. This concept is confusing to a lot of shooters. Why not commit to shoot . . . "make the release happen," and end the shot with followthrough? That's what most people do (or try to do). The problem is, *if* commit or getting on target triggers us to shoot, we will eventually start to *anticipate* this process which ends with followthrough. Remember, we haven't established an end for the followthrough . . . *we follow through to where?* We really don't have a *conclusion* in our sequence. That's the biggest problem for most people. Whoever told you *competitive archery* was *easy* — go track them down and smack 'em upside their head with *this book!*

Anticipation

We will often end our followthrough prematurely because we can (and will!) anticipate *arrival on target* and/or "let-go." Followthrough then gets shorter and shorter until it is nonexistent and we are quitting at the end of "let-go!" Then, we eventually start anticipating "let-go" and end our effort *as the shot is going off . . . before the arrow is clear of the bow!* This leads to erratic shooting, confusion, anxiety and/or the worst scenario . . . target panic or buck fever. Imagine . . . all that grief over anticipation of the release!

So, how do we stop anticipation and therefore prevent its more serious eventualities? Unless we are a Type B (focused) personality . . . we usually can't. As I said before, because we are human . . . *we must think*, and if we repeat any conscious activity enough, we can and will anticipate any or all of its parts. Remember, *any repetition done consciously will be anticipated.* If it is anticipated, then Type A's, analyticals and risk takers, like you and me, will judge it and then analyze it. And, if it is judged and analyzed . . . it will be changed! And, if it's changed . . . even a little . . . how do we expect to hit in the same place over and over? On the other hand, anything done *subconsciously cannot be anticipated . . .* if you don't anticipate it, you won't judge, analyze and change it. If you don't *change it* because you *do it subconsciously,* that means you do it the *same every time.* If you do it the same every time, you can

Bernie Pellerite

compete with the pros . . . Wow, what a concept! Someone should write a book about this someday!

So, does that mean we will *eliminate anticipation?* No, most of us will *always anticipate* (our personality dictates that!), but that doesn't mean that it has to destroy our shot. We can *use anticipation,* instead of *it using us!* Our only hope to totally escape the negative effects of anticipation is to *redirect it* to a place, sound or act that happens *after* the arrow is gone from the bow. We simply *anticipate conclusion!* It sounds complicated, but it's not if you compare it to any other sport. For example, if a golf, tennis, or baseball player stopped their swing one foot past ball contact, can you imagine how erratic their results would be? Even though one foot past contact could be called following through, soon some of the swings would stop eight inches past, and then two inches past, and eventually at contact, or maybe during contact. Can you see the similarities to archery? If they didn't finish their swing every time, they would be in the same trouble we are, wouldn't they? Fortunately though, most of them are taught and practice at swinging all the way through to a set position . . . their "conclusion."

> ⊙ **Key Point #40**
>
> *Most of us will always anticipate . . . our personality dictates that! But that doesn't mean it has to destroy our shot. We can use anticipation, instead of it using us!*

So the secret for us is . . . by ending our physical and mental effort at any one of the sight, sound, or touch conclusions, we change "negative anticipation" of the release to "positive anticipation" of the conclusion. For example, it's okay to anticipate touching your shoulder after the release of the arrow. That anticipation won't affect the release or execution because we've trained ourselves not to end our effort (i.e. quit pulling) until we touch our shoulder and therefore, the arrow has cleared the bow (#7 Conclusion).

> ⊙ **Key Point #41**
>
> *We can change "negative anticipation" of the release to "positive anticipation" of the conclusion. For example, it's okay to anticipate touching your shoulder after the release of the arrow.*

Idiot Proof Archery

Commit and Motors

In further analyzing "commit," it should cause us to . . . *consciously start*, but *subconsciously finish* one of the techniques or mechanisms that we will call "motors." This is how we get from #5 to #7. There are three kinds of motors that people can use: *pullers* start to pull (usually via back tension) while the bow arm maintains (most winning archers nowadays have adopted this technique). *Pushers* are the people whose bow arm pushes while the string side maintains (hardly any use this method now). *Equalizers* or *push-pullers* are those who push with the bow side and pull with the string side (a few good shooters use this technique). Which one you use, depends on which one you trust the most, can duplicate the easiest, and are the most comfortable with. Once one of these is engaged, they will work by themselves without conscious thought, that is, if you *trained them to do this*. I will tell you how this is done a little later.

*Golfers are taught to swing **past ball contact** on their way to conclusion.*

Aiming Moment

As soon as the "motor" is activated (i.e. back tension is started), you now mentally immerse into the *aiming moment*. This is the most important part of "excellent archery." True aiming (mental aiming), is *total concentration* and *concern* for where the arrow is going . . . not thinking about shooting ("let-go"), moving/controlling the sight or push-pull, etc. *These all should happen subconsciously.* At the mental aiming stage, *all conscious thought and focus is directed toward the center of the target.* If you are a Type B, the center of the target **or** the pin **or** aiming dot works . . . Type B's seem to be able focus on either. If you're not a Type B, your mind should be flooded with the image of the center of the target and the sound of your inner voice, *reciting a mantra.* For example, "Aim . . . find the *center* . . . find the *center of the center* . . . aim *harder* . . .

Bernie Pellerite

Your conscious mind should be flooded with the picture of the center of the target and the sound of your inner voice talking you through the aiming process.

focus on the exact center . . ." Any anticipation that you had is *gone* by now because anticipation was *directed toward* and **ended with** thoughts of *"how much* you powered up or got ready to go" . . . *to conclusion*. For example, if you had to jump across a six foot mud puddle on a sidewalk, you would have to get ready for that jump. Therefore, you'd set your muscles to get ready to run and jump six feet . . . you would anticipate clearing six feet! In this example, how much you got ready or powered up for . . . **is your anticipation**, as opposed to the amount of anticipation you would have for jumping two feet! You would have a different amount of anticipation, depending on how far you wanted to go. However, once you started to run to make that jump, all that anticipation *is now gone*. The only thought in your mind is . . . *the dry land* on the other side of the mud puddle (your target). Anticipation for archers is, for example: *how hard* and *how long* are we *going to contract* our back muscles . . . in order to get our hand to *fly all the way back* and *touch* our shoulder. "Touch shoulder" . . . is what we *anticipated*, *not the release or trigger*. The release process/four second motor was started *before* aiming (like lighting a fuse) and is *allowed* to happen here, but is not consciously *thought of* (anticipated) or *caused to happen here!* You just *commit* . . . light the fuse (*start* the motor) . . . *aim 100% until conclusion* . . . *trust* that the fuse will burn on its own (the four second motor *will cause "let-go"*) . . . and followthrough - *until conclusion!*

The Equation For Success

So, if you have *followed this chain reaction so far* (I'll go over it many times later), we should train ourselves to organize

Idiot Proof Archery

our shot (#1, 2, 3, 4) to a maintainable position (#5), through followthrough (#6), to a preset conclusion (#7) while we allow our form and our equipment to function (also #5) without conscious thought . . . while we totally immerse (consciously) into aiming. The "kicker" here is that these principles can't be fully appreciated or absorbed while practicing on a target.

How to Practice "Excellence" You can't aim and think about your release, bow arm, sight, etc., *at the same time*, but most of us try, don't we? There are a few "practice secrets" to excellent archery! The first is the "empty target bale." Here's how it's done . . . take your "new" shot sequence 3-5 yds. in front of any backstop at shoulder height, that will catch 5 or 6 (scattered) arrows safely. Practice parts of your shot sequence with your ego "unplugged," scattering your arrows . . . no target, no aiming, not caring where your arrows go! Do this, *at first,* by closing your eyes at anchor, through the completion of the shot. You can *absorb the new feeling* this way. Then, open your eyes as you practice and you will make astounding improvements . . . if you can handle the mental boredom. That's why I invented the **Laz-Air Shot Trainer** and the **PanicMaster**

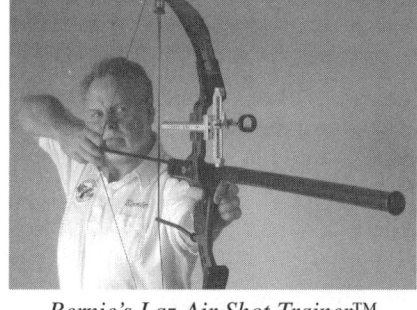

Bernie's Laz-Air Shot Trainer™

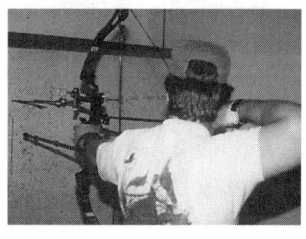

Empty bale shooting

Bernie's PanicMaster and Bow Simulator

Bernie Pellerite

*and **Bow Simulator*** which is much easier because the laser dot gives you the mental reward of where the shot would have hit without the panic of missing the target with an actual arrow *(see photo pg. 119)*. You can concentrate on, pick apart, and analyze any aspect of the shot, one at a time, and absorb the "feeling" of what a good shot feels like. With shot repetition (sometimes a few hundred or, for some, two to three thousand), you can build or replace any part of your form you wish, *to a subconscious level*, through programming "muscle memory." Once on the empty bale, **PanicMaster/Bow Simulator**, or **Laz-Air Shot Trainer** you are also free to experiment or change things. As long as your "change" is trained to the subconscious level *(ground in through repetition*, until it's *automatic!)* before you go back to a target, your practice will still be productive.

Remember, the purpose of all of this is to *free us consciously so we can be immersed totally in aiming* (which is all we wanted to do in the first place) while our shot sequence *works independently and subconsciously.* (I know I said all this before, but without *lots of repetition*, this whole chain reaction, *cause and effect concept* usually confuses or escapes most students or readers.) This concept is the real "secret of the pros," and the heck of it is that I don't know any pro that can explain this concept to you, me or anyone else (even though they can do it better than any of us). To quote Babe Ruth, when a reporter asked what he thought about when he was at bat, he said, "Hell, if I had to *think*, I'd never hit the ball!" Get the point?

The 12 Step Program

Good shooting form (or any discipline) is built around the principle of a sequence. Shot execution is something that is supposed to happen automatically while you mentally do only one thing — aim! So, how do you build your form and get your subconscious mind to do what you want automatically? Just like many other programs, that reformat and change addictions or bad habits into good ones . . . I have a 12 Step Program/ S*hot sequence)* that I teach, which must be installed into your shooting routine.

Idiot Proof Archery

Defense: *Mentally Cautious Attitude* (Steps 1-7)
Step 1   Set Foot Position/Posture
Step 2   Nock the Arrow
Step 3   Hook Up — release or fingers on string
Step 4   Set the Bow Hand
Step 5   Pre-Aim *(and run positive mental imagery program)*
Step 6   Draw to Anchor *(includes putting sight on target and pre-loading trigger, for release shooters)*
Step 7   Position Attainment *(Is the shot in order? Is #1 thru #6 maintainable thru to #12? If not, let down!)*

Offense: *Mentally Aggressive Attitude* (Steps 8-12)
Step 8   Commit (with the anticipation of #12, the conclusion . . . for example, *get ready* to pull until you *touch your shoulder)*
Step 9   Start motor *(back tension or your release method which takes 3 to 4 seconds to cause "let-go")*
Step 10   Aiming Moment *(mentally concentrate and focus on the **exact** center of the target . . . your sight will go there automatically . . . don't watch your sight!)*
Step 11   Followthrough *(this happens automatically because of released tension)*
Step 12   Conclusion *(the predetermined end to #11 that is reached after the arrow is gone)*

This 12 Step Sequence helps separate and expand on some of the compound principles in #5 of Len's 7 Principles. Your sequence can be longer or shorter, but *should at least include the original 7 principles beginning on page 113 and be consistent in cadence and order, and must be brought to the subconscious level through off-target repetition.* The average Type A (Controller/Analytical) will spend about 60 days and 3000

Key Point #42

Your shot sequence can be longer or shorter, but must at least contain the 7 principles and be consistent in cadence and order and must be brought to the subconscious level through off-target repetition.

Bernie Pellerite

shots to get it to the "automatic level." If this sounds overwhelming, this corresponds to 50 shots a day for 60 days or 25 shots a day for 120 days.

The first 7 steps require a defensive attitude on the part of the archer, so I call that part *The Defense*. The last 5 steps require you to think offensively, so I call those steps *The Offense*. We'll start with *The Defense*, then we'll go over *The Offense* in the next chapter. The defensive part of the shot sequence is really the building of a shooting platform. We're not yet interested in hitting anything because we haven't started the "motor" and are not yet aiming. We are *cautious and meticulous at this stage*. We proceed methodically and don't want to rush through this phase. If something doesn't look or feel right, we should start over. It's like packing your parachute before you get ready to jump out of an airplane; you're not concerned with jumping yet and you're not *going to be ready* until your chute is packed perfectly. Remember, whatever happens at *explosion . . . was caused to happen in setup!* So, make sure your setup (like packing your parachute) . . . *is perfect!*

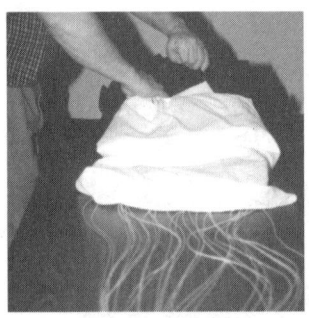

*You're not ready to jump until your parachute is packed **perfectly**!*

 **Key Point #43**

Remember, whatever happens at explosion . . . was caused to happen in setup!

Step 1 Foot Position/Posture
Starting Off on the Right Foot
(Even If You Are Left-Handed)

Compared to other aspects of the archery shot, adopting a proper stance and posture sounds elementary and relatively unimportant. In fact, it really has more to do with proper shooting form than we think. We've all been told that there are three

Idiot Proof Archery

basic foot positions (you should assume I'm talking about a right-handed archer): 1. The *straight* or *square stance (see Fig. 1)* which is to stand toeing a straight line that points to the target; 2. The *open stance (see Fig. 2)* which requires the front foot back somewhat and the body is turned slightly (15-30 degrees) *toward* the target; and 3. The *closed stance (see Fig. 3)* which is when your back foot is behind slightly and your body is partially turned *away* from the target. Unfortunately, most archers just step up to the shooting line or stake without paying any attention to exactly where their feet are from shot to shot, which ultimately cost them points.

Foot Position In the school, I do a demonstration to show how important stance/posture and foot position really are. Four or five student "volunteers" get their bows and stand at the 20 yard line like they are going to shoot at the targets. I have them get ready to come to full draw . . . and then have them turn their heads and look behind them, at me. (This disorients them.) Then, I tell them to close their eyes and turn their heads back around toward the target and draw to anchor with their eyes still closed. Once at full draw, they are told to open their eyes, memorize where their bow is aimed, and then let down, without shooting. The results are usually very interesting! Most shooters are usually off to the right (and occasionally to the left) anywhere from 12 inches to 12 feet!

What this proves is that people have a predetermined idea of where their feet should be planted without regard to which is the most natural or comfortable . . . and therefore, the easiest to duplicate for their bodies. Most people think they should be toeing a line that is pointed straight at the target (the square

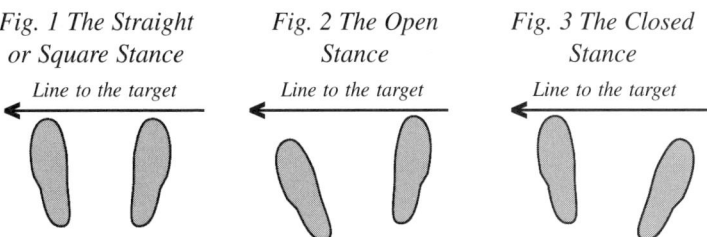

Fig. 1 The Straight or Square Stance

Fig. 2 The Open Stance

Fig. 3 The Closed Stance

Bernie Pellerite

 **Key Point #44**

Our "natural body position" should dictate where our feet should be. We should not plant our feet arbitrarily and draw the bow using muscles to push the bow over or twist the body toward the target.

stance). That is usually *not the case.* Our "natural body position" at full draw, should dictate where our feet should be. We should not plant our feet arbitrarily and draw the bow, using muscles to push or pull the bow over or distort (twist) the trunk of the body to get the bow on target. If you stand on the shooting line or by a shooting stake and look at the target, you will draw toward the target, without being aware of how much you are twisting your hips, torso, or shoulders. The torque or tension you load into your body doing this can guarantee lower scores. By drawing with your eyes closed however, you are "tricked" into drawing the way your *body wants you to draw and hold the bow,* because it's the *most natural and therefore, the steadiest* for your particular shooting form. Simply keep drawing and moving your feet more open or closed, until your sight is pointed at the target every time, when you open your eyes.

Here is an example: You are a right-handed archer standing on a direct line to the target (straight stance) and, after drawing with your eyes closed, when you open your eyes, your sight is aimed 3 feet to the right, at 20 yards. This means that if you had drawn with your eyes open, you would be *unconsciously twisting or torquing* your body around *unnaturally* to get your sight pointing toward the target. This builds in tension and/or pre-loaded torque that will cause unwanted movement that will make aiming take longer and become more difficult. This tension or torque can be responsible for over-holding, because of an unsteady sight picture. This violates your physical comfort zone which is usually 7-8 seconds to execute a shot. It can also cause some unexplained lefts and rights. In this example you should open your stance slightly, which will bring your alignment around to where your sight is pointed toward the target *naturally.* You will be able to get into the center with your sight *much quicker, with less effort, and hold steadier* . . . enabling you to *aim*

Idiot Proof Archery

sooner, hold longer, and to release the arrow *when the sight is at its steadiest*.

Whichever way your bones are lined up and your natural body position allows you to point the bow, is the most "idiot-proof" way for you to stand and to aim. You shouldn't have to recruit any muscles to get your sight lined up on the target.

Key Point #45

Whichever way your bones are lined up and your natural body position allows you to point the bow is the most "idiot-proof" way for you to stand and to aim.

Finding Your Correct Foot Position Once you have your draw length adjusted properly, learned to use back tension, and you are holding with a low, down, and relaxed shoulder, *only then* can you identify *your* correct foot position. To find your correct foot position, as described previously, *disorient yourself first*, and then close your eyes and draw the bow. *Don't try to look at the target before you close your eyes and draw*, as this causes your body to subconsciously point the bow toward where you *were looking* or to where you pre-aimed.

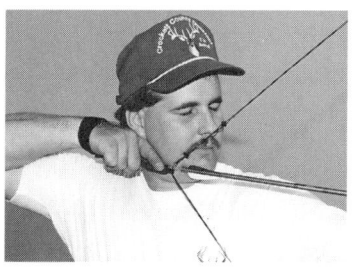

Drawing with your eyes closed is the best way to find your natural foot position.

Once you establish which foot position you should be using, practice it by putting markers on the floor or the ground, until it becomes *automatic*.

Stance Most shooters assume a stance or posture that is too rigid, preconceived, totally artificial, and that eventually breaks down like a "high wrist grip" can during the competition. Your body should be erect but relaxed. Don't stand "at attention." If you do, here is what can happen. When you first start shooting at a tournament, you'll be standing up straight and stretched to

Key Point #46

Your body should be erect but relaxed, in the "at ease" position. Don't stand "at attention."

Bernie Pellerite

Form will break down, eventually, if you start out standing too tall.

Stand erect, but stay relaxed, and good form will last all day!

your tallest for the first 10 to 15 shots. As the day goes by, and you aren't paying attention to your posture, or as you begin to tire, you will automatically start to relax or slump a little. Your body slowly assumes your natural "at ease" position. This is one of the reasons that some shooters have severe differences in their scores between practice and tournaments, or between the first and second half of a tournament. When you are "psyched up" for a tournament, adrenaline is coursing through your bloodstream and that gives you energy to "stand up tall." Then, as you start to relax and you aren't as nervous or revved up, the adrenaline leaves your system and you relax further and . . . you slump a little. When you are at home practicing, there is little or no adrenaline to effect your form. I recommend that you start out, on the very first shot, to stand the way you will be standing on the last arrow . . . *erect but at ease!* You should be mindful of this and utilize it in your practice sessions. Then, when you do go to a tournament, your "tournament form" should be identical to your "practice form."

Your *shoulders* should be *directly over your hips* which should be *directly over your feet (see Fig. D, pg. 101)*. Do not twist your upper body or lean back (usually a sign that your draw is too long). Your weight should be distributed *evenly on both feet.*

Idiot Proof Archery

A common mistake 3-D shooters make is shooting with their ankles together. The feet should be about *shoulder width* apart. This gives you a much wider and more solid foundation, which is important if you want to hold steady. Archers who shoot with their feet together are forced to lean back (away from the target) to get their balance because their bow arm is extended and holding up 5 to 10 pounds of bow. Therefore, they must lean back to counterbalance the bow's mass weight *(see photo)*. Leaning back also happens when the draw is too long, which contributes to the inability to hold steady. Holding steady is impossible now because the *bow arm is tense, which causes movement!*

Archers who shoot with their feet together are forced to lean back in order to counter balance the bow's mass weight.

You see, *everything is tied together!* One thing causes another to happen and then *that* causes something else to happen, etc. If your "shooting platform" is not in alignment or not relaxed, why would you expect the shot to happen naturally, or your body to repeat it over and over again, naturally? However, for those "true athletes" and professional archers out there that practice 2 to 4 hours a day, 5 to 7 days a week, *any form works well*, because it's practiced and reinforced mentally and physically nearly every day. Remember we said . . . you don't have to do it right . . . just do it the *same way every shot!* Having said that, how many true professional athletes do we really have, with practice regimens like the Korean Olympic team (45 hours and 6 days per week)!

Key Point #47

If your "shooting platform" is not in alignment or not relaxed, why would you expect the shot to happen naturally or your body to repeat it over and over again . . . naturally?

Bernie Pellerite

Oh, Kyo-Moon, one of Korea's top archers

No matter what form they use (which happens to be bone-to-bone which I also teach), they practice it so much it always happens the same way each and every shot. Sometimes though, there are champions that succeed with very odd shooting forms. However, when most people try to copy a great shooter with unorthodox form, they fail! The reason is that most people *don't* or *can't* put in that much effort.

That's why, for people *who have real jobs*, I teach "idiot proof" archery, which is *naturally repeatable*. My entire coaching philosophy is adapted for the "nonprofessional" archer to shoot "professional scores" . . . sort of "Better Archery Through Idiot Proof Execution!"

Step 2 Nock the Arrow

This isn't rocket science, but nocking the arrow should be done the exact same way every time. Don't push the arrow up against the nock set one time, and have it a thirty-second of an inch low the next. That will affect both the arrow flight and impact point.

Step 3 Hook Up

The same goes for hooking up your release to the bowstring; it should be done the same way every time. Consistency is the foundation of your shot platform. If you hook onto the string the same way each time, theoretically, the release (or your fingers) will come off the string the same way each time.

 **Key Point #48**

Consistency is the foundation of your shot platform.

If you are a finger shooter, set your tab and fingers using a "deep

Idiot Proof Archery

Deep Hook

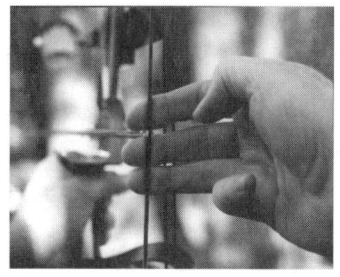

Shallow Hook

hook." This, in my opinion, is the best way to get a clean release. I define a deep hook as one in which the string goes in the first finger joint or beyond. Shooting off your finger tips guarantees poor shots because it causes tension and fatigue in your fingers and tension in the back of the hand. A relaxed "back of the hand" is key to a good finger release. This can't be done with a shallow hook (more on this in chapter 9).

Key Point #49

A relaxed "back of the hand" is key to a good finger release.

Step 4 Set the Bow Hand

Get a Grip! Years ago when Jan and I had our pro shop, I remember a fellow who came in totally frustrated. He had spent hours and hours tuning his bow and arrows, but was still having trouble getting consistent groups. This guy was a real enthusiast that could recite every detail of his setup. He matched his arrow weights to within $1/10$ of a grain from each other, fletched his own arrows, measured, calculated, and researched every possible item of his setup, *ad nauseam*. I checked his arrows and equipment, and everything was okay. I watched him shoot a few shots and his form looked acceptable. He was using back tension and not punching the trigger. I continued to question him and watch him shoot a few more shots. When I asked him how he put his hand in the bow, I got a blank stare . . . "Huh?" As it turned out, this fella was doing most everything right (to the point of being totally obsessive), but never paid any

Bernie Pellerite

attention to how he was putting his hand in the bow.

Have you ever watched a professional golfer when they gets ready to tee off? They'll do what's known as a "waggle," which is a pre-swing routine that includes getting their hands on the club in precisely the same place each time. Ever watched a major league batter? . . . it's the same thing!

Your bow hand is the last thing that makes contact with the bow after the string is let go. Think of the shot in slow motion. The release, or your fingers, let go of the string first; the nock is still in contact with the string; the arrow and string move forward together to brace (and beyond), and the string and arrow finally part company. As the arrow continues forward, it is touching the rest; your hand is still on the bow handle, therefore, is still able to influence the flight of the arrow! If your hand grabs, twists or torques, crab claws, drops, pushes, collapses, slips, heels, or changes position *in any way* . . . you will mess up a perfectly good shot. As with all phases of archery, *consistency* is the name of the game.

Different Types of Hand Positions

The High Wrist Grip The high wrist grip could be described as having the web between the thumb and index finger as the pressure point against the bow grip, and no part of the palm of the hand touching the bow grip. For a long time, due to the influence of some top recurve and longbow shooters, the "high wrist" hand position *(see photo)* was thought to be the best, by many shooters. It was believed that the less hand in contact with the grip, the better. So, a lot of shooters were taught to shoot with this hand position. The problem with this, for the average archer, is *lack of repeatability!* I won't tell shooters not to use a high wrist grip if it works for them, and they can do it consistently. Top professional archer Terry

High wrist

Idiot Proof Archery

Ragsdale, comes to mind as having perfected this style of shooting but Terry has very thick, strong wrists with "Popeye" size forearms. However, there aren't too many Terry Ragsdale's out there and the average archer, who isn't as strong or doesn't practice enough to perfect this technique, will have trouble duplicating this hand position from shot to shot. Due to fatigue, the hand position on the sixtieth shot will usually not be the same as on the first shot.

The Medium Wrist Grip I would probably describe the "medium wrist" grip or hand position as being any hand position that attempts to have most of the palm pressed evenly along the length of the grip. This description in itself should tell you how many variations there could be . . . too much top hand pressure on one shot . . . too much low hand pressure on the next. It's nearly impossible to spread the *exact* same hand pressure over 4 to 5 inches of bow handle on every shot. Consistency, consistency, consistency!

The Low Wrist Grip The "low wrist" position has the base of the thumb, on the thumb side of the lifeline, touching the grip. This is the hand position, I consider "Idiot Proof!" It is the most easily duplicated, takes the least amount of thought, and requires . . . *no muscle!* There is only one low wrist position . . . just heel the hell out of it! However, the medium and high wrist positions have varying versions. Also, you can shoot with the low wrist grip with your bow

Medium wrist

Key Point #50

The low wrist grip is the most easily duplicated, takes the least amount of thought, and requires no muscle involvement.

Low wrist . . . This is "Idiot Proof!"

Bernie Pellerite

hand *more relaxed*. More muscles are used in the medium and high wrist grips and remember . . . *tense muscles cause movement* . . . thus an unsteady sight picture.

Another reason I recommend the low wrist grip is for shooting up and down hills. If you "heel" the bow (low wrist) all the time, your shots should be consistent, regardless of whether you are shooting up or down hill. On the other hand (excuse the pun), if you normally shoot medium or high wrist and have to shoot up hill, what can happen is (and usually does), you will "heel" the bow to help elevate it, but not go back to your normal hand position before the shot goes off. This "pre-loads" the shot and can cause you to have unexplained high arrows that "blow out the top" of the target.

I tried an experiment one time. I shot arrows from 20 yards with varying hand positions, from low wrist to ultrahigh wrist, (moving the pressure point up continuously, about $1/8$" per shot). I was able to "walk" my arrows down the target 6" to 7" ($1/2$" to $3/4$" per shot), *without adjusting my sight!* Imagine how much it would be at greater yardages. Don't you have enough trouble trying to shoot well at tournaments, without having to worry about this being added to the formula, too? If you are buying into my prescription for **Idiot Proof Archery** . . . try a low wrist grip.

Pre-Loaded Torque

I just explained where some of your high and low arrows might be coming from. *Pre-loaded hand torque*, which is any *preset rotational or twisting force* applied to the bow handle *before the shot is released*, can cause a lot of unexplained left and right arrows when the explosion of the shot occurs. What you need to do is find a *"torque-free" hand position*. The best way to do that is to wet or lubricate your hand (try some baby oil) and try several different hand positions. This will simulate a nervous or sweaty hand or a rainy day. This allows your hand to "seek its own position" on the bow grip. Your hand should be free to slip all the way up into the grip until it can slip no more (up, down, left, or right). Try shooting several shots at five

Idiot Proof Archery

yards, with different hand positions while watching the tip of your long stabilizer (or tape an arrow on to the end of your short one), until the tip of the stabilizer jumps straight out toward the target and does not kick to either side. Once you have found that "torque-free" position, mark your hand and bow grip with "alignment marks" and practice it until it feels natural and happens automatically. It's not a good idea to use a glove or a nonskid wrap on your grip, as this will "camouflage" and/or promote pre-loaded hand torque. Also, there are a few popular bows that come from the factory with a modified high wrist grip. Some are so high that the hand slips off to the side, causing severe torque. Fortunately, most manufacturers now offer, as an option, the more popular "low wrist" handle. If your bow's handle doesn't allow you to adopt this grip, you can take it off and use the riser, or you can grind the handle down flat to fit your new, low-wrist hand position.

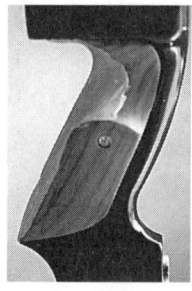

This grip was sanded down then built up with auto body epoxy! The important thing is to get the shape right for your hand (not the looks)!

I used to watch my wife shoot with my back to the target. Without turning to look, I could tell from which way her stabilizer kicked, where the arrow went. If the stabilizer kicked to the left and up, chances were real good, the arrow went high left. If the stabilizer kicked straight forward, I could almost guarantee that she put it in the center of the X. Think about it . . . the arrow is pointing in the same direction as the stabilizer, so normally, wherever the stabilizer goes . . . so goes the arrow!

Correct Hand Position

My good friend and top Olympic-style archer, Ed Eliason, learned a long time ago of the importance of a consistent hand position. He has gone so far as to put a tattoo on the back of the web of his bow hand, that lines up with a mark on the grip *(see photo A)*. This gives him a repeatable point of reference for his

Bernie Pellerite

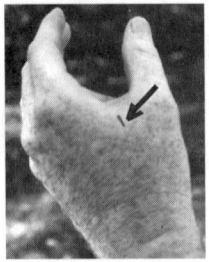

A. *You know you're serious when you get your hand tattooed with alignment marks.*

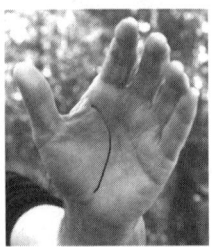

B. *Palmar crease*

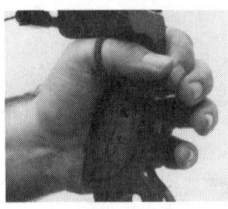

C. *This grip has too much hand in the bow.*

hand placement. Years ago, my wife, Jan, was an accomplished shooter with numerous state and sectional championships. But, before she became really competitive, she used to have trouble finding a consistent hand position, so she came up with this idea — she taped the tip of a rubber eraser (about the size of half a pea) on her grip where she could feel it in the same place, in the middle of the "lifeline" of her hand, each time. Her scores went up immediately, because her lefts and rights, from hand torque and inconsistencies, went away. Some shooters take the grip off the bow so they can feel the edges of the riser, thus giving them a repeatable point of reference.

The bow handle should stay on the *thumb side* and should not cross the "lifeline" (the *palmar crease*) of your hand (see *photo B)*. Although there are a few excellent shooters that are able to shoot well "crossing the lifeline," *(see photo C)* I don't recommend it for most archers. The first reason why is that there are muscles on either side of the crease that can influence the shot if flexed or not flexed. On the "little finger" side of the lifeline (the *hypothenar eminence*) is a complex of muscles you want to avoid. If you keep the grip on the thumb side (the *thenar eminence)*, there tends to be more consistency because there's only one set of muscles contacting the bow handle. Second, if you saw a cross section of your arm and wrist, you would find the two bones in your forearm (the *radius* and *ulna*) terminate at your wrist. The larger one is the radius and is behind the thenar eminence *(see photo D)* and is a solid point to put against

Idiot Proof Archery

the bow grip. This is what is called "bone-to-bone" or, in this case . . . "bone-to-bow" form in which the least amount of muscles are used, and this alignment provides you a solid, consistent position that gives you the calmest possible sight picture. Remember, muscles cause you to shake from tension, fatigue or nerves . . . bones are not affected by any of these. At full draw, the lifeline should point straight up and down. Don't "shake hands" with your bow. Extend your arm and put up your hand like you are gesturing to stop, with your index finger and thumb forming a "V" (tilted toward 1 o'clock when looking at the back of your hand). Put the bow in your hand, on the thumb side of the lifeline and let the fingers drop down in a relaxed manner *(see photo E)*.

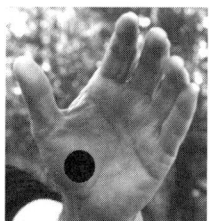

D. The radius bone is behind the thenar eminence and is a solid pressure point to put against the bow grip . . . **bone-to-bow form.**

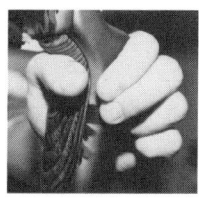

E. Put the bow in your hand, on the thumb side of the lifeline and let the fingers drop down in a relaxed manner.

Grabbing the Bow

Most archers know that "grabbing the bow" is a big no-no! It is a form of "dynamic torque," which is torque *at or during the release*. I'm sure a lot of you know that it's a tough habit to break if you have it, but there are some simple remedies. When we video each student in the school and play it back later in slow motion, quite often we will "bust" someone "grabbing the bow" *before* or *during* the release *(see photo F)*. Can you imagine how much you can influence the flight of an arrow if you move the bow by grabbing it right at the moment of release? Most shooters who shoot-and-grab don't influence the shot all the time because some-

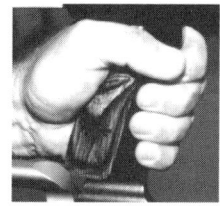

F. Grabbing the bow at any point in the shot guarantees a poor shot.

Bernie Pellerite

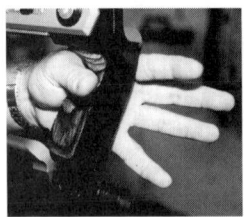

G This grip...
it's a "grab"
waiting to happen!

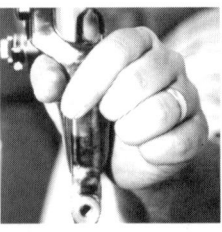

H. Tuck and relax your 3rd, 4th and 5th fingers against the bow handle. Leave only the index finger and thumb out...
it's the most Idiot Proof way!

Freddie Troncoso
Top Coach and founder of Golden Key-Futura

times, the arrow is gone *before they grab*. But frequently, because of anticipation, they'll *grab-while-shooting or grab-then-shoot!* This is usually where they get some of their unexplained "fliers." Occasionally, you'll see archers with their bow hand fingers sticking out straight and tense *(see photo G)*. I guarantee that they used to (or still do!) *grab the bow . . .* and this is their solution.

One of the best solutions is to tuck and relax your 3rd, 4th and 5th fingers in against the grip. Leave only the index finger and thumb out. This is a great hand position and a lot of top shooters shoot this way. Lightly touch the front of the riser with the tip of your index finger *(see photo H)*. This will give you a secure feeling without affecting the shot. Whatever you do, *don't pinch or "crab claw"* the bow handle with your hand . . . you're defeating the whole purpose. Tucking three fingers under will also help you keep from putting too much hand in the bow. Consequently, the *forearm is not as close to the string* and therefore, there is less chance of hitting your arm.

Professional archer, Frank Pearson, taught me this grip and Freddie Troncoso, top coach and founder of Golden Key-Futura, taught it to Frank. Rumor has it that way back, a r-e-a-l-l-y long time ago . . . Robin Hood taught it to Freddie. Just kidding! Freddie actually developed this grip while he was coaching his wife, Eva, to six national championships. Besides, Freddie is not nearly *that old* but

Idiot Proof Archery

since *he is an archery historian* (sixty years of archery experience), I thought Freddie and Robin could handle the humor!

Use a Bow Sling

I highly recommend that everyone use a bow sling. They are inexpensive and can help you have a good, clean release. The way it fits you is important, though. If it's *too tight*, it can cause torque. If it's *too loose*, you'll continue to grab the bow . . . because *you won't trust it!* Sort of like having an 11 foot safety rope in a 10 foot treestand! The sling should allow the bow to jump out of your hand, no more than about ¾ of an inch. Any more than that and you won't feel secure and you won't trust it. There are three common types *(see photos)*. I use the finger type sling, which is simply a loop around the thumb, and around the front of the bow, then attached by another loop to the index or middle finger. Another type is a rope sling that is looped around your wrist (like a lasso) and the loose end has a hook on it that you pass between your fingers, around the bow, and hook on to the loop on your wrist. The third and probably most common is the kind that attaches directly to the bow. It's usually a strap or a plastic or rubber tube that you simply slip your hand through when gripping the bow. These, however, were originally designed for hunters and are usually the ones that are either too tight or too loose and can cause more

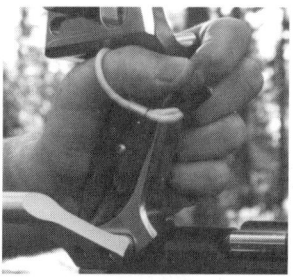
Finger Sling

Rope Sling

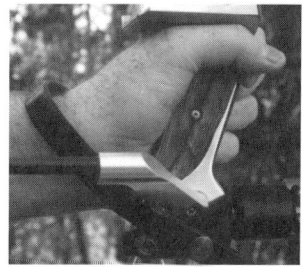
Bow Sling

Bernie Pellerite

problems than they solve. If you have this type or want to use this type, make sure it is adjusted properly. **Note**: You may find it needs to be much looser when hunting, so you can get in and out of it more quickly.

The grip of the bow is sort of like the seat of your car. Regardless of what's under the hood, if that driver's seat fits you and feels good, you'll probably like the car! I've known guys who have traded in a perfectly good bow, "because it didn't feel right in their hand." Chances are it was just the bow grip and there are quick and cheap remedies! You can take the existing handle off completely or put a different one on. Or, just modify the one you have by building it up or sanding it down.

Step 5 Pre-Aim

In order to get the bow shoulder in the correct position, which is down and relaxed into the socket, you should bend forward at the waist with most of your weight on the front foot, while pointing the bow above the target with your bow hand at about eye level *(see picture)*. **Note:** At this point you will want to run a *mental program* that is called *positive mental imagery*. This is a technique used by many top athletes such as Olympic divers, high jumpers, long jumpers, and others in various sports. They simply visualize themselves doing their chosen discipline *perfectly* in a sort of mental commercial. Right after they have seen themselves *doing it correctly*, they simply imitate what they have just seen in their mind. This technique takes only a moment of real time and will help keep you on track for the rest of your sequence (more on this in chapter 12). As soon as this is done, while the

To pre-aim . . . bend forward at the waist, point the bow above the target with your bow hand at about eye level.

Idiot Proof Archery

bow is still at eye level, sight across the bow and pick a place on the target to draw to. Then as you draw, straighten up and your bow hand will drop to the proper level, with the shoulder set in the correct position. Your draw hand will come back at eye level and drop into your anchor. Make sure your weight is evenly distributed on both feet at full draw. Most people waste valuable time getting onto the target with their sight. If you pick a spot to pre-aim at just above the spot or bullseye, you will be ready to aim sooner and will become less shaky, because you didn't waste energy and time getting to the target. Always pre-aim 3" to 5" above the spot and, once at full draw, drop down to approximately 12 o'clock, at the *top of the spot* and *"put on the brakes," momentarily* . . . then *relax slowly, down into the spot.* It is much easier to relax down into the spot than to use muscle to wrestle it upward. Remember, if you are trying to draw right at the spot, when you start to *relax*, chances are you'll drop down out of the spot and either *freeze there* or have to *"load the muscles"* in your shoulder to "pick the sight back up" . . . which takes longer and is a lot *shakier!*

Key Point #51

Always pre-aim above the spot, because it is easier to relax down into the target than to use muscle to wrestle it up into the spot.

Step 6 Draw to Anchor

As you draw to anchor, don't forget to breathe! (I highly recommend it!) The best way to do this is, as you draw back . . . inhale! At full draw, let about a third to one half of the breath out (whichever works best for you). If you don't have a one-cam, really definite stops or a "hard wall" on your bow, you should now visually line up the *draw marks* on your cables to make sure you are at your *exact* draw length. Then lock in your four anchors. For example, the tip of your *nose on the string* . . . *the knuckles* or bones in your hand *locked in to your jaw line* . . . . your *eye centered in the peep* . . . and finally, align the *aperture into the center of the peep sight.* Check the bubble level (if you have one), and *center*

Bernie Pellerite

the target spot in the aperture . . . this is called calibration! Don't worry about hitting the X-ring or the kill zone yet. It is really important that you understand that you are *not* aiming at this point; you are merely *calibrating (sight acquisition)*, or aligning the sight where you want to start out, so you can start the aiming process later.

You **also** have to have your finger/thumb on the trigger of your release, with **half the trigger pressure pre-loaded** or fingers on the string **stretched out** and **as relaxed as possible!** Then, with the draw arm and the bow arm aligned and relaxed, **everything else should be ready to release the shot** . . . **except activating back tension** (or your particular motor system).

By the end of this stage, you will have used up about *four seconds* from the time you raised your bow to draw.

Step 7 Call Shot to Order
(Position Attainment)

At this point, you want to ask yourself some questions, "Do I have the previous six steps under control? . . . Does everything feel right? . . . Can I athletically keep this shooting platform stable for at least four more seconds?" . . . if the answer is yes . . . then you change your attitude from being defensive and careful . . . and *go on offense.* You have *brought the shot to order.* This step is also called "position attainment" . . . you have organized the shot platform into a maintainable state that will *remain stable through* the rest of the shot (about four more seconds) to Step #12, *Conclusion.* If you answered, *no* to any of those questions . . . then *let down* and start over.

There seems to be a "magic number" of *four seconds* to complete the rest of the shot, for most shooters. Four seconds is merely the average time *for most people.* Young shooters or archers in really good physical condition may be able to hold a little longer than four seconds. Conversely, senior shooters and archers who are out of shape may only be able to hold for

Idiot Proof Archery

another three seconds. Your "magic number" will depend on your *physical comfort zone. See chapter 12.*

From raising the bow to the conclusion of the shot should take approximately *eight seconds*, for most. Have a buddy put a stopwatch on you and time five or six shots. If you are way faster, or more than a few seconds slower, or your timing varies more than two seconds from shot to shot . . . you have work to do! Remember, for your conscious mind to *trust this sequence,* it has to have, not only the same *steps,* but the same *timing* and rhythm *(cadence)!*

Key Point #52

From raising your bow to the conclusion of the shot should take approximately 8 seconds, for most people.

Key Point #53

For your conscious mind to trust this sequence, it has to have, not only the same steps, but the same timing and rhythm (cadence)!

Matt Setzer, of New Brunswick, NJ, after reading some of Bernie's articles, organized and attended two NFAA Shooter's Schools. He spent a lot of time learning Bernie's techniques and reprogrammed them into his subconscious on an empty bale. He has since won 2 State Outdoor Field and Hunter rounds, and set 2 new state records in the bowhunter freestyle division. Since then, he went on to win 2 more state championships and 4 Neeta World Championships. Matt also became an NFAA Advanced Level Certified Instructor and regularly coaches shooters on proper shooting form and mental techniques.

Bernie Pellerite

Bobbie Metzler, *has been a professional archer for many years, shooting on the pro staff of two major bow manufacturers. Along with her husband, Don, they owned and operated a pro shop in Elkhart, IN. After attending two different shooter's schools on the west coast, three to four times each, in a period of six to eight years, Bobbie was still having problems shooting high and low at long distances. She was shooting FITA rounds (for women that's 30, 50, 60 and 70 meters). While hosting the NFAA Shooter's School at their pro shop, Bernie discovered that Bobbie was drawing an inch and a half past the valley of the bow causing her to "pull into the limbs." As Bernie pointed out to her with a draw arrow and the bow scale, when she elevated her 40 pound round wheel bow to shoot 77 yards (70 meters), her draw length was slightly shorter by about one quarter of an inch, causing her to have one to two pounds less holding weight at full draw. This caused her to miss low at 70 meters because draw length becomes slightly shorter when the bow is elevated and vice versa. After correcting her draw length and giving her tips on shooting form and release techniques, Bobbie has since won numerous NFAA and NAA National tournaments and titles. She has set fourteen new records since attending the shooter's school and using Bernie's proven program.*

Chapter 8

The Shot Sequence
A 12 Step Program, Part Two — The Offense

We now come to the offensive part of the shot sequence. This causes more problems than all the rest put together, i.e., letting go of the string . . . what do I do? . . . what do I think? . . . and what do I anticipate? This vital concept that I touched on in chapter 7, gets so complex that it is difficult for most people to grasp it the first seven or eight times they *hear or read about it!* So this is where you need to get out the aspirin bottle and note pad . . . pack a lunch . . . put your therapist on speed dial . . . and see if you can follow the "bouncing ball" concept again! As the first *offensive step* — commit — is begun, thoughts and actions twist and turn and interweave, totally involving both the conscious and subconscious mind. It evolves from an affirmation of position attainment (bringing the shot to order) . . . to the ignition of a four second *"let-go" system,* like back tension. We call this system a *motor!* It is consciously started, with the anticipation of *reaching the conclusion* (example: anticipate touching your draw shoulder). It then evolves into a subconscious takeover of the rest of the physical motor that eventually causes release of the arrow in three to four seconds. **NOTE:** "Let-go" is *allowed to happen* here . . . not *caused to happen!* Also, followthrough is *allowed to happen* . . . because, the **anticipation of conclusion** you had at commit, **has subconsciously carried you past explosion and followthrough** . . . and *caused you to reach* the preset end or conclusion of the shot (touch your shoulder). I know what you are thinking . . . easy for me to say, huh!

Bernie Pellerite

Anticipate touching your shoulder will keep you from anticipating the release.

Put another way, commit causes us to go on automatic *physically* . . . after a millisecond of *conscious* ignition (i.e. start the motor/light the fuse). The physical part of the "let-go" system or motor, is then continued by the subconscious mind which *frees the conscious mind* to totally focus and immerse into conscious aiming . . . *mental concern for where the arrow is going!* This only works if the conscious mind **trusts** and completely gives up control of the rest of the physical motor program, to the subconscious (usually via back tension) . . . which takes us through to conclusion! As I pointed out before, any *anticipation* we had should be in the form of the *amount of effort to power up* . . . to **reach** conclusion. For example, anticipation is *purposely put* or *directed to the preparation to reach a destination* . . . how much you pre-load your muscles to reach your draw shoulder with your draw hand **before** you start back tension (motor). Therefore, this allows commit to **carry anticipation . . . way past explosion**, so it can't interrupt or change how or when our subconscious "causes" the release to happen. As you can probably tell by now, since this is pretty complex and is the *real secret* and the *virtual Rubic's Cube* of *excellent archery*, I'm going to have to go over it many times from different "angles," so I don't leave anyone behind. First

the basics, then with the element of back tension emphasized, and then with the various releases you may be using, including just your fingers.

In Step 8 of the shot sequence we are going to go boldly ahead. Up to this point you have been extremely careful and cautious. Just as if you were going skydiving! Like I said, the *"defense"* is like

Idiot Proof Archery

packing your chute. You would be extremely cautious and meticulous because your life depends on it! If you *didn't feel confident* that it was *absolutely perfect*, you would probably *start all over*, wouldn't you?

But now, your parachute is packed perfectly . . . no more caution! You are now, "offensively *committed*" to jump.

Step 8 Commit

Now that you've at least been introduced a couple of times to some of the complexities of the sequence, I will begin at the beginning of this *offensive process* once more. At this point, if you haven't let down, you *commit to the conclusion* of the shot.

As I said, commit is really a *mental trigger* that starts a four step process:
- Motor
- Aiming moment
- Follow through
- Conclusion

Commit ends with conclusion. (I have seen fit to break my shot sequence down into twelve individual steps, but some people can, and do, combine them into fewer steps.)

Commit to conclusion sounds like a simple concept, but it evolves into one of those *convoluted chain reaction processes*, so allow me to "chase this rabbit" again for a moment. It is *absolutely vital* that you understand that we commit and anticipate the complete end, or *conclusion* of the shot. We don't commit and anticipate the *release*, or "let go." Why? Like I've said, for most personalities, if you do any repetition consciously, you have to anticipate it. Therefore, *most of us will anticipate, judge, analyze . . . and then change it!* Remember, the essence of any discipline is *a sequence* that you have to do *the same* over and over. You *can't change it!* Competitive archery is like assembly line work . . . the same thing over and over. If you

Key Point #54

If you do any repetition consciously, you have to anticipate it, for most personalities. Therefore, most of us will anticipate, judge, analyze . . . and then change it!

Bernie Pellerite

keep trying to *improve it* by changing things all the time, it would be an *art form* . . . like making hand-carved statues . . . each one slightly different. So, the key here is to understand that if we know we will *have to anticipate something* anyhow, then we should get smart and *move our anticipation* as far away as we can from the action, i.e., release and followthrough. We simply anticipate (on purpose, if necessary) something that happens *after* the arrow has cleared the bow . . . by then, it's too late for us to "screw up the shot." We just anticipate, for example, *touching* our draw shoulder. Because, by the time our hand gets back to our shoulder, the arrow will be 5 to 10 yards *past the front of the bow.* Also, if we occasionally fail to reach our conclusion *completely* . . . no big deal . . . we had some room for error built in to this conclusion! For instance, if we once in a while stopped our draw hand one inch before we touch our shoulder (and, by no means, is that *permission to, or forgiveness for* **not** reaching the conclusion) . . . the arrow will still be *well past the riser* . . . *fail-safe!* What a concept . . . sorry, I didn't mean to chase that rabbit quite so far! Oh well, back to the subject, uh, let's see, oh yeah . . . COMMIT.

The reasons *not to commit*, are many and varied. But the result of not committing, should be the same . . . *LET DOWN and START OVER!* Most good target archers will let down 20% to 30% of the time when under pressure and 10% to 20% of the time in practice. This is nearly always because they don't reach Step 7, position attainment, in time. So, if you only let down three times in a 60 arrow round, then that must mean *you are better* than the top professionals. If you are wondering where some of your missed X-rings or tens come from, chances are, you ignored *the opportunity to let down.* Something didn't look or feel right, but you went ahead . . . held a little longer, and shot the arrow anyway. Top shooters *do not gamble* . . . if the shot isn't right, *they let down.* This step is one of the more important in

Key Point #55

The reasons not to commit, are many and varied. But the result of not committing, should be the same . . . LET DOWN and START OVER!

the sequence and it is usually ignored. We are all guilty of this. That's why you'll *never hear* someone say, "Gee, I wish I *hadn't* let that one down!"

Chances are, you won't let down in a tournament unless you get used to it in practice. The next time you practice, let down every other shot, whether you need to or not. The feeling you are looking for is, "Boy, I'm glad I didn't shoot that one!" Start every warm up session at competitions by letting down your first shot. Often that is all you need to remind yourself that *not every shot is worth shooting!* Remember, top shooters don't gamble . . . they only shoot good ones!

Key Point #56

You'll never hear anyone say, "Gee, I wish I hadn't let that one down!"

Key Point #57

Remember . . . top shooters don't gamble . . . they only shoot good ones.

Step 9 Start Motor

If you commit to the completion of the shot (conclusion), that "mentally triggers" you to start your motor. The motor is a *technique* you use (or fuse you light) that *causes a delayed release of the shot* . . . 3 or 4 seconds later, consistently! The motor can technically be one of three methods *(as I mentioned on page 117):* 1) **Push-pullers** or "equalizer" . . . pushes with the bow arm toward the target and pulls with the string hand. **WARNING:** If you don't have equal weight on both hands (i.e., 10 pounds pushing and 10 pounds pulling), you will always have trouble with lefts and rights. For example, if you get 9 pounds pulling and 11 pounds pushing, right handed archers will push the shot to the left and if it's vice versa . . . you will pull it to the right. 2) **Pushers** . . . hold and push: This method is not popular any more, but there were a few who used to hold with the string hand and push with the bow hand, usually pushing through a clicker, then *"dropping the string"* with the draw hand (dead release). 3) **Pullers** . . . hold and pull method: This is, by far, the most popular today. You hold or

Bernie Pellerite

maintain pressure with the bow hand while you *pull with the string hand*. For most personality types (except some Type B's) back tension is the method used to "pull with the string hand" and is the *fuse that we light* which *eventually causes a delayed* "let-go" (in three to four seconds)! It is usually the only method to achieve a repeatable subconscious motor that is *unable to be anticipated* (*see chapter 9, Anticipation, Back Tension and Your Release*). *Truly* focused Type B's can use practically any method or motor system, such as slowly squeezing the trigger until release occurs. The rest of us would call this a "controlled punch." We would anticipate *that motor* after about five shots. The Type B's can somehow focus completely on aiming *while* they subconsciously squeeze the trigger slowly and never anticipate, think back, wonder when, try to help, or hurry the release (top professional, Tom Crowe, uses this method). Go figure! It just ain't fair . . . is it?

Step 10 Aiming Moment

Once you can get your elbow, *via the back muscles,* to move and fire your release (or *rip* your fingers off the string) in about four seconds every time, *automatically*, then all you have to do mentally (after you start your back muscles in motion) is *immediately stay "hooked up"* to, and *focused on,* the *exact* center of the target for five seconds. The release will happen in four seconds. *Surprise!!!* You are probably familiar with the sequence, "Ready, Aim, Fire," when it comes to shooting rifles. Shooting a bow with a subconscious release is more like "Ready. Fire. Aim. Aim. Aim," . . . or more precisely, "Ready . . . start back tension . . . Aim. Aim. Aim." Since the motor sequence is trained to take about four seconds, it *relieves your conscious mind of* anything to do but aim . . . **aim finer!** . . . **Aim Harder!** Aiming should always be the *last thing* you were thinking about consciously, right before the shot goes off with a rifle or a bow!

 **Key Point #58**

Aiming should always be the last thing you were thinking about consciously, right before the shot goes off.

Idiot Proof Archery

That Ain't All Folks!

Most archers struggle with the concept of conscious aiming with a subconscious release while they anticipate their conclusion. This is because they fail to understand how they are tied together and how one thing affects the others. In other sports, we are taught to *power up*, to swing or concentrate *past* the point of contact. For example, a long jumper may anticipate powering up or preparing to jump 28 feet, if he wants to succeed at 24 feet. A tennis player or golfer is taught to swing past or through the ball contact. Karate champions and boxers learn to strike or punch past or beyond the board or face they are trying to break. Their concentration and anticipation is on a *preset conclusion,* which is past the goal they wish to attain. In golf, one of the most common woes when putting is called the "yips," where golfers see their putting ability disintegrate (especially on putts of six feet or less). This is due to their anticipation of the putter hitting the ball rather than anticipating the *completion of the stroke* (their conclusion). They therefore, make a *defensive move* toward the ball, trying to *not miss* the putt instead of trying offensively to *make* the putt. Golfers can only succeed *by stroking through the ball offensively,* to a preset conclusion, with the club. This is true whether they are on the green, fairway, or on the first tee with a driver. For example, don't try to hit the ball, just try to swing the club! The ball is *usually* in the way . . . and *accidentally gets hit!* Archery should be the same but, unfortunately, most archers mentally and physically "conclude" their shot *at the explosion* and not well past it. They are trying to (defensively) "not miss the bullseye" instead of trying to (offensively) hit the exact spot . . . in the *center of the center.*

I also cure golfers of the "yips"(golf target panic) . . . through committing to conclusion!

Key Point #59

Most archers "conclude" their shot at the explosion and not well past it. They are trying to (defensively) "not miss the bullseye" instead of trying to (offensively)hit the exact spot . . . in the center of the center.

Bernie Pellerite

Most people, try to hit the center with the *worst possible* aiming system for their personality. They should not try to *keep the sight in the center.* This causes them to over-hold and over-control and obsess over *the perfect sight picture,* as I said before. Therefore, *reciting a mantra or chant* such as . . . where's the center? . . . find the center! . . . find the center of the center . . . *deeper into the center!* . . . etc., will help keep "analytical types" and "controllers" *focused and hooked up mentally* and *out of the release sequence!* They have usually been programmed to *put the pin* in the middle! . . . hold it there! . . . keep it there! But, as we discussed in chapter 5, they don't understand that we have a *natural arc of movement.* They don't trust their built-in, *self-centering subconscious mechanism* that we all have. *It will always keep returning* the sight to the spot we *think about* or *concentrate on.* We don't have to have the sight in the *exact middle* when the shot goes off for the arrow to *go in the exact center!* This is because, if the sight is slightly off the exact center when the shot goes off, by the time the arrow clears the front of the bow, the subconscious (through hand-eye coordination) will have moved the bow arm and sight back to the center! *It will always put the sight in the center, without your help* . . . **IF the mind was focusing on the center in the first place!** Not understanding this is the basis of the program that causes the punching and/or the snapshooting scenario.

I'll tell you a story that I tell in school that helps my students aim really, really hard. The story goes like this . . . Once upon a time, there was an old man coaching his grandson on how to shoot a bow. They were in the middle of a big field with a huge hay barn off in the distance. The young archer was grouping his arrows so tightly, at about 25 yards, that he was breaking the nocks off. As he was shooting, a neighbor came over to watch. After several minutes he remarked to the old man, "Boy, I wish I could shoot like that . . . but I can't hit the broad side of a barn with a bow and arrow." The wise old archery coach turned to him and said, "It's not all that hard. You just have to know how to aim." The neighbor said, "What do you mean

Idiot Proof Archery

. . . know how to aim?" The old man says, "Look at that barn out in the distance and I'll show you how to aim." The neighbor says, "I can see the barn, so what?" The old man says, "Look really hard. Can you see the crack between the two barn doors?" The neighbor squints his eyes a little and says, "Yeah, I can see it." The old coach says, "Look a lot harder . . . can you see the lock hasp about half way down in the crack between the two doors?" The neighbor squinted a little harder and said, "Yeah, I can *just* see that." The old man said, "Now concentrate and focus really hard, and see if you can see the lock hanging on the hasp." The neighbor squinted really, really hard and said, "I can *just barely* make out the lock from here." The old man says, "You're not concentrating hard enough. Focus really, really, really hard. . . and see if you can see the hole in the middle of the lock." The neighbor said, "Wow, that's really hard to see," and he squinted and he concentrated, and he *focused r-e-a-l-l-y hard!* After about three or four seconds he said, "There it is, I can *just barely see it!*" Then the old man turned to him and said, "See, that's the secret of aiming . . . if you aim at the hole in the middle of the lock . . . *you'll always hit the barn!*" Cool! Is aiming an awesome concept, or what?

Step 11 Followthrough

Most people have some type of followthrough in their shot sequence which, unfortunately, they consider to be the end of the shot. Followthrough is simply the involuntary, dynamic reaction of the body to the release of tension, at the moment of execution, *on the way* to conclusion.

However, we too often end our followthrough prematurely and at different points because we *anticipate* followthrough. Eventually, the duration of our followthrough begins to grow shorter and shorter, until it no longer exists. At that point, we are physically and mentally quitting the shot at the moment of "let-go." Our effort is end-

Key Point #60

Followthrough is simply the involuntary dynamic reaction of the body to the release of tension at the moment of execution on the way to conclusion.

Bernie Pellerite

Key Point #61

Most personalities will naturally anticipate anything done on a repetitive basis.

Key Point #62

Our only hope to totally escape the negative effects of anticipation is to redirect it to a place, sound, or act that happens after the arrow has cleared the bow.

ing *before, or as the shot is going off . . . while* the arrow is still on the string! This leads to erratic shooting, mistrust, more anticipation, and confusion.

How can we stop anticipation? I'll say it again! *Most of us can't*. As thinking creatures, most personalities will *naturally anticipate* anything done on a repetitive basis. It's the same in any other sport. Golfers focus on the ball and anticipate finishing with their hands and/or the club touching their shoulder or back (see below). This takes them past contact all the way around to a preset point. Tennis and baseball players focus on the ball and anticipate swinging all the way around. It's the same in archery. Successful archers learn to aim or focus on the target . . . and pull through the shot subconsciously . . . to a *preset conclusion*, such as touching your shoulder. If you understand this concept . . . half the battle is over!

Step 12 Conclusion

As we said in chapter 7, conclusion is where we predetermine or pre-measure the duration of our followthrough and the end of our mental and physical effort. There are three basic forms of conclusion . . . sight, sound, and touch. There

Conclusion!

are many variations of each of them, but whichever one you choose, they must *take longer to do* than it takes for the nock end of the arrow to clear the front of the bow. Examples are, the draw hand ripping straight back and *touching* the shoulder, or *seeing* the arrow hit the target, or *hearing* the arrow hit the target. All of these occur *after* the arrow is gone and we can no longer affect its flight. You should choose the one you trust the most and can repeat the most consistently, as the conclusion of your shot.

Chapter 9

Anticipation, Programming, Back Tension, and Your Release

As you should have learned by now . . . professional level archery teaches us that you don't have to do it right . . . you just have to do it the same every time! But, understanding this simple concept can be complicated. The best way for most people to do it the same every time is to *keep the conscious mind occupied with something else* and let their body release the arrow automatically, through *"muscle memory."* This "muscle memory" is really a previously learned and stored program that is on the shelf in a huge warehouse, inside the memory section of the subconscious mind. Thousands of these programs are stored there and, when we need to do a particular set of actions like walking or writing your name or shooting an arrow, our conscious mind selects the one we need. It's loaded into the huge master computer in the *motor movement section* of the subconscious mind. The conscious mind then pushes the button to start the program, forgets about it, and then operates the *guidance system* (which would be aiming in this example).3 This program is delivered to the muscles through the central nervous system. Thus, the term "muscle memory" is really a misnomer . . . muscles don't really have a memory! So, if we *trust* this program to work on its own, then our conscious mind can be *free to focus* on aiming and not go back and push the *manual override button* and take the program

Key Point #63

If we hit the target, we judge that we did it right and . . . if we miss the target, we judge we did it wrong . . . and then we must fix it.

Bernie Pellerite

away from the subconscious. These so-called, "muscle memory" programs are capable of duplicating a set of actions so closely that, when you sign your name, a handwriting expert can pick *your signature* out of a thousand others every time! However, if you try to write your name with your other hand that you didn't have a program for, you have to *direct that hand consciously*. Every time you wrote your name with the un-programmed hand, it would be a little different (until you developed a subconscious program with that hand). Can you see now how important these programs are to any discipline, especially archery! Remember . . . *everything done consciously will be anticipated,* and if you anticipate it, you will judge it. If you judge it, you will change (fix/correct) it. Also remember . . . anything done subconsciously *cannot be anticipated*. You breathe over 25,000 times a day. How often do you anticipate that? Other than the breath you are about to take, to see if you'll really anticipate it!

Anticipation causes us to think about and, therefore, change the execution of the "let-go" . . . which usually destroys everything we want to accomplish. Most of us are predisposed to repeat this scenario because we have this John Wayne, *goal-oriented mentality*. Therefore, if we *hit* the target, we *judge* that we did it right and . . . if we *miss* the target, we *judge* we did it wrong . . . and then *we must fix it!* And since the archery gods say, "Thou shalt not always hit! . . . Thou shalt eventually miss" . . . we are *doomed to shoot until we miss and* then *change something* . . . do it a little faster or slower or push more, pull more, etc.

If, on the other hand, the release program is subconsciously run . . . because you trust it . . . it happens exactly the same way every time! The solution here is to practice our shot

Key Point #64

You should commit to touch . . . not commit to let go! This keeps any anticipation on an action that takes place after the arrow is gone and you can no longer affect its flight path.

Key Point #65

Anticipation, in this case, is how much and to what extent we "power up" to go. It's how much powder we use when we "light the fuse" (start the motor.)

Idiot Proof Archery

sequence and release method off target until we trust it, it becomes *automatic,* and *is ingrained subconsciously.* Only then should we *test it on a target.*

After *consciously* starting the "physical motor" program that eventually causes release in about four seconds, *we immediately immerse ourselves mentally into aiming* (and make sure we stay there!) . . . so our conscious mind won't *interrupt* or *modify* the "let go." Ideally, aiming should *totally occupy* our conscious mind. However, because of our controlling, analytical, and/or risk-taker personalities, most of us will usually *anticipate* "let go" *before we start,* or as we *try to start,* focusing on aiming. So, if we are compelled to anticipate something . . . then it should be something that won't affect the outcome of the shot. The secret to that is a technique that I told you about before called "commit to conclusion." If we choose a *touch* conclusion, for example, we must understand that *before we start aiming,* any anticipation we have is on *powering up to touch* our draw shoulder. So we *commit to touch* . . . not *commit to "let-go."* Again, if we commit to, or anticipate touch, our *anticipation carries us mentally* well past the point where the arrow clears the front of the riser and we can't affect the arrow flight any more. Anticipation, in this case, is *how much, or how far,* and *to what extent we "power up" to go!* It's *how much powder we use,* when we "light the fuse" i.e. start pulling. It is the amount of *tension in this "state of readiness,"* and therefore, it is used to make sure you don't "under-prepare" when you *get ready to start your back tension.* However, as soon as you start contracting the back muscles, your *conscious mind* left the powering up stage behind (and any anticipation) and focused on the goal . . . the middle of the target!

Key Point #66

You simply commit to conclusion and immerse into aiming and everything will happen correctly.

So, "start the motor" with the anticipation of reaching your shoulder. We could actually change #7 in the Shot Sequence *from* Commit *to* . . . Anticipate Your Conclusion, for most of us. It would logically follow that, if you always *committed to*

Bernie Pellerite

your conclusion, at some point, you *had to allow* (not cause) "let-go" and followthrough to happen . . . as you anticipated your hand touching your shoulder. Therefore, you couldn't anticipate, analyze, change or assist the release . . . *and* the arrow would be well past the front of the bow *before you stopped pulling.* Wow! What an idiot-proof concept! This concept *ensures* that "let-go" happens, *the same way every time.* You simply commit to conclusion and immerse into aiming and everything will happen correctly.

The Role of Back Tension in Your Motor

Everyone has heard by now that "if you want to win . . . you have to shoot with back tension." However, back tension seems to be a mysterious feeling that most archers never understand or experience.

First, why do you want to shoot with back tension? As you probably know by now, the real reason is because nearly all of us *will anticipate* the release if it's not a surprise, and back tension is the easiest way to effect a *consistent surprise release.* The mind can only focus on one thing at a time . . . it's either aiming or it's "doing the release," so pick one . . . it can't do both! If you're *"doing the release,"* your mind is on the release, not the target and you'll lose *control of the pin* (or "sight picture" for instinctive shooters). If you want to keep the pin in the middle (except Type B's), your conscious mind should continuously *focus on the spot you want to hit* . . . not *try to hold* the sight in the *middle of the target!* This causes most people to try to *overcontrol the sight* and leads some uninformed coaches with big resumes to preach that *conscious aiming is the problem* . . . not the solution. Their solution is . . . *focus consciously* on your *release* or *back tension,* etc. . . . and the sight will *subconsciously stay*

Key Point #67

If you want to win and you don't have a Type B personality, you need to shoot with back tension.

Key Point #68

Back tension is the easiest way to effect a consistent surprise release for most archers.

Idiot Proof Archery

in the middle! But, for 99% of us . . . *your eyes can **put** the sight in the center, but they **can't keep it there**! The **mind** is the only thing that can keep it there!* This is true for nearly all shooters, because of their personalities.

Different Coaching Philosophies

The only people that can consciously focus on their execution or their back muscles, etc., while they subconsciously aim . . . would be (at least in the U.S.) that one in a thousand, totally focused, Type B personality, that has no natural desire or impulse to anticipate, analyze, control or gamble! Therefore, since most of the great champions were/are usually Type B's, it's easy to see why some of these misguided coaches rationalize that they should tell their students to do everything the way those champions did or do it. This is especially true if they were exposed to the Korean Olympic program (nearly all Type B's). Oriental cultures have a much different mindset and less diverse personality range than the western countries. Also, I think some coaches teach this way because they were *also champions*

Key Point #69

If we commit to the conclusion of the shot, we can't anticipate the execution of release

and/or Type B personalities themselves. The problem with that is, for example, if they won the nationals by concentrating on their execution (release) and *not the target*, then eventually they are convinced that their way is right and quit exploring other coach's philosophies or methods . . . *they stop learning!* Then they start teaching and preaching *their way,* because it worked for them! But eventually, they find out that there is only a very few (five or ten) people that are capable of winning by not aiming! Since these Type B coaches are not analytical themselves, then they would probably have to buy this book to find out that they're not analytical and that their way won't work for 99% of the shooters on the planet! But, I'm pretty sure (because I *am* analytical) that they won't buy this book, because they don't think anyone could out-think or out-coach them, either . . . a vicious circle, isn't it! That's one of the biggest

Bernie Pellerite

problems with archery. As I mentioned in the Introduction, the overall perception is that you can't be a great coach if you weren't a world champion shooter. That's really absurd if you consider that champions usually don't or can't analyze . . . great coaches *have to!* Champions are seldom Type A's . . . great coaches are *nearly always* Type A personalities! Champions are not emotional people . . . great coaches are *always emotional!* Think about it . . . great coaches are usually analytical, Type A's that communicate with a lot of emotion . . . Bobby Knight, Vince Lombardi, Woody Hayes, Bela Karoli, etc. . . . get the point!

Analyzing the Release

A surprise release is pretty tough to achieve if you do it the way most shooters do. Since a finger or thumb are in contact with the trigger on the release aid, or in the case of a finger shooter directly on the string, it's impossible for most of us *not* to anticipate the release, because of the thousands of tactile sensory receptors on the tips of our fingers. These receptors are so sensitive that they can feel the difference between one and two sheets of paper that you are holding between your index finger and your thumb. That's 0.002" (two thousandths of an inch)! So obviously, they can feel when a trigger on a release moves even slightly, and sends a message to the conscious mind to "Get ready! It's going to go off" (creates anticipation). When that message, sent by what I call "the smart muscles" hits the brain, it alerts the senses and the entire body. It interrupts and overrides any concentration you may have had on aiming, and you lose control of the sight picture (again, because *your mind was controlling it, not your eyes).* Now, your mind has left the sight picture (Elvis has left the building!), and has gone directly to the "let-go" or trigger system. It has shut off the automatic subconscious program, and is now going to run it manually (consciously) so as to be able to *control it!* That's what screws up the shot. Of course, we've all been there, haven't we? If somehow we had a way to set it off without any warning . . . well, that's why most everyone who wins does it with back

Idiot Proof Archery

tension. That's because the back muscles have comparatively few tactile receptors and they aren't in direct contact with the release trigger or string. They can't accurately calibrate exactly when and where the trigger is, and therefore call or command the attention of the mind, at any given point in the execution part of the shot, like the fingers can. These "stupid muscles" as I call them, help keep our conscious mind from "anticipating the explosion," by not calling attention to themselves. Pulling with the back muscles can, with a focused and repetitious training method, be put on the *trusted, subconscious level,* thus freeing the conscious mind *to do nothing but aim!*

What Does Back Tension Feel Like?

The next question is usually . . . how do I feel back tension? This is where almost everyone gets stumped. The best way to feel it is first to know where the muscles involved are on your body and what they are supposed to be doing. The muscles you are trying to feel, are a group called the rhomboids *(see diagram)* that we discussed before, located between the spine and the scapulas (shoulder blades). They are *under* some other major muscles *(the trapezius)* and work together with the levator scapula muscles, which I won't get into here and is not important in this example. I've discovered that, to technically define exactly which muscles are involved in back tension using medical techno-babble that only third year medical students and doctors can understand, won't help the average shooter. So, the point here is that the muscles (rhomboids) between your shoulder blades . . . actually *just the one between the spine and draw arm shoulder blade* (the other should be relaxed), are what we're trying to get you to feel.

You can feel this muscle in a number of

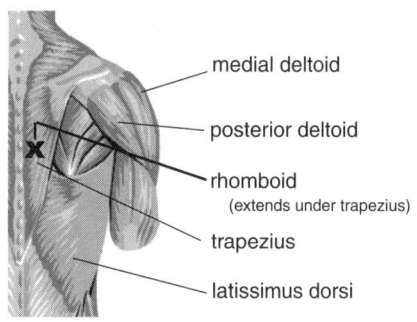

medial deltoid

posterior deltoid

rhomboid
(extends under trapezius)

trapezius

latissimus dorsi

Bernie Pellerite

ways . . . one way is to elevate your draw arm elbow to above shoulder height and put the palm of your hand flat against your chest, with the tips of your fingers touching your breast bone (sternum) — see Figure A. While keeping the finger tips in contact with your sternum, try to move your elbow, which should remain above shoulder height, to a spot behind your head without moving your fingers away from the sternum. You should feel some muscles contracting between your spine and the tip of your shoulder blade . . . those are the ones! Here's another way: grab each end of an arrow with both hands and raise it above your neck. Now with both fists gripping opposing ends of the arrow, try to pull the arrow apart, using only the muscles between your shoulder blades *(see Figure B)*. The third way is to have someone put their finger on the draw arm side of your back between the spine and the tip of your shoulder blade and firmly press in while you try to squeeze their finger tip with your back muscles *(see Figure C)*. You can also back up to a doorway and put both elbows above shoulder height, against the door jam and push yourself out of the doorway *slowly*, by squeezing your shoulder blades together which will contract the rhomboids and drive

Figure A

Figure B

Figure C

Idiot Proof Archery

both elbows rearward. One of these techniques should help you to feel these muscles. But, just because you can feel the right muscles, doesn't mean you can use them properly.

Setting up for Back Tension

The rhomboids can't help you unless you get the *draw length short enough to elevate the bow arm elbow*, at least as high as your nose *(see photo chapter 3 pg. 44)*. **NOTE:** *Some people need to raise it as high as their forehead to be able to make this process work.* You see, the idea is for you to squeeze the draw arm side rhomboids *only* and cause the elbow to move very slightly (½" to 1") . . . *without* using the upper arm *(biceps)* or shoulder *(deltoid)* muscles. If you can't get the elbow to move when you contract your rhomboids, then you can't proceed to the next step. **Caution:** *Some people will erroneously tell you to squeeze your shoulder blades together using the rhomboids on both sides of the spine . . . that's back tension. You don't need to squeeze the bow arm side . . . it doesn't operate the release . . . however, it could make your bow move to the left! . . . and make your score move down!*

Now that you can make your elbow move by contracting your draw arm side rhomboids, you are ready for the *hard part*. This would be getting the release hand, wrist, and forearm positioned correctly to make the shot go off, without *thinking about doing* anything else, or *moving* anything else, except the back muscles.

Your hand positioned on your release (or fingers on the string) should be in a stretched out and relaxed position at full draw, (take out all of the slack in the system) so the next ½" or so that the elbow moves up, back, and behind your head will cause the shot to go off . . . **without thinking about it** or having to move any fingers, wrists, or any other body part! **Caution**: a lot of people think that the elbow should move two to three inches before the shot goes off . . . not true! If that happens, it will cause your bow to move sideways off target or pull your arrow back farther on the rest, and you'll be spraying shots left and right all day long!

Bernie Pellerite
Different Applications Of Back Tension

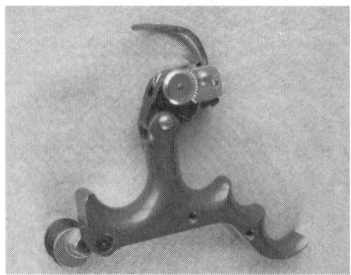

Bernie's Missing Link a new safe-draw, back tension release.

Slow motion video reveals that "back tension" shooters usually rotate the handle with their fingers or wrist.

Triggerless Releases (**Bernie's Missing Link and E-Z Back**, Stanislawski, Carter, Scott, Tru-Ball, Zenith, etc.) These releases have a half moon cam in them which, when rotated under tension, causes the release to trigger *(see photo)*. The older style need to be pulled to anchor, almost entirely with the index finger and thumb to keep from prematurely firing them which earned them the nickname of "mouth buster" releases. To prevent this they were often set up with a lot of travel in them. They need to be set *very quick* (light) if you want to use *back tension only* to set them off. *Nearly all* archers shoot this type of release incorrectly. These people may have *some* back tension but they really set the release off by *rotating the handle with their fingers or wrist*, because the release was set up *with too much travel* to be done with *just the back muscles*. Jan and I have proven on video, in slow motion, that 99.5% of them squeeze their fingers or rotate their hand or wrist to get the shot off. This technique will only work for, (you guessed it) . . . a few "Type B" personalities. The rest of us will find this is really just a *"controlled punch"* that

⦿ Key Point #70

A triggerless release should be activated with back tension only (unless you are a Type B). You should not be triggering these releases by rotating them in your hand . . . the most common mistake people make.

Idiot Proof Archery

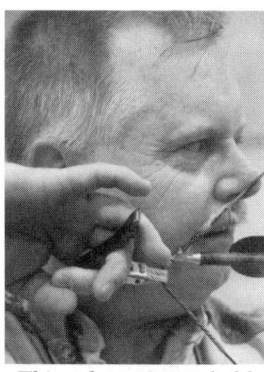

*This release is not held properly to set it off with **back tension only**.*

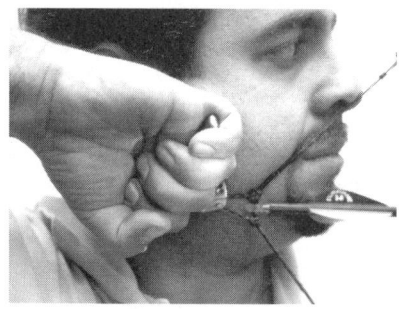

*Hook **really deep** on this type of release, (like brass knuckles) and make a relaxed fist. This keeps you from **cheating**!*

is inconsistent at best. It will not get us winning scores . . . if we ever try to leave our local zip code.

At full draw, most archers need to hook *really deep* on this type of release, (like brass knuckles) and make a relaxed fist. This keeps you from "cheating" by using the fingers to *crank* or *squeeze* it, to *help the shot go off* (see photos above). The fist should be about 45 degree angle to the ground. This angle matches the movement of the nose-high elbow tip when you contract the rhomboids on the draw side. **IMPORTANT:** The squeezing should move the elbow *up* and *back* and behind the head, just about ½" to ¾". This *very slight* and *slow movement* (which *takes 4 seconds* to make it *move only* ¾") should be enough to move the lever off the half moon cam *by itself, if it's set up properly*. If not . . . it's set up too slow! **Note:** Set up with the elbow **slightly outside** of perfect arrow alignment (see **Click-Cam**™ alignment in diagram on pg. 164). As back tension is applied, the elbow is drawn into perfect firing alignment with the arrow . . . which is when the release should go off. However, if you start out "in line (firing position)," as your elbow rotates behind your head, it will end up left of (or inside) the line when the shot goes off, and you'll get left arrows (and vice-versa if you're right of the line). Remember, people who squeeze the back muscles **and** rotate the handle with their fin-

Bernie Pellerite

Contract rhomboid muscles, string side only. This moves elbow into perfect firing alignment at explosion.

Firing Position
Click-Cam Position

If the draw elbow is rotated too far behind the head, inside the firing position, this will cause the bow to break left at explosion (resulting in a left arrow) and vice-versa if the elbow is not rotated enough.

gers and/or wrist, will eventually *mentally calibrate* where the end of the handle travel is . . . and then they will, once again, anticipate the moment of release. To eliminate this I have invented two "safe draw" back tension releases called **Bernie's Missing Link** and **Bernie's E-Z Back** *(see pg. 94, 162 and Appendix)* that can be drawn to anchor using all the fingers without fear of a bloody nose or premature release. Once at full draw, the shooter rotates the handle on the **Missing Link** until a pin in the handle drops into the link thereby making the release functional then back tension is used to execute the shot. The **E-Z Back** has a "dual index finger hold" that keeps the handle in a safe position until anchor at which time the index finger is dropped down to a lower finger position rotating the handle into the ready position. Both releases come standard with a "clicker" type groove machined into the edge of the half moon shaped cam (this may be reversed and shot without the clicker). Both releases may be shot directly off the string loop with an included rope that wraps around the string. With either of these "safe draw" releases, once at anchor, shooters simply rotate the handle until it clicks (see diagram **Click-Cam** position) and then rotate the elbow behind the head about one inch (using back tension) and the release will fire. **No pain! No blood! Idiot Proof!**

    Thumb Releases The biggest mistake people make with a thumb or index finger release is to set them up with *a hair trigger!* When set up like this, these releases *cannot be set off slowly (4 seconds) with your back muscles.* The trigger pressure

Idiot Proof Archery

needs to be *3 to 7 lbs.*, not 3 to 7 ounces (except for Type B's)! You will probably need to send your release back to the manufacturer and, probably for a small fee, get heavier return springs put in the trigger mechanism so it becomes firm-to-heavy, *without any detectable creep or movement,* before it releases. Check with your individual manufacturer. The heavier trigger pressure will allow you to put the tip of your thumb ahead of the trigger *on the case* of the release. Then, put firm pressure (about *half* of what it takes to set it off . . . pre-load) on the trigger with the middle section of your thumb. At this point, you need to have all the kinks and bends out of the wrist, with everything in line from the tip of your elbow to the tip of your arrow *(see photo on previous page).* Because the trigger is firm, you now can *"pre-load it"* without fear it will prematurely fire. **(Note:** This has to be pre-loaded and the sight must be on target *before* you ever commit or start back tension. These two steps are done as a part of anchor.) At this point, all you have to do is *relax* the rest of the hand while keeping *medium pressure* on the case with the tip of your thumb (and still keeping the one half *pre-load* on the trigger), then . . . activate the back muscles and "slowly push your elbow *up* and *straight back behind* you . . . into an imaginary wall." The movement will only be half an inch or so, but if the hand is relaxed, this will cause it to hinge at the knuckles and force the middle section of the thumb *in* toward the middle of the hand *naturally* and fire the release in about four seconds. Since you don't have to *think* about the hand hinging or the finger moving, because it happens naturally, all you have to do is *preset* everything mechanically, pre-load the

Key Point #71

On a thumb release, put the thumb on the case, not on the trigger.

"Pre-load the trigger by putting firm pressure on the trigger with the middle section of your thumb."

Bernie Pellerite

trigger and back tension will do the rest without thinking! ***Caution!*** Don't try to rock the release trigger into the thumb to make it go off (a method I used to recommend). We've found out by experimenting in the shooter's school that this method will eventually develop into a controlled punch, because you have to think about your fingers and wrist to make them move (if you're thinking about that, you're not thinking about aiming)!

Index Finger Releases There are also a few secrets to shooting this release with back tension. First of all, it must fit your hand properly and there are some things that you *can and cannot do*.

1. At full draw, the trigger should just fit into the first joint *(crease between the first and second sections of the finger)* of the index finger. The finger tip pad should *not* contact the trigger.
2. On the other hand (no pun intended!), it should not be so short as to enable you to wrap too much of the finger around the trigger, so the tip of the finger is pointing toward your rear foot at anchor. Nor should the trigger be put in the second joint, or section, of the finger.
3. You should pull the string back with the wrist strap, not by grabbing on to the barrel of the release and pulling. At full draw, the only place you should feel any pressure is on the wrist strap and in the first joint (or crease) of the index finger where the trigger is, when you get ready to start back tension.
4. The tip of the index finger should *just be able* to make it over the trigger and should *point straight down*. This puts just a tiny bit of pre-load or pressure on the trigger by stretching out the finger to get the first *crease* or *joint* on the trigger. The rest of the finger should have a sort of "flattened out" arch to it (because you reached out *slightly - see photo)*. Everything between the elbow and the first joint should be *relaxed*.
5. The wrist should be straight . . . no curve or "hump" in it. You should be able to draw a straight imaginary line from the tip of the elbow to the index finger.

Idiot Proof Archery

't put your thumb behind your
. This puts a kink in the wrist
causes pre-loaded torque upon
sion. I used to shoot that way
trust me, I know! (See #15 of
ter 11.)

ing: The trigger should be set
ith **absolutely** no slop or
!, and should be very firm . . .
nd three to four pounds —
, if you can get it! Having a
nairy trigger is one of the indirect causes of punching and full blown target panic! A firm trigger with no travel is very important. You should also move the finger as close to the barrel of the release as possible. This will cause the trigger to be harder to set off. At full draw, with the hand, wrist, and forearm relaxed, squeeze off (or pre-load) about one half of the trigger pull. At this point, the hand is completely relaxed and your finger is like a fish hook on the trigger . . . with a tow line tied to your elbow (see diagram. pg. 168). All the slack must be out of the line before you start! As you activate back tension, it tows your elbow rearward, (and here's the secret!) your release hand (which has to be relaxed) will stretch out and collapse slightly . . . and actually start to slip a little through the wrist strap (sort of like trying to slip your wrist out of a set of handcuffs). This will cause the "hook" in your index finger to "tow" the trigger back, causing the release to go off . . . but **only** if you **pre-**

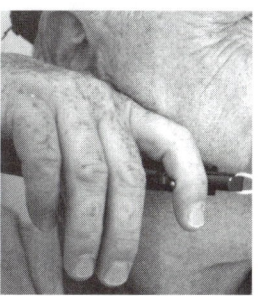

Trigger should be in the first crease, not on the pad of the finger. Fingertip should be pointed straight down and the rest of the hand should be relaxed..

Key Point #72

There should be no slop or creep in the trigger. This will warn you and attract the attention of the conscious mind which should be aiming.

Key Point #73

Having a hairy trigger is one of the main causes of target panic! A firm trigger with no travel is very important!

Bernie Pellerite

Hairy triggers will make most archers TERRIFIED of touching the trigger at all, so they "pounce" on it (punch it) from ambush.

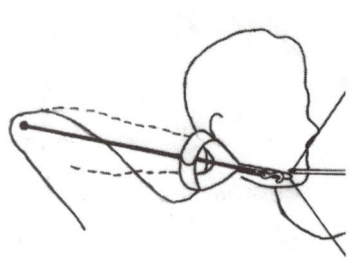

Your finger is like a fish hook on the trigger with a tow line tied to your elbow.

loaded *the heavy trigger* **at least halfway** *and* **relaxed** *the rest of your hand!* If you didn't, you'll just draw the arrow back *farther on the rest.* **NOTE**: If it goes off in one or two seconds, you pre-loaded the trigger too much. If it doesn't go off for ten or twelve seconds, or you start drawing the string back further, or think you have to "help it go off" with more pressure of your index finger . . . then obviously you *didn't pre-load it enough.* When done properly, all releases that you use this technique on should go off between three and five seconds. *(Four seconds is what I consider perfect, for most shooters!)*

An Index Finger Alternative In an effort to stop the *irresistible urge* that most personalities have to punch the trigger, but still keep the index finger caliper style, with *back tension automatically added*, I invented and patented a *release system* called the **Bernie's Can't Punch™**, which is now made for me by Scott Archery Manufacturing. My good friend, the late Bill Scott, designed and patented the famous Scott Caliper release, the world's most popular caliper release. When using my **Can't Punch Release**, it is not necessary to set the trigger pressure heavy, because it has a second, *stationary trigger* that is adjustable called *The Captivator (See Fig. A).* It is mounted below and slightly forward of the "real" trigger or *Activator.* Since the *Captivator* does not move, the index finger can press on it as hard as the shooter wants *(see photo).* This keeps the sensory receptors on the end of the index finger in a state of "sensory

Idiot Proof Archery

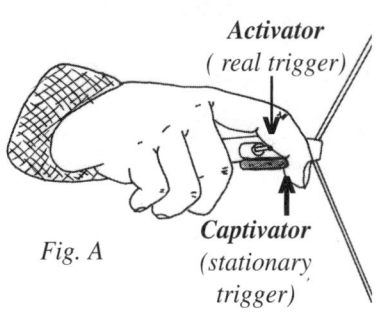
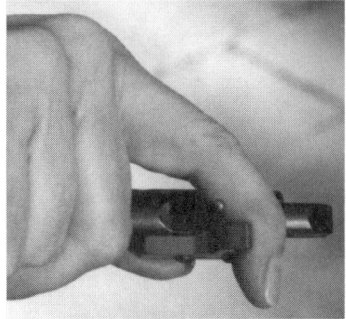

Fig. A

Activator (*real trigger*)

Captivator (*stationary trigger*)

Bernie's Can't Punch™ Wrist Strap Release by Scott

overload," and therefore unaware of the "real trigger." As the shooter activates back tension, which in turn pulls the elbow rearward, the hand starts to slip *slightly*, through the wrist strap, as in the previous example. This pulls the curve in the index finger out *slightly*. The middle pad of the finger is then pressed harder against the real trigger and sets it off . . . without anticipation. If the archer tries to punch it, the curve in the index finger arches forward and away from the *Activator* or "real trigger." This makes it impossible to punch or "hammer" the way

Paul Arnold, Marshfield, WI, writes:
Dear Bernie,

    After attending your school and shortening my draw length by 2", and changing numerous other things, I went back home and started shooting the empty bale. It took me 2000 arrows to get the feeling I was after. Next, I shot your reduced target bridge program for a month and then went back to shooting targets. You said that my scores would go down before they came up and they did! But, after about a month my scores started coming back up. Soon I was at my old average, then above it . . . 300 with 45Xs, then 55 Xs, and one day 300-60 Xs - I shot it with your **Can't Punch Release!** I now shoot carefree archery thanks to you. Hi, my name is Paul Arnold and *I **had** target panic!* Thank you, Bernie.

Bernie Pellerite

Tommy Ray, Dixmont, ME *(age 8) had target panic so bad, he was unable to draw his bow. With the help of **Bernie's Can't Punch Release** and his dad, Tom (a shooter school graduate), he was cured and has gone on to win many tournaments. At the World IBO Championships he finished with (a perfect score) 100 points with 9 out of 10 X's, and a robinhooded arrow! He also went to Africa with his dad and harvested 3 warthogs and an impala with his **Can't Punch Release**.*

you can with ordinary index finger releases *(see Fig. A, pg. 169)*. Also because the wrist, forearm, and elbow have to be relaxed and in a straight line pointing directly away from the target to make the release fire properly, the shooter's *left and right misses practically disappear!*

Hey, what about us finger shooters? Okay, I said I'd include you guys! One of the keys to successfully shooting with back tension and a finger release is to *make sure that the back of the hand is completely relaxed, stretched out, and flat . . . not cupped.* The three fingers (or two) should contact the string in the first joint or, *preferably,* deeper *(see Diagram A)*, not the fingertips *(see Diagram B)*. This allows the fingers and the back of the hand to be relaxed, and as the hand travels rearward, the

*Mike Martin of Niagara Falls, NY, a shooter's school graduate, has won two IBO Indoor Worlds, two Canadian National Masters and the CFAA Nationals Team 300 Round Championship, in the Senior Pro Division, while using **Bernie's Can't Punch Release**.*

Idiot Proof Archery

fingers hinge out of the way of the string at the *second joint*. If you try to hook shallow on your fingertips, this will cause the back of the hand to "cup," which causes tension throughout the rest of the hand and wrist, causing much more string oscillation during "let-go." It can also cause the arrow to come off the rest while drawing the bow. **NOTE:** Most successful finger shooters draw to anchor with all three fingers, then "drop" or "drag" either the top or the bottom finger before starting back tension. The direction of pull should be in a straight line directly opposed to the target. Again, the back of the fingers, hand, wrist, and forearm must be *relaxed*, and stretched out on this imaginary line or "direction of pull." This is not always possible for some shooters, but by getting the elbow back as far as possible behind your head, this will eliminate a lot of inconsistencies and excessive string

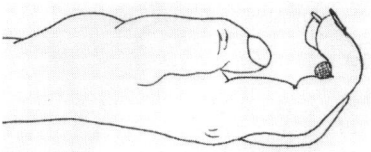
Diagram A - Deep Hook

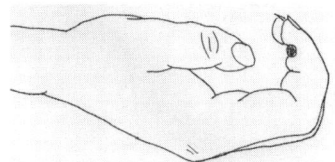
Diagram B - Shallow Hook

Key Point #74

One of the keys to successfully shooting with back tension and a finger release is to make sure that the back of the hand is completely relaxed, stretched out, and flat, not cupped.

Triple robinhood from 40 yds. for finger shooter Norm Lewis, TV Weatherman, Baltimore, MD. Norm shot his first perfect 300 winning the NFAA Mid-Atlantic Indoor Sectionals (SFSL Division) not long after attending the NFAA Shooter's School. He has since won Atlantic City Classic, 2 outdoor nationals, 2 indoor nationals, and 7 state championships, all in 2 ½ years. Who says you can't teach an old dog new tricks!

Bernie Pellerite

oscillation such as "plucking the string." The last thing, and probably most important, is the *anticipation* and *amount of acceleration* that is used with this "motor system." The fingers are "ripped off the string" on the way back to conclusion (for example, touching the back of your neck or shoulder with the index or ring finger). *Don't try to "let go" of the string!* If you try this method, as your fingers start opening, the string actually moves ¼" to ¾" *forward* . . . *before the string comes off the fingers.* This is actually called *creeping* and is a Form Flaw (see chapter 11, #42). It's very inconsistent, because you always think about it . . . and therefore change it slightly, shot to shot.

Instead, as you *rip it back to your shoulder* . . . "*refuse to hold it!*" . . . as famous Olympic coach Al Henderson put it. For example, before you start back tension, and you are *anticipating touching your shoulder* with your index finger, *you "power up" with enough back tension* to drive your elbow up and back through an imaginary wall. The elbow will drag the "whole unit" straight back . . . *ripping your fingers loose* from the string . . . keeping your index or ring finger *in contact with your face*, all the way back, until you *touch your conclusion* (neck or shoulder). Therefore, the *tips of your fingers will actually come in,* toward your face, as they are forced or pulled off the string . . . *they shouldn't pop open* or *flip open* away from your face, which is called plucking . . . another Form Flaw, see chapter 11 #30). If you pull until you touch your conclusion . . . I'll bet you have to let go of the string somewhere along the way! . . . but you let go *subconsciously,* because you anticipated the *conclusion,* instead of the "let-go."

Clickers If you shoot FITA competition with fingers and a recurve bow (out to 90 meters for adult men), chances are you will put a clicker on your bow. The same technique of *"rip it back,"* can be used successfully with a clicker *(see clicker photo on page 95).* Just set up your draw timing to where you *slow down your motor,* right before the clicker (but don't stop). At this point you should be *calibrated,* with your sight on target and . . . as you *commit* . . . you *accelerate through the clicker*, ripping your fingers rearward toward your "touch neck" or

172

Idiot Proof Archery

"touch shoulder" conclusion. Gold medalist and national champion Butch Johnson, and 7-time National Champion Ed Eliason, have successfully mastered this technique. If you stop at the end of the draw cycle, right before the clicker . . . you can develop *"clicker panic."* This stalls your "motor system" completely and freezes "your motor," making it almost impossible to pull it back any further. You then resort to jerking it through the clicker to release the string . . . not a pretty picture!

NOTE: Finger shooters, in particular, will find that if your elbow is slightly higher than your nose (one or two inches above), it is easier to use back tension and easier to get through the clicker.

If you can master "back tension," you will completely eliminate anticipation of the release and you will be free to (and be forced to!) . . . really *aim hard!* Remember, *aimers will always win!* . . . shooters can only play!

Whichever release method you choose, you need *to ingrain a* three to four second contraction of the draw side rhomboids (light a four second fuse), that will cause "let-go" subconsciously.

Key Point #75

Whichever release method you choose, you need to ingrain a three to four second squeeze of the back muscles (this is called lighting the fuse or starting the motor), that will cause "let-go," subconsciously.

The Subconscious Release

Many people spend years and years trying to figure out how to squeeze the trigger of their release, instead of jerking or punching it. Squeezing the trigger (for 99% of us) is *not* the answer either. This method is merely an attempt to "control punch" the trigger and keep the "motor" in the hand, instead of the back muscles. Therefore, the release will still be anticipated. The most common problem of my students is that the majority of them "control punch" or just plain "hammer the trigger" (or pluck the string) or have another form of release malady, which can be directly related to *consciously* releasing the string. Although there are no overnight cures, there are some easier ways to develop a *subconscious release* that *can't be anticipated*.

Bernie Pellerite

First, it helps if you understand the psychology behind it.

The Problem with a Conscious Release When your conscious mind *knows* or can *reasonably predict* the instant of release, because of feedback from the "tactile sensory receptors" in the finger(s), then the rest of your body reacts in anticipation of the shot, as does your mind, which causes you to stop aiming . . . and *start thinking about the impending release*. The secret of avoiding this is to *keep the mind immersed in aiming . . .* **which is the *only thing* that *keeps* the sight in the middle** while "let-go" happens automatically. That sounds hard, and it is, if you try to learn this technique by continuing *to practice on a target*.

Building a Subconscious Release As long as there is a target on the bale and the eyes are open, the eyes will focus on what they see . . . which is the target. And, *as long as you* are looking at, and therefore thinking about, a target, you cannot practice, learn, absorb any other change you want to make, including a subconscious release.

Remove the target. Stand about three feet from an empty bale, which is at shoulder height. By the way, if you have more than one problem in your form or release method to work on, practice only one at a time. Once it becomes subconscious, then work on another problem you have. (If you had to eat an elephant, how would you do it? All at once, or one bite at a time?)

A subconscious release is like having two people shoot the bow. The guy in front (the conscious) does nothing but aim and point the bow at the target, and never turns around to check on the other guy. The guy in the back (the subconscious) doesn't care about anything that's happening up front. He's just gonna pull and pull and finally . . . let go in four seconds. Therefore, if the guy in front *really trusts* the guy in back to do his job . . .

 **Key Point #76**

As long as there is a target on the bale and the eyes are open, the eyes will focus on what they see . . . which is the target. Therefore, as long as you are looking at and thinking about a target, you cannot practice, learn, or absorb a subconscious release.

Idiot Proof Archery

what do you think the guy in the front will be doing for the next four seconds?? . . . Aiming his butt off! The correct release technique for you will vary some, depending on which type of release you choose, but all of them have the same thing in common. The conscious mind *directs*

It takes two "minds" to achieve predictable accuracy!

the draw side back muscles to *start to contract* (then **trusts** them to continue) . . . and then the conscious mind *immediately starts aiming!* As the contraction increases it slowly moves the elbow back, forcing more pressure on the trigger (or for finger shooters, stretching out the fingers on the string, causing them to start losing their hold). This should cause release in about four seconds with *enough **stored tension** to reach your conclusion.* The only thoughts allowed are of focusing harder and harder on the *exact middle* of the *target!* If your conscious mind leaves aiming (even for an instant) and goes to check on "the guy in back," you should let down and start over.

This technique must be practiced daily on an empty bale or bow simulator, by drawing to anchor, centering the pin or scope in the peep sight (pre-load the trigger on thumb or index finger releases) and then *close your eyes.* Contract your back muscles (on the draw side) so you can *internalize* what that *feels like* without being aware of anything else, except *that feeling* . . . which builds muscle memory. It is important to practice this first, to familiarize yourself with, and later ingrain things like . . . how much pressure you can put on the trigger without

Bernie Pellerite

setting it off, or how much elbow rotation or elbow drive (not wrist rotation) and back tension it takes to accomplish a slow, steady, *dependable* technique that will activate the release (or pull your fingers off the string), *in approximately four seconds.* Some push/pull shooters also push with the bow arm side at the same time that they are rotating or pulling with their string arm elbow. This push/pull might make it easier for some people to get the release to go off *(if they can keep both the push and pull even).* Whether you choose the hold/pull (preferred) or the push/pull method, this should be done one to two times a day (in 30 to 50 arrow sessions), over a period of three to four weeks . . . until it becomes *totally automatic.* **NOTE**: At first (for three or four days) close your eyes half the time, then *when you are sure of the "feeling" you are trying to absorb, keep your eyes open all the time.* But, if you can't resist picking a hole or something on the bale to aim at . . . take the *sight off!* You may want to use the **PanicMaster and Bow Simulator**, if you *can't handle* the boredom of the bale . . . most people can't. Nearly all shooters think because they did it right five times in a row . . . that they've got it! So, they can't wait to put up a target to see if this works! **It won't!** I'll guarantee you . . . **you don't have it yet** . . . you just, "bumped into it" five times in a row. When you "bump into it" five hundred times in a row, **perfectly** . . . **then you've got it!** For most, it takes 2,000 to 3,000 shots for *back tension* to become automatic, and a *minimum of 21 days!*

These methods are illustrated in more detail in **Volumes 2** and **3** of the NFAA Shooter's School Videos and in **44 Form Flaws** of the Shooter's School Master Series *(see Appendix).*

If you don't ingrain the release to the subconscious level, most personalities will eventually experience more serious consequences. S-H-H-H! Don't say it out loud! You might catch it *(see chapter 10)!*

Chapter 10

"Hi, My Name is Bernie and I've Got Target Panic!"

This chapter is for those of you who need a refresher course, didn't get the videos or get to the shooter's school in time, and already have target panic. The first thing you need to know is that you can relax . . . *there is a cure!*

**Target Panic and Denial
(Denial Is Not Just The River In Egypt!)**
In my opinion (and in most informed industry leaders' opinions), the single greatest underlying cause for the loss of participation in target archery, bowhunting, and 3-D . . . is target panic. Until recent years, when I started doing surveys and compiling questionnaires in the NFAA Shooter's School, there was no accessible data on the soon-to-be extinct "endangered species" known as *Festivasaurus Toxophilus Rex*, commonly known as the *competitive tournament archer*. Having surveyed and worked with over 1,600 students (a third of them have already won state through world championships), we now have sufficient data to make some definitive statements and draw some inescapable conclusions about the habits, backgrounds, preferences, psychology, and mind set of the average and the advanced level tournament archer and bowhunter. It's amazing to discover that approximately 25% of these students admit they came to the shooter's school, primarily *to cure their target panic*. Another 10%, after some discussion, think they might have "just a touch" of it. (That's kind of like being *"just a touch" pregnant* . . . either you is, or you ain't!) In

Bernie Pellerite

1998, I started another experiment. I asked the students, who believed they had target panic, to get up from their seats and stand in the back of the room in a group. Usually about three quarters remained seated. I then went through the list of symptoms of target panic . . . like freezing, snapshooting, flinching, and punching. I ask the seated students, "Out of the last five hundred shots you took, did any of you . . . *freeze below or to the side* of the spot and couldn't get the sight in the middle of the target . . . and then tried to jerk it into *or through the spot* . . . shooting as the sight crossed the X?" (Sort of a "drive-by" shooting!) Usually several students would then join the "panic group," standing in the back. "How about shooters that *freeze in the middle* of the X, but can't shoot?" Once again, a few more joined the standing students. "How many shoot as soon as the *sight touches the bullseye* or spot on the 3-D animal they're aiming at (snapshooting)?" Again, a few more joined their counterparts. "How many *flinch* while trying to release?" A few more would join the standing group. "How many recurve shooters freeze up on the clicker *(clicker panic)?*" A few more would go to the back. "How many *punch the trigger* or *pluck the string*, in an effort to get it to go off at the *exact moment the sight is in the middle?*" Even more of them would join the group. "How many can shoot 3-D animals, but *not spots?*" A few more go to the back. "How many can shoot dots, but can't shoot accurately when it's a *trophy buck* (buck fever)?" Same results as before. Usually by then, all the remaining students have joined the others . . . *leaving all of the chairs empty*. Occasionally, in about one out of five schools . . . there would

Idiot Proof Archery

be one person left seated, who after some real hard probing by me *confesses . . .* or his buddies in the back would tell on him . . . "He does it, too! He just lies about it!" Or, he grudgingly admits to having a problem ". . . *only in tournaments!"* Well, Duh! Isn't that the point? Are we tournament archers or *practice archers? (You don't really want to know the answer to that question! We'll talk about that in chapter 14.)* Anyway, at the end of this experiment, there is usually no one left seated (once in a great while there is one person, who truly doesn't have panic). The people in the back are usually all smiling or laughing out loud by now, because they are so *relieved* to find out that they are all in the same boat and *the guy sitting down is really the odd ball . . .* not them! It has figured out to more than 97% of my students have identifiable target panic with one or more of the above symptoms (either all of the time, most of the time, or once in a while). The problem is, most people don't think . . . or don't want to think, that their symptom (punching, freezing, etc.) . . . is really *target panic . . .* which to them is fatal "Archery Aids!"

Most are astounded to find such a high percentage are infected and, maybe more important, that most shooters are in *complete denial* about their target panic. Furthermore, most don't really understand what target panic is! They don't realize that punching is a symptom of panic, or don't realize that freezing, snapshooting, or flinching are all symptomatic of panic . . . and "tournament nerves" is simply *target panic in tournaments,* etc. I've also heard "I don't have target panic . . . I just freeze below *sometimes."* It is *very important to note* that panic, like most afflictions and addictions, has various degrees of severity. One thing they have in common (in the beginning stages at least) is *denial . . . I don't have a problem!* When

Key Point #77

More than 97% of my students have some form of identifiable target panic . . . the stats are even higher for the general archery public!

Key Point #78

Most shooters are in complete denial about their target panic.

Bernie Pellerite

dealing with alcoholics for example, there are many stages of *functional alcoholism;* from the stock broker who has three martinis for lunch, but *doesn't have a problem,* because he can still *function* in his job . . . to the housewife who hides vodka bottles all over the house and is tipsy by noon, but still manages to get the kids off to school, clean the house, and put dinner on the table. In archery, we also have thousands of shooters that are *functional,* so to speak, and *don't really have a problem* (they insist) because they "only flinch" *once in a while* . . . or "only *froze twice* in the last tournament." We also have plenty of snapshooters and punchers that can *"control punch"* a 295 out of a possible 300 indoors, or a 180 out of 200 on a 20-target 3-D course. To hear them tell it, they *"don't have much of a problem"* and they can *"control it!"* . . . *RIGHT!* If you believe that, I've got some swamp land in Florida I'd like to sell you!

As both alcoholism and target panic progress, partially because of *denial,* the frequency and severity of their symptoms increases. Soon, *"denial"* turns into *"despair."* In alcoholics, it is called *debilitating alcoholism* . . . that would be the wino that lives in a refrigerator box, and ends up dying of the disease. Archery also has . . . *debilitating target panic.* This is the guy who *flinches* eight out of ten times that he draws the bow, or the guy who *freezes* below the target every time and jerks it up and *snapshoots* in a futile attempt to get it into the center. Or, the girl who "hammers the trigger" as soon as the sight touches the target . . . they all are *completely destroyed mentally!* They can't have any fun shooting the bow any more. Let's not forget the bowhunter who can't put the pin on the vitals of the deer and ends up missing or, even worse, wounding several animals. All these people are in the same boat and end up *quitting!* **Note:** I helped "bowhunting rocker" Ted Nugent through a similar problem. He couldn't put his pin in the vitals of an *antlered* whitetail buck . . . he was okay on non-antlered deer. But, because bowhunting was *practically Ted's life* . . . other than music . . . he was *smart enough to get help,* before it got so serious that *it* took him out too!

Idiot Proof Archery

Ted Nugent, bowhunting rock star said the following after Bernie cured him of his target panic, "The only real remedy I know of is Bernie's **Detox Exorcism Program (Tedism!)**. The program is tough, but it's the only way. If you can't absolutely lock on to the target, look into Bernie's proven program. Bernie has produced a series of great videos that deal specifically with this target panic hell. Combined with his laser-sighted training device, Bernie's PanicMaster and Bow Simulator, it has changed archers' lives across the land."

Unfortunately, the guy who shoots 300 with 50 Xs (possible 300 with 60 Xs) *in practice* . . . but shoots 299 with 48 Xs in tournaments, has the *same problem*. However, he doesn't even want to admit he has any problems . . . i.e., "my release misfired!" . . . or "my peep sight keeps turning" . . . or "my scope is loose!"

Regardless of the symptoms it manifests, target panic really boils down to not trusting your subconscious "let-go" system — trying to do two things with the conscious mind at once, . . . control the sight on the target and control the finger on the trigger, or "let-go" system . . . both at the same instant! It is3 actually a *loss of confidence in the shot sequence because it is either out of order, incomplete, incorrect, or nonexistent.* The archer is slowly programming through a defective and defensive shot sequence how to "punch" while trying to aim, or freeze below the target, etc. This is because they are afraid of missing the target, by trying *defensively* not to miss it, instead of trying *offensively* to hit the middle of it! In a nutshell, the cure is really the reverse of this "target generated programmed response." As I

Key Point #79

Target panic is trying to do two things with the conscious mind at once . . . i.e. keep the sight on target and operate the "let-go" system. It is actually . . . mistrust of the shot sequence . . . which is either out of order, incomplete, incorrect, or nonexistent!

Bernie Pellerite

Jon Stephens of Inkster, MI, after attending a shooter's school, at the age of 19, shot his first 300 under the pressure of the toughest and biggest indoor tournament in the world ... the Las Vegas Shoot. His personal best before the school was 285 and he was frustrated to the point of quitting archery.

touched on before, it involves offensive reprogramming off target! ... which retrains your release ("let-go" system) to the point that you *trust* it, and therefore don't have to think about any part of it, except to start it. (Like you really don't have to think about walking or driving a car most of the time.) Once you trust your motor system, all your mind has to do is . . . aim! Nothing but aim! If your conscious mind has to "check up" on, or "assist" what's happening with the "let-go" system . . . you haven't got it trained. Or, more probably, you don't *trust* that it is trained well enough to work by itself without your direct thought or control. *(I have repeated this concept before and will again by the end of this book . . . because that's how important it is and — repetition is the only way for some people to grasp it!)*

Coming Out Of The Closet —
It's Normal To Develop Target Panic

You must understand that (because of our training methods) target panic is *normal* . . . not an exception to the rule! Therefore, you should realize that you are not all by yourself and, in fact, it is quite typical and understandable that you have this disorder. It's really *abnormal* if you don't ever develop target panic unless you are 1) a

 **Key Point #80**

You must understand that target panic is normal . . . not an exception to the rule.

Idiot Proof Archery

beginner, or 2) a recreational archer who really doesn't care where the arrows go, or 3) you've been brought up in archery from the beginning, with a qualified coach who truly understands the problem. These coaches were almost nonexistent, until recently. Because so few were really conversant with the causes and symptoms of target panic, in 1999 I started giving free seminars at several major events like the AMO (Archery Manufacturer's and Merchants Organization) convention/show, the Las Vegas World Archery Festival, the NFAA Indoor Nationals, the ASA World Championships, and other shoots . . . just to get the word out. The response has been amazing and very liberating for hundreds of shooters and shop owners who come to these seminars and finally confront their "demons." Hopefully, if this trend continues, it might be okay or even fashionable someday to admit you have it, and we're all in the same boat. That, in fact, is one of my main goals. That's why my opening statement in these seminars is, "Hi, my name is Bernie, and I've got Target Panic!"

We lose participants who feel that they cannot master the "sport" because they can't get past their panic, can't enjoy it any more, and are ashamed and embarrassed to admit it out loud. They're actually *afraid to find out* they have it, because they think it's always "fatal" (incurable) and/or there's always been a stigma attached to it. Most are in denial because of their macho, Type A egos and fear they will be laughed at, ridiculed, or embarrassed in front of their friends. They'd sooner tell their buddies that they like to dress up in women's clothes than admit to having *the problem!* So, they lie and alibi and fabricate the reasons for their lousy scores or wild

Bernie introduces the industry to the target panic epidemic.

Bernie Pellerite

misses. "That stupid string loop slipped, again." . . . "It's my bow. It just jumped out of time. I think I'll get a one-cam!" . . . "My pin sight is loose!" . . . "My serving separated.". . . "My nocking point slipped up!". . . "Somebody must have screwed around with my rest." etc., etc. I have compiled over 100 reasons why I missed (I had target panic for over three years!) If anyone needs some really ingenious and inventive excuses, just e-mail me at *AskBernie@aol.com or go to my web site www.robinhoodvideos.com* . . . I'll sell them pretty cheap!

The Cause . . . How we learn

One of the main causes for all this lies with *our training method*. As with most people in America, archers tend to want *instant gratification* and *results*. We are more interested in the "bottom line" or end result and in having fun, while we are learning. We are hooked on seeing the arrow fly and/or hit the target or animal . . . it validates our fragile egos . . . "Look what I did!" Trying to master any shooting sport however, depends heavily on *repeatable constants* in form, aiming and execution. As I said before, excellent archery is a learned discipline . . . like a good golf swing or solid tennis backhand. It is not something we are born with and all three sports normally require years of practice and considerable instruction and supervision by a qualified expert to master them.

We could learn a valuable lesson from the Korean archers who dominate international archery competitions. Their training program for beginners starts with a month of drawing and shooting an *imaginary bow!* They stress that your mind can only do *one thing at a time*. . . you can *learn form*, or *you can aim* — but *not both at once!* You can't think about your back muscles or bow arm while you are aiming; something has to give. The second month, they draw and release a rubber stretch band. The third month, they are given a very light, unbreakable bow (with no *arrows)*, to draw and release. This is how they learn to pull and release it subcon-

Key Point #81

Koreans learn their form and technique off the target first!

Idiot Proof Archery

sciously, with the correct muscles and form in place. **NOTE:** Students proceed at different levels, depending on their innate skill level. They are not allowed to proceed to the next step before truly mastering the previous steps!

They are not confused at this point, with trying to aim at or hit a target. By the time they get to shoot arrows with a tournament bow, they have ingrained their form and release into *"subconscious muscle memory."* Consciously now, all they have to do is aim. . . and the rest happens automatically.

This training method is much the same in other sports. When we first learn golf, tennis, or boxing, we don't try to compete against an opponent, or in competition. As beginners, we don't go to a golf course and get in a foursome . . . we go to the driving range, hit numerous buckets of balls into an empty field and hopefully get some advice from a pro or an instructor. In tennis, we don't try to score and compete while we learn how to swing the racket. We hit thousands of balls against a blank wall or back to an instructor. In boxing, we don't begin fighting against opponents, we learn on a punching bag with a coach, and then spar with a noncompetitive opponent.

Unfortunately, for the vast majority in archery, the first shots we take are at a target . . . *which is our competition. You can't learn any sport or discipline while you are competing!* But, because of our upside-down training methods, we are forced to try to aim and do multiple complicated physical tasks simultaneously . . . all with our conscious mind. As our sight aperture is just reaching the center of the target, our mind anticipates that we must now hurry up and hit the trigger (or let go of the string) . . . as the sight arrives on target . . . or before the sight moves away from the center . . .

Key Point #82

In archery, our competition is the target . . . you can't learn how to do any sport or discipline while you are competing!

Bernie Pellerite

or before we start to shake from holding it too long. This comes from the misguided belief that we need to have a "rifle sight picture," and we must have the sight in the exact middle when we release the arrow for the arrow to go into the middle! We fail to realize that we all have a "natural arc of movement" and no one has a perfectly still sight . . . it always moves in and around the spot continuously. Therefore, when we see the sight in the exact center, by the time we release . . . the sight is on its way *out* of the center! Not understanding this is why, during the shot process, our mind oscillates back and forth from target to the fingers on the string, or the release trigger finger several times, in an attempt to time the release while the sight picture is perfect! Is this what we call a practice method? It sounds like we are trying to program ourselves to subconsciously shoot while we arrive on target, or shoot while we are leaving the target . . . not while we are staying on target! Obviously, this learning method eventually sets up and programs all kinds of mistrust and other undesirable reactions that we have to de-program later . . . snapshooting, freezing, punching, etc. That's why you are reading this chapter, *isn't it?*

Now that you have heard the basics and how the components of the shot work several times, I will try to go through the entire target panic scenario again. Now, let's see if you can finally wrap your head around this entire *enigma wrapped in a contradiction!* Good luck! If it was easy to understand, I wouldn't be writing this book and the book wouldn't be so long!

As stated at the beginning of the chapter, one of the working definitions of target panic is *consciously trying to keep the sight on target and cause the release of the arrow . . . both at the same time!* This concept is obviously impossible . . . *because the conscious mind cannot process two thoughts at once.* Also, because we *try* to think about both things at once, the symptoms of target panic (punching, snapshooting, etc.) develop because we slowly program an incorrect, out of order or incomplete shot sequence into our subconscious mind (or we don't have a sequence at all). Because we end up with a bad (or non-existent) shot sequence that we have *no confidence* in, we get inconsistent

Idiot Proof Archery

or bad results . . . which causes our conscious mind to *mistrust the sequence* even more and *reinforces the belief* that we have to do the aiming and the "let-go" *both* with the conscious mind . . . which is *impossible* because you can't do two things . . . etc., etc. A vicious circle, isn't it! The circle eventually gets *tighter and tighter* until we can't do anything right any more . . . and we just give up and go get a fishing pole!

As we discussed earlier, this chain reaction is perpetuated because we are lead to believe that *we aim first, then we shoot!* But actually, we should *shoot, then aim!* . . . Remember? *Shoot, then aim!* Light the fuse (start the motor), then AIM! Since the motor causes a *delayed release* in three or four seconds, that's really the same as shooting a rifle. You squeeze . . . *then* you aim! Aim *has to be* the last thought you have . . . to get an excellent rifle shot . . . or archery shot . . . or baseball pitch . . . or basketball shot . . . or golf swing . . . or tennis serve, or any one of a hundred athletic exercises. They all work like shooting a bow . . . and shooting a bow works just like all of them! Think about it; if you were throwing a baseball, what is the last conscious thought you should have before releasing the ball? . . . the catcher's mitt! You shouldn't think about or look at the ball as you are throwing it, should you? You start the windup *consciously,* and then let it continue *subconsciously,* as you cock your arm. When your arm is about to come forward (to make the ball release from your fingers), I'll bet you are thinking about or concentrating on (aiming at) the middle of the catcher's mitt (target) . . . not *how or when* the fingers should release! Here is a typical scenario of when a pitcher gets into trouble (pitcher's target panic). It's the bottom of the ninth, 2 outs, bases loaded, score is tied, with a full count on the batter (3 balls and 2 strikes). Now he's in deep mental doo-doo! He's *afraid he'll miss* the strike zone and walk the winning run in (fear of missing with severe consequences, the same as us)! So now he doesn't *trust* himself or his subconscious throwing sequence. Now, he can't just look at the mitt and rear back and fire the fast ball, like he's been doing in practice, and has been taught to do, and has been doing for the whole game . . . up

Bernie Pellerite

until now! He's got to be r-e-a-l-l-y careful (he thinks) to make sure that he doesn't miss and walk the winning run in! So, what does he do? Probably the same as you and I . . . he tries not to miss the huge strike zone (a defensive throw) as opposed to focusing on and hitting the exact center of the catcher's mitt (an offensive throw). He tries to carefully guide it (consciously control on-target and "let-go") . . . *two thoughts at the same time.* (Target panic, in baseball vernacular . . . he's gonna choke!) His last thoughts were mixed between . . . make sure to snap the wrist and "God, I hope I don't hit him in the head!" Let's see . . . snap the wrist and don't hit him in the head . . . Where do you think the ball will go? That's right, probably right at the batter's head or maybe in the dirt, because he was trying to be really careful and think about snapping his wrist (which he could always do before now . . . without thinking!). But as I mentioned many times, anything you do consciously will be anticipated, judged, analyzed, and changed (just a little) . . . to try and make it better! You see, everybody in any of the above sports gets target panic, too (they just call it *choking!*). If you've ever see Shaquille O'Neal *try* and shoot a freethrow (he only makes 30% of his foul shots) . . . it's not a pretty picture!

Programmed Release Problems

Punching the Trigger Every time you see someone playing any sport in a pressure situation and they *choke* . . . that's the same feeling that archers have had for years. They won't trust their "motor program" to work on its own — like they trained it to — while they concentrated on aiming. They don't trust their throw, swing, stroke, pass, pitch or whatever, to happen automatically, while they *focused* (conscious aiming) on the front of the rim, receiver's chest, catcher's mitt, incoming ball, or middle of the gold, etc. But, because they don't throw the exact same pitch, or swing at the exact same fast ball, or shoot the exact same jump shot over and over and over . . . like we shoot the exact same shot, exactly the same way . . . they don't anticipate *all* of their shots, pitches, swings, etc., like we do. Therefore, they don't develop *choking* (their form of

Idiot Proof Archery

target panic, except maybe Shaq) to the same degree or with the same frequency that we do. This is because they have another team, player or different types of shots in their sport which changes their strategy, sequence, delivery and/or rhythm continually. For instance, take the different shots in golf . . . a driver off the tee . . . a 3 iron off the fairway . . . a wedge from the sand . . . a long putt, or hopefully, a short putt . . . all done with a different club, with a different club head speed or swing angle, which *keeps anticipation to a minimum*. Plus the fact that, all of them have professional coaches that keep them on track with a *sequence* that is *reinforced with drills* (repetition), *done without the competition present*, which keep them from ingraining or learning *bad habits* or *bad sequences*. Like trying to shoot a freethrow while you are trying to think of the front of the rim and how to make the fingers come off of the basketball . . . both at the same time! (By the way . . . does anyone have Shaq's cell phone number? I'll bet you I could get him from 30% up to 70% shooting from the foul line!) Anyway, because *archers do ingrain* these "two thoughts at once" concept, we end up with a lot of problems with our "let-go" systems, such as **punching the trigger.** We call it lots of names . . . thumping it, hammering it, jumping on it, pounding it, jerking it, popping it, triggering it, banging it, dumping it, and the most common one . . . punching it! All are nicknames for *doing it wrong* or *choking!* The conscious act of "punching" can usually be traced to one common source . . . *fear!* When we first learned to shoot, most all of us used our fingers to release the bow string. Most of us discovered that this was not as easy as it looked. Then, we probably saw another archer, whose groups were one-third the size of ours shooting a release, and said, "What's that thing in your hand?" . . . and were introduced to an "easier way." From that moment on, a mechanical release became part of our standard equipment. Some discovered quickly that it wasn't for them, but most of us stuck it out. At the beginning level, we usually fell into one of two Groups:

    The not-sure-I'm-gonna-stick-with-this-release-thing-so-I-don't-want-to-waste-a-lot-of-money-on-one Group, or The-I-

Bernie Pellerite

Can-Make-This-Work.-I-Just-Gotta-Make-This-Thing-Go-Off-Quicker-When-I-Want-To Group.

The Cheap Release Syndrome A lot of us fell into the first group. We were unsure about whether or not to stay with this "newfangled gadget," so we didn't want to invest very much money into this "iffy experiment." So, we usually ended up buying from K-Mart, Wal-Mart, discount catalogs, or the low-end section of the display case in our local archery shop. This was the beginning of the end for a lot of us. Why? Because a lot of cheap releases, (especially in the past) have too much travel in their triggers. If you set them firm or stiff, you almost have to jerk the trigger to release the arrow. Since trigger punching is directly related to fear and anticipation, which these things cause, most of us didn't have a chance.

To clarify this, it is necessary to understand that most of us first punch the trigger because we are scared to death that it will go off *when we are not ready* and/or if *the sight's not in the exact center of the target*. So, we don't put much pressure (if any) on the trigger, until we want it to release . . . then we "dump it" all at once . . . *punch it!* Most of us have experienced this first hand. This "pre-loaded fear" makes it nearly impossible (except for Type B personalities . . . remember them?) to squeeze the trigger, without anticipation. This leads to anxiety and more anticipation, which are all factors that prime and program us for the "conscious jerk method" of activating the trigger. The number of archers shooting well on a long term basis with a release like this, is as small as the number of lotto winners. Because they have stiff triggers with a lot of trigger travel, or too much trigger travel, period. . . they warn us . . . and *make sure* that we anticipate explosion! But, we still *think* we can control the instant of explosion, thereby controlling the impact point of the arrow. To most, this seems much less frightening and more logical. You just set your muscles for the shot, aim until the sight gets

$14.95 release with a plastic case

Idiot Proof Archery

where you want it . . . and then "punch it!"

The Hair Trigger Syndrome This second group is a bit more sophisticated and, being a "deep thinker" myself (plus I already tried the other way!), I was proud to be a member (and past-president) of the "Hair Trigger Association of America." Our numbers were considerably more than the "Trigger Travel Association of America" because our theory was much more imaginative. Since we recognized early on that a hard trigger with a lot of travel obviously caused more bow movement and w-a-y too much warning, we figured we'd "sneak up" on the problem. Through the purchase of a more expensive release (and therefore superior, we reasoned), with travel and pressure adjustments, we were able to super tune these "magic wands," until the trigger travel was less than a human hair and the trigger was so light, that the sound waves created by a squirrel farting in a nearby tree would set it off! That way, whenever we finally maneuvered the sight into position, we just simply "touched it off." Unfortunately, there was a flaw in our theory. As with most things we try in archery, *everything new works* . . . for about three days. Usually, a few days later, we would put an arrow in the water heater, almost kill the German Shepherd three houses away, or nearly drive a tooth through our bottom lip as we tried to draw to anchor. Then, in a club shoot or tournament, we suddenly realize . . . we are completely terrified to touch the trigger at all! To do so creates the same anxiety and anticipation as swimming naked at night, in a pool of snapping turtles! *Now, that's anxiety!* So now, we either pump our finger up and down on the trigger . . . you know the "ready, get set, go" method, or set up with our finger a half an inch away from the trigger and then "pounce" on it from ambush. Either way, *we were doomed!*

Key Point #83

As with most things we try in archery, everything works . . . for about three days.

Some Nasty Side Effects of Release Problems

With both methods, because they involve the conscious decision to set off the release, this anticipation eventually sets

Bernie Pellerite

up an "involuntary reflex reaction," which can vary from archer to archer, but usually involves the tightening of the bow hand at the moment the brain makes the decision to hit the trigger. This "reaction" usually causes additional bow torque, because we sometimes *grab* the bow or start *tightening* the muscles in the bow hand *before,* or *at the same time* we move our trigger finger or thumb on the trigger. As a result, we end up torquing the bow and/or the bowstring. We punch the trigger and torque the bow handle because we anticipated the "punch," which will usually evolve into more serious problems such as flinching, snapshooting or freezing. All of these examples of loss of control, including punching ("plucking the string" or "dead release" for finger shooters), are symptoms of target panic. They're all factors in the formula that we program into our subconscious. It goes something like this: *bad form = shaky sight picture = fear of missing, anxiety, and anticipation = triggering (punching or plucking) upon arrival on target = bow torque = total mistrust of your shot sequence = judge it(to be bad), analyze it (what did I do wrong?), and change something (every time we miss) = punching gets worse and/or additional symptoms develop (freezing, flinching, snapshooting) = can't enjoy shooting any more = total frustration = buying a fishing boat!*

Taking The Cure

So with all this in mind, I finally realized that the only way to get through to most people is to first get them to admit they have it! As you learned in the previous pages, there are a variety of symptoms and severities to most programmed addictions or afflictions. Remember, this is a mentally programmed "disease" and you *will not* and *cannot* accept the cure until you *admit you have it.* So, in the shooter's school, I now have the group in the back of the room (that admitted they have target panic, remember them?) take **Step #1** together. I say, "Repeat after me . . . Hi, my name is (your name), and I have target panic!" This admission gets them to commit, just like AA (Alcoholics Anonymous) and the other successful anti-addiction programs to **Step #2** — Reprogramming . . . another 12 Step program!

Idiot Proof Archery

Only I have a 12 step shot sequence that usually takes 2,000 to 3,000 off target repetitions on an empty bale or with my **Bow Simulator** or **Laz-Air** (the easiest way), until you trust it completely and it happens automatically, and *you can't remember how you used to do it!* (I explained these in chapters 7 and 8, but I'll list them again, for continuity's sake.)

D	**Step 1**	Set Foot Position/Posture
E	**Step 2**	Nock the Arrow
F	**Step 3**	Hook Up
E	**Step 4**	Set the Bow Hand
N	**Step 5**	Pre-Aim *(pick a spot to draw to and run a*
S		*positive mental preview)*
E	**Step 6**	Draw to Anchor *(includes putting sight on target and pre-loading trigger)*
	Step 7	Call Shot to Order *(am I in control of Step 1 through 6 and can I keep it through Step 12 for 4 more seconds? If not, let down!)*
O	**Step 8**	Commit *(anticipate going via your motor to*
F		*conclusion)*
F	**Step 9**	Start Motor *(start back tension or your release*
E		*method)*
N	**Step 10**	Aiming Moment *(mentally concentrate on and*
S		*talk yourself into focusing on the exact center of*
E		*the target, for five seconds. Your sight aperture will go there automatically)*
	Step 11	Followthrough *(this happens automatically because of released tension)*
	Step 12	Conclusion *(the predetermined end of #11 and the shot, that is reached only because you anticipated and powered-up to get here in #8, Commit)*

Done properly, installing this program off target (blank bale, **Laz-Air** or simulator) removes the cause of the panic . . . a bad or nonexistent shot sequence. Again, your sequence can be longer or shorter, but it must include the previous concepts

Bernie Pellerite

🎯 **Key Point #84**

As I stated over & over, in the final analysis, excellent archery is not a sport, it's a discipline!

and be consistent in cadence, duration, and order. Then, the little known but all important **Step #3** . . . is a *bridge* program, that *slowly builds* up *trust* in your new shot sequence . . . *on a target with a bow!* This starts on a large target at close range and eventually ends up on a regular size target at tournament distances.

The Missing Link . . . A "Bridge" From The Empty Bale Back To The Target For most personalities, shooting at three or four yards away on an empty bale, **Laz Air** or **Bow Simulator** then going immediately to a target at 20 yards or more, won't work. Moving back that quickly will usually shock your system severely and make you lose faith in your program, because *you didn't build up enough trust in your new sequence on a target yet!* Therefore, your target panic will return! Going back to the target, from the blank bale or bow simulator, should be *bridged*, or *done gradually*. It should be done in stages so your conscious mind can develop *confidence* in your new sequence and can adjust *slowly* to the difference between shooting at a blank bale and shooting at a target at tournament distance. A typical bridge program would be the **"21 Day Program."** After shooting the blank bale or simulator for 21 to 30 days, you might try shooting one arrow at a time, at 5 yards at a nine inch bullseye (no X ring), for three days. (Paper plates make great targets.) Don't worry about not hitting the exact middle of the plate (bullseye) or the arrow hole from your last shot. If you can't resist aiming at the same hole, use a new paper plate for every shot. Shoot one arrow only, then pull it, and start again (make sure you shoot it *correctly,* i.e. commit to conclusion, etc.). Any place on the nine inch bullseye is okay! Spend a minimum of three days, 30 to 60 shots per day at this yardage and target size . . . *don't cheat!* After that, move back to 7½ yards and reduce the bullseye to eight inches. Spend at least three days at this yardage. Every three days, move back 2½ yards and reduce the bullseye one inch. Continue in this manner and at the end of 21 days, you will be shooting from 20

Idiot Proof Archery

yards at a three inch bullseye. ***Caution:*** If you feel the target panic creeping back *at any time* at any of the yardages, go back to the previous yardage and spend three more days there before moving to the next yardage. You must *execute perfectly every shot,* for at least three days at each yardage, before moving back. For a very few less severe cases, you may be able to cut down the time spent at each distance to two days, which would get you to 20 yards in 14 days. **Note:** This is *not permission* for most of you to shortcut the 21 Day Program. This alternate program assumes that your reprogramming was particularly successful on the first part . . . the blank bale or bow simulator shooting. In some cases, you might want to try another drill, called **Rotational Aiming**, before shooting the empty bale or bow simulator. This would make some shooters go through a 3 Step Deprogramming process: 1) Rotational aiming. 2) Blank bale or bow simulator. 3) 21 Day Program. Rotational aiming was developed by Freddie Troncoso, to help people with severe *freezing* or *snapshooting.* Here's how it works. Take a large target and place many dots, randomly on it *(see photo).* Stand at 5 yards, draw, pre-load the trigger, aim at one of the dots . . . *but don't shoot.* Hold for 4 to 6 seconds (depending on your comfort zone) and let down. Draw and let down this way, 30 to 60 times a day (aiming at a different dot each time in no particular order) for 3 weeks. This will reprogram you so you are not subconsciously afraid of holding on target and you don't freeze off target and/or don't have the urge to snapshoot, as soon as you are on target. Eventually, you will be able to hold anywhere on the target you want and for as long as you want. This drill can be modified to fit your particular schedule or problems. For example, professional archer Jimmy Despart, one of the nation's top target

Rotational aiming

Bernie Pellerite

Photo by Arlyne Rhode

Pro archer Jim Despart reprogrammed his shot sequence using rotational aiming and the empty bale which cured his target panic. Jimmy has since shot two perfect scores at the Indoor Nationals, among other accomplishments, and is a top competitor.

archers, used this solution for his problem. The following is paraphrased from a book called, ***Professional Archery Technique*** by top pro Kirk Ethridge *(see Appendix)*. Kirk was the first pro to ever shoot a perfect score (600 with 120 Xs) at the NFAA Indoor Nationals. Kirk writes that, Jimmy had severe target panic several years ago and stopped shooting all together, which was a necessary component of the cure. For one full month, he simply drew his bow and aimed at the target, and then let down . . . *never firing*. By practicing aiming alone, he removed the stress of scoring (and fear of freezing).

For month two, Jimmy shot using no sight or target. He only practiced the mechanics of the *perfect release*, without having to worry about where the arrow hit. He fired arrows into blank bales of hay, and occasionally shot blindfolded at point-blank range. His entire focus was on the feel of the shot and followthrough (muscle memory).

During month three, he began to combine the two disciplines. Perfect aiming was mated with the perfect release and followthrough. Shooting for score, he allowed himself to get back into the game of archery. If he began having problems either aiming or releasing, he would return to the previous solutions for an entire practice session.

At the end of three months, Jimmy's target panic *demon was exorcized*, he never had a problem with target panic again.

In combination with the empty bale or bow simulator, one or both of these drills should get you back on track. **Warning:**

Idiot Proof Archery

In some cases your panic will *not go away*, or if it does, *it may return*. The following are some of the main reasons why.

Some personalities fail to trust the programming, because it is *not set deep enough* into the subconscious, in the first place (usually because of lackadaisical, halfhearted shot executions or insufficient reprogramming sessions). The blank bale is simply to catch your arrows, so you can concentrate on learning, changing, analyzing, or exploring parts of your sequence or shot blueprint that you think need improvement or that you don't trust. Remember, there are two very important things about this process, whether it's on an empty bale with a bow, or my **Laz-Air** or **PanicMaster and Bow Simulator**: 1) They won't give you the right answers . . . unless you ask the right questions! 2) After you've discovered the answers to whatever it was you wanted to find out, you must now commit to the task of *ingraining* or *grinding* them into your subconscious, through repetition, *until they happen automatically.* That's not easy and it won't happen in 100 shots. You must trust them *completely* to work on their own, without conscious thought on your part. That usually takes *at least 2,000 - 3,000 well thought out shots* . . . *done correctly!*

Key Point #85

The blank bale or bow simulator won't give you the right answers . . . unless you ask the right questions!

Shooting On A Blank Bale Alone, Won't Cure Your Target Panic If you don't reprogram the shot sequence that you had before . . . and you continue to shoot your "normal" shot sequence on an empty bale . . . it will not cure your panic. Remember, your old shot sequence was either incomplete, out of order, incorrect, or nonexistent. So consequently, the "bad" shot sequence that you have will simply be further ingrained by practicing it on the blank bale. Using the blank bale this way, may have a "placebo effect" for a short period of time, but your panic will almost always come back with a vengeance. Because in this case, the root cause of the target panic, as always, was the shot sequence, not the target. The faulty sequence

Bernie Pellerite

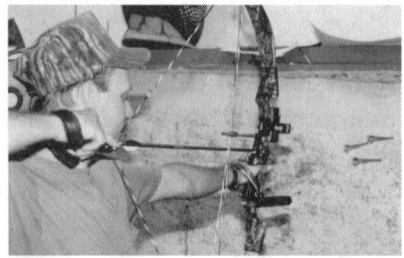

🎯 **Key Point #86**

The root cause of target panic, as always is the shot sequence, not the target.

caused you to fear missing the target, and removing the target, *removed the symptoms only.* Therefore, you will probably get only temporary relief from your freezing, punching, snapshooting, or flinching . . . because the cause is still there! A correct sequence, absorbed and trusted to the subconscious level is the *only way* you'll ever be panic free!

You Didn't Shoot The Blank Bale Exclusively This is a pretty common reason for not succeeding on the empty bale or simulator. Most shooters are not willing to give up tournaments or leagues to get rid of their target panic. The empty bale or bow simulator should be shot, *without interruption*. A complete sabbatical should be taken from shooting any and all tournaments, leagues, or targets for at least 42 days (simulator or bale for 21 days and then a 21 day bridge program . . . at least!), 30 to 60 shots per day. A lot of personality types need 90 days or more to reprogram their sequence correctly. If you try to shoot tournaments, etc., it will take much, much longer (eight months to two years), or it may not help at all. The shooter should concentrate on ingraining a specific program or personal shot blueprint. Shooting targets between empty bale sessions only serves to neutralize or reverse the reprogramming you're trying to accomplish.

🎯 **Key Point #87**

It takes a minimum of 21 days to change any habit, or to ingrain any subconscious program. Plus, you have a 2 step or 3 step program to do . . . so expect to take at least 42 to 63 days to succeed!

Note: If you think you have to shoot tournaments to please a sponsor, remember, you probably won't keep the sponsor very long anyway if you keep your target panic . . . so pick one! Nevertheless, if you think

Idiot Proof Archery

you must shoot these tournaments, then spend as much time as possible on the blank bale. Keep in mind, though, it will take a lot longer, possibly three to ten times as long!

You Didn't Shoot The Empty Bale Long Enough
Some shooters may stay on the empty bale (or bow simulator) for two to five days, not really understanding how long they *have to stay*, or what they're trying to accomplish. As soon as they think they have discovered the solution to their form, sequence, or execution problem (after maybe, two or three days), they quit the bale . . . *because they found the answer!* . . . *and then go right back to shooting targets. The problem is, they failed to ingrain and build confidence and trust in the change or solution they found* into their subconscious *completely*, and make it part of their total shot blueprint. They find their "new solution" still has to be done consciously (because they don't really trust it yet), and they are *not mentally free to aim!* They soon develop the same or similar symptoms of target panic they used to have. Then the cycle starts again. They try to treat the symptoms again . . . punching, freezing, etc., not the cause — a bad shot sequence! That's why most psychologists agree that on average, it takes a *minimum* of 21 days to change any habit, or ingrained subconscious program, depending on personality. (Some hardheads will take much longer!) As an example, if you write left-handed and decide you want to be right-handed, it should take around three weeks before you could comfortably write with your right hand (assuming you only used your right hand, *exclusively*, and wrote a great deal . . . one or two hours every day). Similarly, if your left hand were broken and was in a cast and you couldn't possibly write with it, you would learn pretty quickly to write with your right hand, if you *repeatedly* and *exclusively* practiced with it. If, however, your hand was not broken and you decided to learn to write with your right hand *just when it was convenient*, it might take 10-20 times longer to learn to write comfortably (subconsciously) with your right hand (if you ever learned at all!).

You Shot With Your Eyes Closed All Of The Time
Shooting with your eyes closed will help you internalize and

Bernie Pellerite

make you really aware of the details, techniques, and *"feel"* of the individual parts that make up your shooting form and program "muscle memory." This is good, if you are working on feeling some new aspect of your form, such as back tension, etc. However, shooting with your eyes closed for every shot, won't cure target panic, in most cases. Usually, as soon as you open your eyes, you *have to look at a target* at tournament distance, for the first time, with your new program. Also remember, *visual input* was not part of the practice routine you were working on. Since you didn't slowly develop trust for your new sequence with your eyes open and/or slowly bridge back from the bale or simulator to regular size targets at longer distances, the panic will re-develop for most shooters. Most forms of target panic are activated by a visual trigger, such as target acquisition or "on-target" sight picture. Therefore, shooting with your eyes closed all of the time *will not cure* most people permanently. You should shoot with your eyes closed about half of the time *at first*, to ingrain a particular feeling (muscle memory) that you want in your new program. Then later, toward the middle and the end of your final programming and bridge program, keep your eyes open *all the time*. And as mentioned previously, if you find yourself aiming at a straw on the empty bale, or an arrow hole, *remove your sight*. This will help you keep from redeveloping some types of target panic, such as snapshooting or freezing.

Eyes closed half of the time at first for feeling.

You did not use a bridge program Moving back to a target from the bale or the bow simulator too quickly will cause your conscious mind to mistrust your new shot sequence because it has not yet been proven on a target. Therefore, you need to use a bridge program, as we just discussed, to gradually reintroduce your new sequence

Idiot Proof Archery

to your conscious mind and build trust that it can and will succeed on targets of tournament size and distance. The problems I just mentioned are the main reasons why the program, *if not done correctly,* may fail to cure your panic permanently. This failure can be a contributing factor to *why so many people quit archery.* I discovered another main reason, which may come as a total surprise to most people.

Key Point #88

You must gradually introduce your new shot sequence to the target with a bridge program.

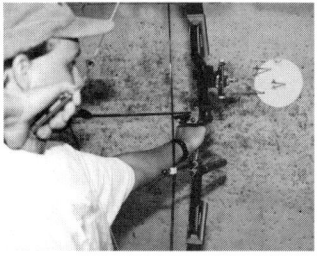

21 day bridge program

Understanding The Average Shooter's Profile

I've found through numerous surveys, that most people interviewed believe that archers, in general, are competitive and probably played other competitive sports in high school. Thus, if they played football, baseball, or any of the other organized sports, they would usually turn to a coach if they ran into problems with their sport. Surprisingly, out of all the archers surveyed with target panic, *less than 20% actually played any organized sports!* This amazing stat explains why most of them never looked for or relied on a coach or a coaching solution and didn't even realize the advantages of having a coach. They would then, quite predictably, become isolated and develop low self-esteem issues. When they start having trouble with their archery game, they think it's their fault that they can't shoot well, but don't want to admit they need help. So, they try to solve their problems by buying a new gadget, a new bow, or a dozen new arrows. After all, the *archery industry does push products . . . not education! It **is** run by manufacturers . . . not teachers!* A lot of archers don't know there are coaches and instructors out there that can help them with their head problems or their form. They can, however, always find someone willing to help them tune their bow or help support the status quo by pointing out

Bernie Pellerite

If they played football, baseball, or any of the other organized sports, they would usually turn to a coach if they ran into problems with their sport.

that this new whatchamacallit will probably get rid of your problem . . . which is where our real problem usually lies!

Typically, a competitive team sport athlete will try to improve themselves by getting a coach to help them with their problems (or buying a book or video). Unfortunately, as I have discovered, there's only about 20% in the category. Most archers have the philosophy that, if I can't win (or at least be competitive after buying six or seven bows and dozens of other accessories), I'm probably not cut out for this! . . . I think, I'll just quit! The majority of these people don't know the value of a coach or what other solutions are available. These troubled archers internalize the problems and eventually turn to another non-team sport, like fishing . . . something they feel they can't fail at.

I Understand That Not Everyone Will Listen Having been given all of these coaching solutions in baseball, golf, archery, or any other sport, not everyone will take "the medicine that the doctor prescribes." In the shooter's school, only about one quarter to one third of the class actually have the discipline, guts, time, or interest to bear down and take the cure for this affliction. The cure typically takes six weeks to three months of reprogramming and boring, tedious, non-fulfilling, off-target practice, which is why I developed the **PanicMaster and Bow Simulator.** They don't seem to hate this "laser-equipped gadget" nearly as bad as an empty bale, because the laser shows them where they would have hit, if there was an arrow in the bow. It comes on when they draw (and projects a dot on the target) . . . and goes off when they release. So wherever the laser dot was when it went off . . . that's where their *arrow would have hit!* Therefore, they can get some instant gratification for doing it right (or doing it at all!). However, at the same time,

Idiot Proof Archery

they soon realize it's just a simulator with a laser dot and their fear of missing soon subsides! However, the remaining archers who don't have the patience or dedication to take either cure, can continue to shoot bad or mediocre archery . . . and that's okay too, because now they have smiles on their faces. That's because they understand *why they miss* and aren't frustrated, confused, and at a loss for solutions. There is now much less chance of them quitting the sport because they now realize, "It's okay not to win!" They now know *why* they don't win!

It sort of works like this in other sports, too. I took golf lessons, but I still play really bad golf! (I figure, I might as well *see the whole golf course* . . . water,

Joe Church of Toledo, OH, had target panic and was snapshooting. He bought **Bernie's PanicMaster and Bow Simulator** *on Thursday and won the IBO World on Sunday. The next weekend he won the ASA World in the barebow division. Joe raised his average* **15 points in two days** *using the Simulator.*

sand, trees, deep rough, bushes, etc.) I have been shown the way to hit the ball correctly, and been given the drills . . . my cousin was a pro! But, I *chose not to put in the hours* of practice, hitting thousands of balls at the driving range, sand traps, and putting green that it would take to improve my game to a competitive level. The difference now is, I can continue to play bad to mediocre golf, but now *I enjoy the sport.* Before I took lessons, I was confused and mad all the time . . . threw my driver in the lake once! I couldn't figure out why that sucker sliced to the right all the time. Now, I laugh when I hit it in the lake, instead of throwing my clubs in! I made a conscious choice *not* to hit 1,000 balls a week at the driving range, like my cousin did. I now don't have to win at golf to enjoy it! If you really think

Bernie Pellerite

about it, archery is really *just a game* (like golf). And remember, we play games to have fun and . . . **If you're not having fun . . . you're doing it wrong!**

Don Williams, *works at Schupbach's Sporting Goods in Jackson, Michigan. By the way, Don is Bernie's tallest student at 6'9" and was stuck at an average of 300 with 50 Xs for over two years. I know a lot of you out there would like to be stuck at 300 with 50 Xs but Don was not a happy camper! After organizing a shooter's school and getting some personal coaching from Bernie, Don began his reprogramming. Bernie asked him to chart his scores after he came back from shooting the empty bale and began to keep score on targets again. Bernie told him his scores would probably go down before they came back up again . . . and he was right. Don later reported that when he returned to shooting leagues, the first few weeks dipped down to 295 or so with 35 to 45 Xs. As the weeks rolled by, his score came up and by week six Don's scores had returned to 300 and 50Xs. By week seven they were at 54-55 Xs. By the end of the eighth week, they were at 56-58 Xs. His indoor scores now average 57 Xs and, in 3-D, he is averaging 30 points higher since the school. He is presently in the top twenty of the IBO MBR and in the top ten to be Shooter of the Year in 2001. At the school, Don also became an NFAA Advanced Level Certified Instructor and a couple of years later became a Certified NFAA Master Coach. Don loves to coach and teaches what he's learned to anybody that needs help. Besides his regular duties at the pro shop, Don also coaches 170 kids in a winter league. Don says, "Keep up the good work, Bernie. This stuff really works!"*

Chapter 11

44 Form Flaws
When Things Go Wrong

The following is a list of 44 different form flaws, that I have identified in my coaching career. I will tell you how to identify them and also how to correct them. The correction is based on achieving "idiot-proof" form, which is much easier to do the same way every time, because it is natural and logical *(see photo)*. It also holds up much better under pressure, is less practice-intensive, and not as hard to absorb to the subconscious level, as some of the more unorthodox ways of shooting are. These 44 are the

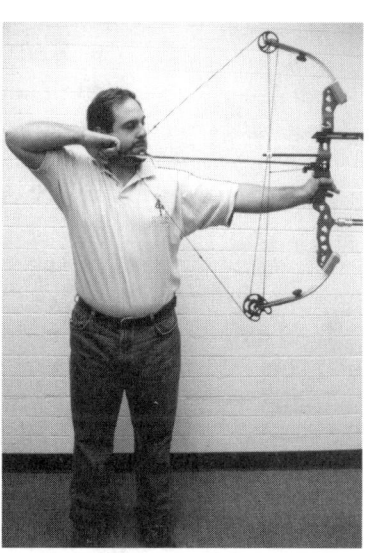

"Idiot Proof" Form

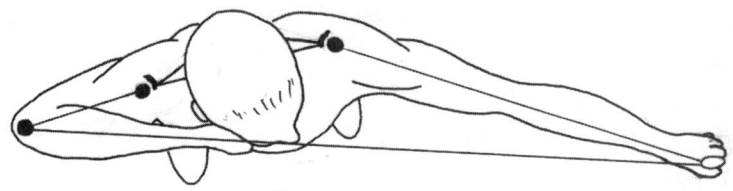

With a slightly open stance, you will probably find it easier to achieve "Idiot Proof" form.

Bernie Pellerite

The overhead mirror we use in the shooter's school, will reveal most alignment problems.

most common that I have noticed. However, I'm sure you can probably add to the list.

The list is broken into the following general categories: Stance, Alignment, Bow Hand & Grip, Anchor, Bow Arm, Finger Release and Mechanical Release. The assumption will be made that you are a male (so I don't have to say he or she every time), right-handed archer (so we don't have to say vice versa for lefties), shooting a release. The opposite will be true for left-handers. (Sorry southpaws, you need a better union!)

Take the information below and critique your form. Get an inexpensive 12" by 48" mirror (about $5.00 at a discount store, *see photo)* and suspend it overhead, with the front end hanging about one foot lower than the back. Put a video camera behind it and point it up at the mirror. Stand under the mirror and film yourself shooting. Or, prop the mirror up in front or to the side of you, so you can come to full draw and peek out of the corner of your eye to observe your form. Also, you can set up a video camera to tape different angles of your shooting form and play it back, using freeze frame or pause, to analyze and correct your form. In the shooter's school, we tape each student from three different angles, which has yielded outstanding results. First, an overhead shot (with the mirror), then a profile shot (from the side), and finally, a "laser shot" (laser mounted on the bow) to show aiming patterns. After we correct their form, we tape another profile shot (sort of a before and after), for them to keep for future reference. You can use this technique to see if you can recognize yourself in any of the next form flaws, and compare it to the picture of *good form* on the previous page. We also completely illustrate all these flaws on our video **44 Form Flaws** (see Appendix).

Idiot Proof Archery

Stance

1. **Feet Too Close Together** (ankles touching or almost touching.) This is a common flaw, especially among 3-D shooters. If your feet are too close together, it promotes leaning back, away from the target (another flaw). This is because you are holding out a bow that weighs 4 to 12 pounds in your left hand and you have to lean back, just to keep your balance. When you lean back, your bow shoulder comes up, which causes you to use the shoulder (deltoid) muscle instead of your back muscles. This *causes an unsteady sight picture.*

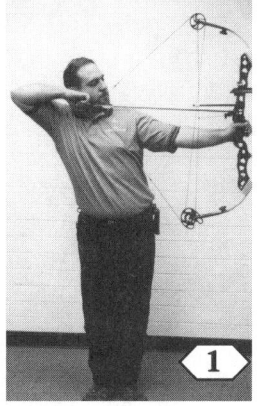

As you can see, one flaw can cause several more flaws, and conversely, correcting one flaw can help clear up other problems you might be having. Your feet should be shoulder width apart, with weight evenly distributed on both feet. This should also help with inconsistencies you might encounter in shooting up and down hills.

2. **Leaning Back** Looking from the side at the profile of an archer at full draw, there is sometimes a tendency to throw the left hip toward the target and lean back with the upper body. This is usually caused by having your draw length too long. This can cause the draw wrist to bend and throws the draw elbow into too low of a position, which makes back tension nearly impossible to achieve. This is because the pivot point in your back is at a much higher point (in your upper back) instead of between the shoulder blades

Bernie Pellerite

(see photos in #6 of high and low elbows). It also promotes rolling the bow shoulder, which creates tension in the bow arm and a shaky sight picture. Feet, hips, and shoulders should line up, one above the other. The aiming eye should be over the belt buckle and the buttons on the shirt should run straight down when looked at from a side view *(see photo, pg. 205 for example).*

3. **Leaning Over The Bow** Looking from behind the archer, he would appear to be bent slightly forward at the waist, shoulders and/or neck. Leaning over the bow causes premature fatigue, promotes creeping and erratic arrow groups. The head and neck should be relaxed on a straight spine.

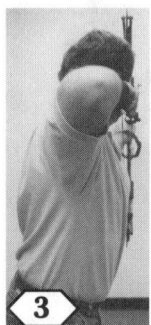

4. **Body Profile In "Z" Formation** This is a combination of several form flaws. Looking from the side at the profile of an archer at full draw, an archer will throw his front hip forward, the trunk of the body is leaning back, and the head is bent forward into the bow string, creating a zigzag or "Z" formation of the spine. It is nearly impossible to exactly duplicate all of these angles each time, especially when shooting up or down hills, thus making shooting form inconsistent. Once again, it is important to align the spine, head and neck in a straight, relaxed line.

5. **Twisted At The Waist** (feet open, shoulders closed) Looking from behind the archer, the feet would be slightly open, (15-30 degree angle), but the upper body would still be straight on a line to the target. This frequently happens when an archer changes his foot position to a more open stance, but doesn't adjust the upper body to line up with the feet. He sets his feet in the new position, but draws the bow back with his shoulders aligned "straight to the target" the way he is used to, especially if he has (or

Idiot Proof Archery

used to have) *too long of a draw length*. A symptom of this problem is sometimes a pain or cramp in the lower kidney area from being twisted at the waist. It is important that the *hips are directly above the feet*, and the *shoulders are directly above the hips*.

Alignment

6. **Draw Elbow Too Low** Ideally, the tip of the elbow should be about as high as the nose (or higher), to get proper back tension.

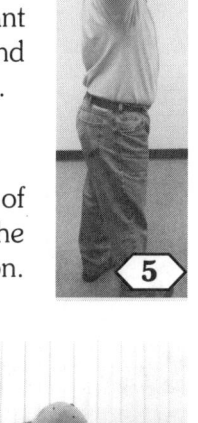

On an archer's back: if you draw an imaginary line from the tip of the elbow to the spine, it should end right between the shoulder blades at the rhomboid muscles - *(see photo 6A)*. If the elbow is too low, and you draw the imaginary line, it will end up in the upper shoulder area, a few inches below the neck *(see photo 6B)*. This will cause the bow to be pulled with the upper shoulder muscles and the arm muscles. For proper back tension, the bow should be pulled primarily with the *rhomboids*, located

A high elbow will help you use the rhomboids as the pivot point.

A low elbow will cause you to have your pivot point too high above the rhomboids.

at a point about 1" from the tip of the right scapula (shoulder blade on the string side, *see illustration of muscles on*

Bernie Pellerite

page 159). The elbow is operated with the *draw-side rhomboid back muscles only*, which acts as the pivot point to hinge the *entire in-line unit* from the rhomboids through the shoulder, and through the upper draw arm, to the tip of the elbow.

7. **Draw Elbow Too High** Some coaches will say that it is impossible to have the draw elbow too high, and most of the time I am tempted to agree with them, but there are exceptions. If the elbow becomes so high that the *draw wrist bends*, this can cause tension, and string torque problems. Also, if the elbow is *artificially high* (not naturally high such as an abnormally long upper arm) it would also elevate the draw shoulder much higher than the bow shoulder, causing tension and would be very hard to duplicate the same position shot to shot. In general though, higher is better than too low . . . as long as it is natural.

8. **Draw Elbow Out Of Line With The Arrow** If the tip of the elbow is outside (to the right) of an imaginary line through the arrow to the target, it can cause the release hand to *fly out* and away from the face, (causing string torque) instead of straight back, like it should. If the elbow is too far inside, (toward the archer's back at full draw, looking from behind the elbow) this can also cause bow and string torque. The draw elbow should be in line (or very nearly so), behind the arrow at the moment of explosion of the shot. (The exception to this is for some finger shooters and a few others who can't get their elbow in line because of limited range of motion or other physical limitations.) However, it's better to be a little too far inside the line, than outside.

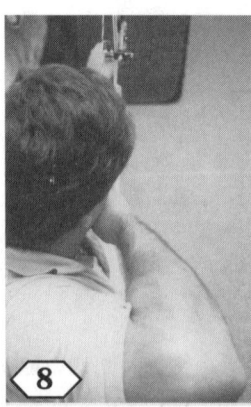

Idiot Proof Archery

9. **Draw Wrist Bent** (Release Shooters). Some archers bend their wrist because they are using the wrist and hand muscles to help pull the bow string back, instead of the back muscles. Ideally, the fingers should only be used to "hold on." The pulling should be done with the back muscles, which moves or rotates the elbow back. Unfortunately, some mechanical release models, such as a "concho type" release *(see photo 9A)* can only be shot with a bent wrist, because the barrel won't line up with a straight wrist *(see photo 9B and photo 2 on page 207)*. Other reasons for the wrist to bend are that the draw length is too long, or some shooters will collapse into the back of their neck, and/or put their thumb behind their neck (also see #15) at anchor, upon coming to full draw. Therefore, at the moment of explosion, the hand-wrist-arm unit sort of "springs back," causing string torque, which in turn causes unexplained lefts and rights, undesirable paper tears, etc. The wrist should be straight, expanded, and relaxed, regardless of whether you shoot with fingers or a mechanical release.

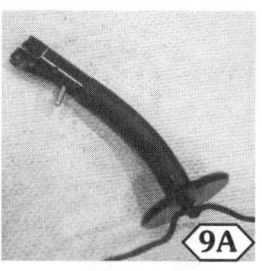
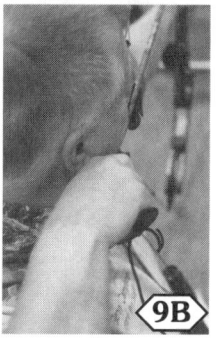

Bow Hand And Grip

The bow hand is a part of form that is much more important than most people realize, because *it is the final place that the human body touches the bow and can influence the bow's effect on the arrow, before it clears the front of the riser.*

10. **High Wrist Grip (Hand Position)** This hand position or grip is actually considered, by some, preferable to the low wrist grip that I recommend. The logic of the high grip is that there is less hand on the bow to influence the shot. In practice though, the average archer will find it nearly impossible to *duplicate* the exact same hand position and pressure on the bow handle *consistently,* over and over and over. There are a handful of well-known archers who have mastered the high wrist grip, and do quite well with it. However, it takes very strong wrists and many, many hours of practice to perfect it. More muscles are used in the high wrist grip than any of the others and therefore, causes more tension in the hand, which can cause an unsteady sight picture. When an archer starts to get tired, distracted, or starts to relax, the bow hand will usually start to "break down," and he will experience high and low arrows. I recommend the low wrist grip, because it is already as relaxed as possible, thereby much easier to duplicate over and over, regardless of the physical condition of the archer or the amount of practice put in. The pressure should be on the bone at the base of the thumb, on the thumb side of the lifeline. It should be directly in front of, and as an extension of, the radius bone (big bone in the forearm, *see photo D, page 135), not* on the web of the hand between the thumb and index finger.

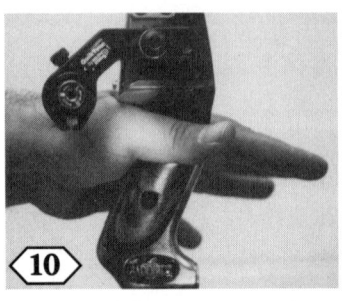

11. **Grip Across Lifeline** (too much hand in the bow). With a few notable exceptions, most top shooters prefer not to have the bow handle cross the lifeline or *"palmar crease"* on the hand. The reason for this is, there are muscles on both sides of the crease. They are called the *"thenar eminence"* (thumb side) and the *"hypothenar eminence"* (little finger side). If the grip crosses this crease *(see photo)*, four different reactions can be experienced at explosion:

Idiot Proof Archery

flex both muscles, relax both muscles, flex one muscle and relax the other, and vice versa. The handle should be placed on the thumb side of the crease with a relaxed bow hand (bone-to-bow contact, *see photos D and E on pages 135)*. There is also less chance the string will 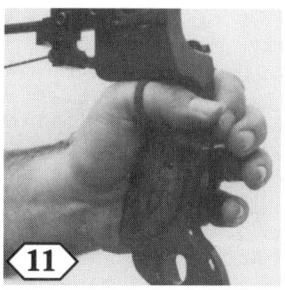 hit the bow arm, and less chance of bow torque with this position. To find a *torque-free hand position*, lubricate your hand or bow handle with water or baby oil, and try out many, slightly different hand positions. Find a torque-free hand position that will allow the stabilizer to jump *toward* the target, not left or right upon explosion.

12. **Too Much Thumb** (not enough hand in the bow). Just the opposite of #11. The handle is placed too far out on the thumb where only soft tissue (ligaments, tendons, and muscle) are holding the bow. This grip is very unstable, inconsistent, and causes bow torque (usually to the right). This hand position 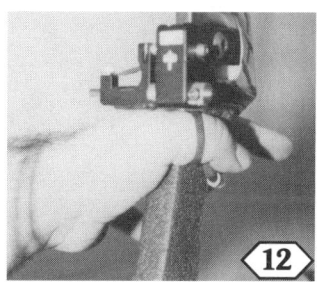 is sometimes used to try to avoid string contact with the wrist or forearm, which is more easily avoided by shortening draw length, opening stance, and/or not rolling the bow shoulder into the bow. Again, the bow handle should be placed against the bone next to the palmar crease, on the thumb side. This is solid, relaxed and easily repeatable.

13. **Grabbing the Bow or Gripping Too Tight** Grabbing the bow *upon release*, is generally caused by a conscious release or punching of the trigger, which "telegraphs" to the body and the bow hand, that the explosion is about to happen. When playing my student's videos back in

Bernie Pellerite

Grabbing the bow

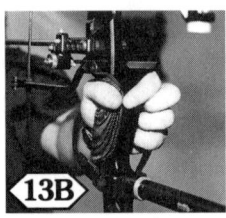

Freddie Troncoso invented this grip. It will keep you from grabbing and will also give you better string/arm clearance.

slow motion, we have witnessed, on many occasions, archers grabbing the bow *before* the arrow is completely clear of the arrow rest. They will usually punch and then grab, but sometimes they grab . . . then punch. Another variation of this flaw is gripping the bow too tight in the first place. Both of these problems will end up causing bow torque and unexplained misses. The use of a sling and/or tucking three fingers in *(see photo 13B)* can help eliminate these problems. Tucking the three fingers will also encourage proper placement on the bow handle. Leaving the index finger out (to lightly touch the bow), will give the archer a certain sense of security. If you are using a sling (and you should be), the hand should not be able to move more than ½" to ¾" away from the bow handle . . . any more than that and you won't have confidence in the sling; any less than that could cause some torque from the sling. The hand should be relaxed and you should let the bow *shoot* out of your hand, through your fingers . . . and let the sling catch it! So, you need to experiment and find out what works for you. Your new hand position should then be tested and practiced until it becomes automatic. This should be done, as with any new form change, on a blank bale, three feet away, or with a bow simulator!

14. **Fingers Spread And Tense** Spreading the fingers of the bow hand at full draw is usually a futile attempt to *stop grabbing the bow* upon release. The tension in the hand and bow arm will cause bow torque and an unsteady sight picture. Again, the more muscles that are involved in the shot, the more unsteady the sight picture becomes. Let the fingers of the bow hand completely re-

Idiot Proof Archery

lax. Upon release (as in #13), the bow should shoot "through the fingers" and the sling should catch the bow. Just like grabbing the bow, this bad habit should be retrained on an empty bale or bow simulator, until the habit is gone. Come to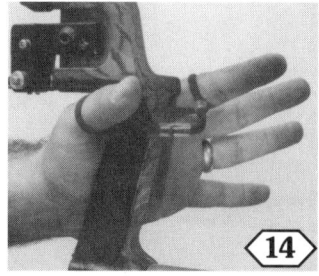
full draw normally and, instead of looking through the peep sight, simply stare at your bow hand while you execute the shot. Notice what your hand does . . . 100 to 300 shots later, you will have trained yourself to *relax your hand and trust the sling.*

Anchor

15. **Thumb Behind Neck** This causes the wrist of the draw arm to kink or bend. Upon release, the wrist recoils and returns to its original straight position, which in turn creates sideways, pre-loaded torque in the wrist and hand and is, therefore, transferred to the bow string. Putting the thumb behind the neck also allows the archer to collapse into the back of the neck, thereby *negating any back*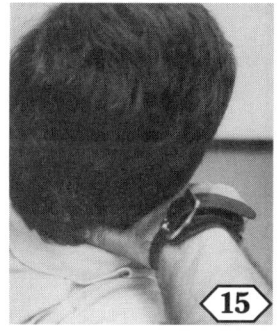
tension the archer may have had. A straight, relaxed and expanded wrist/forearm/elbow unit (in line with the arrow) is the most forgiving, "Idiot Proof" method in archery.

16. **Head and Neck Too Far Forward** As in the "Z formation" mentioned in #4, when the head and neck are pushed forward into the bow string for peep alignment, it creates tension in the neck. This is not conducive to consistent shot execution. The head should be upright and

Bernie Pellerite

relaxed, and only slightly tilted to the side to accommodate peep alignment. The string should *just touch* the tip of the nose. (Archers that wear glasses may have to touch the *side* of their nose in order to see past the frames.) If you can't reach the string with your nose without tipping your head forward, either your draw length is too short or, more likely, your anchor is too low.

17. **String Too Tight Into Face at Anchor** Pulling the string

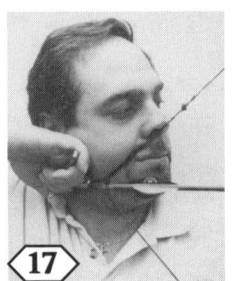

into the skin of the face or side of the cheek causes left and right string oscillation (resulting in left and right misses) and inconsistent anchor. Adjust your draw length, release rope, string loop, and/or anchor up or down until the string just *touches* your nose.

18. **String Doesn't Touch Nose at Anchor** A solid and consistent anchor is imperative for good shooting, and is especially true when shooting up and down hills. The more points of reference you have, the more consistent your shots will be. (I recommend at least four.) Your scope or *pin on target* is one anchor . . . your eye looking through the *peep* is a second anchor . . . the *tip of your nose on the string* is a third . . . and the *knuckles* of your draw hand solidly touching and/or *locked into your jawbone*

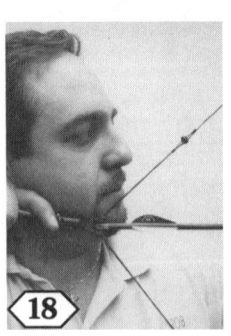

is a fourth. A *kisser button* is an optional anchor, but *it's not necessary* if you use a peep sight. **Note:** If you have trouble touching the tip of your nose with the string *(see photo)* without bending your head forward, try raising

Idiot Proof Archery

your anchor farther up the side of your face until the string naturally comes up under your nose.

Finger shooters tend to use fingertips in contact with the corner of their mouth. This is *not as solid* as locking the bones of the string hand into a place on the jaw bone. Different shaped faces accommodate different anchor points. Find one that is comfortable, relaxed and touching at least two places on your face (plus the front and rear sight *aligned)*, like your hand locked into the jaw bone and your nose touching the string.

19. **Moving Lips To Touch Kisser Button** A kisser button is used *instead of a peep* and really shouldn't be "kissed"! Moving your lips over to "kiss" a kisser button is not a consistent anchor, because the *lips can be moved* into almost any position. If you insist on using a kisser button, make sure it is anchored into something solid, such as the corner of an upper tooth . . . the lower jaw moves.

Don't "kiss" a kisser button

20. **Floating Anchor - Draw Hand Doesn't Touch Face** Your draw hand should be *locked in* on the side of your face where you can feel the bones in your hand mesh or interlock with the bones in your face (jaw). Most archers find placing one or two knuckles behind the jawbone is solid and easily repeatable, regardless of whether you shoot with your fingers or a mechanical release.

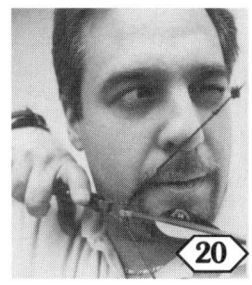

217

Bernie Pellerite

Bow Arm

21. Bow Shoulder Too High This is one of the most common flaws that I see. One of the reasons for this is because a lot of us learned archery on a recurve bow, or we were taught by a recurve shooter that needed all the muscle they could get to draw the bow back. This bad form is passed down from shooter to shooter. Another reason is pulling too much bow weight. This causes the deltoid muscle on the top of your bow

shoulder to be used to push the bow out, and is tense at full draw (like some recurve shooters), which in turn, causes the sight to shake. The bow shoulder should be down and locked in the socket but *relaxed*. It should be level with the other shoulder. This is bone-to-bone form *(see photo on page 205)*, as opposed to using muscles to keep the bow pushed forward toward the target. If it is done properly, the upper arm bone (*humerus*) will slip down and lock into the shoulder joint and the shoulder blade in the back will actually jut out *(see diagram page 205)*. All of the bones in the arm unit including the hand, wrist, elbow, and shoulder should all line up *(see diagram A and D page 101)*. This produces a much steadier sight picture and will be much less tiring, because you are using bones to hold the bow, not muscles.

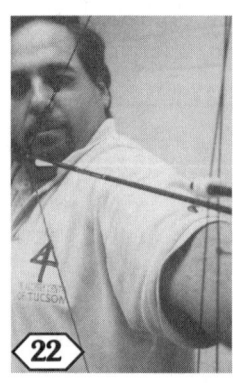

22. Bow Shoulder Rolled Into The Bow Similar to #21, this causes tension and excessive sight movement which can lead to anxiety, fear of missing and later to punching and/or snapshooting. It is also hard to duplicate, and usually will break down over time. It is a symptom that

Idiot Proof Archery

the bow is being held with muscles instead of bone, and the shoulder is not down and locked. It also frequently goes hand in hand with shooting with a bent bow elbow. See #23.

23. **Bow Arm Elbow Bent** This technique has been mastered by a very few archers, but most shooters will find it almost impossible to duplicate the bend in the elbow, *exactly the same way every shot*, especially shooting  up and down hills. Sometimes the degree of bend in the elbow causes a slightly different draw length and the archer can't really tell if he is exactly against the wall or slightly into the valley of the bow, from shot to shot (unless you use a clicker or marks on your cables that ensure the same draw length). Now the bow is, once again, being held with muscles, because you must also use the deltoid (shoulder muscle) to support this "bent elbow style." This can cause a shaky sight picture. Also, shooting with a bent elbow probably requires two to three times more practice than shooting with a *straight, but relaxed bow arm*.

24. **Bow Arm Elbow Locked And Tense** This is the opposite of #23. If the elbow is hyperextended, tense and locked, it also can create tension in the shot and movement in the sight. It is important that this elbow remain *relaxed, but not bent*. You may find it easiest to pull the bow with the elbow locked, but once

Bernie Pellerite

you get to full draw, "unlock" it *but don't bend it!* All bones from the lower part of the hand all the way up to the shoulder socket should be aligned as much as possible, to support both the mass and draw weight of the bow.

25. Bow Wrist Bent This is when the archer bends the wrist 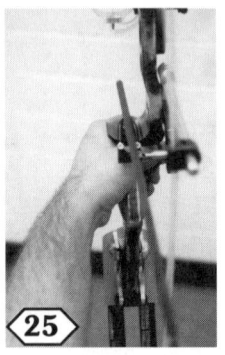 out away from the midline of the bow, sometimes in an attempt to keep the string from hitting his bow arm. As in #12, the handle of the bow is too far out on to the thumb where only soft tissue, not bone, is holding the bow, plus there is excess tension in the bent wrist. This shooting position will almost always give the right-handed archer pre-loaded right bow torque (resulting in right arrows). Again, the bow wrist should be straight and relaxed and the bow handle should contact your hand at the base of the thumb.

26. Bow Arm Fully Extended If the bow is pushed to the  full extension of the bow arm, all the way toward the target, then upon explosion, the bow hand and arm unit has no more forward extension available to expend energy from the bow. This is known as "pre-loaded" torque. What happens is, for right-handers, the bow will kick or swing to the left *immediately* upon release, before the arrow clears the rest, causing left arrows. This is frequently a symptom of too long of a draw. As stated in #21, the bow shoulder should be down and locked into the socket but relaxed. Upon explosion, the bow arm will jump forward along with the bow, towards the target. This allows the arrow to clear the bow before the arm reaches the "stops" (end of the arm extension) and *then* swings to the left . . . which is a normal part of followthrough, because the shoulder is in a ball socket.

Idiot Proof Archery
Finger Release

27. Wrist Bent/Tense (String Hand) If there are muscles used in the wrist or back of the hand as the archer draws to anchor, then as the fingers attempt to release the string, a "sideways torque" or "pluck" is applied to the string (causing excessive string oscillation and therefore, exaggerated arrow paradox). The wrist and the back of the hand should be completely relaxed, expanded in a straight line and in line with the forearm *(see diagram 29C,* 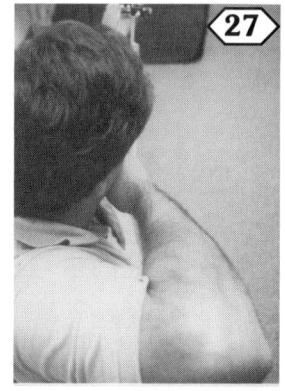 *Deep Hook).* From the elbow to the back of the hand should be as close to being in a direct line with the arrow as your body's geometry and range of motion allow. This will produce the least string amplitude and the most consistent release.

28. Dead Release A shooter with a "dead release" tries to hold whatever ideal position he thinks he has, and then consciously relaxes the fingers in an effort to release while the sight is on the target. This, unfortunately, requires complete control of  *when* the shot goes off and therefore interrupts the aiming process. This technique in slow motion, reveals that the string actually moves forward ½" to ¾", before coming off the fingers . . . which is actually another form flaw called "creeping" (see #42). This leads to trying to "drop the string" or *snapshooting at the exact moment of*

Bernie Pellerite

target acquisition, (as the pin touches the bullseye). Because the mind will always know when the fingers are about to "let-go," anticipation and anxiety build up. Fear of missing then replaces aiming. Plucking, freezing or snapshooting then usually takes over completely. Plucking the string is the equivalent of "punching the trigger" on a release. The dead release *requires the impossible* (if done without a clicker) . . . thinking two thoughts at once . . . *aiming and "let-go."* The opposite and more *repeatable,* for 99% of us, is a *dynamic release* which causes the hand to come straight back automatically, because back tension has *pulled* the fingers off the string. It subconsciously loses control of, or "refuses to hold," the string *as the hand is being ripped back, to touch the shoulder. Anticipate pulling until you touch your shoulder — commit to conclusion.* (See chapters 8 and 9.)

29. **Hooks Too Shallow/Cups String Hand/Lifts Arrow Off Rest** Archers that try to grip the string between the tip of the fingers and the first crease, do so in an effort to have a smoother release *(see photo 29A).* However, the end result is often just the opposite. Because there is no pivot point in the fingers at this location on the fingers, the archer ends up having to *cup his hand* to maintain control of the string. This utilizes the muscles and tendons of the fingers and back of the hand *(see diagram 29B).* Frequently, a direct result of this is the right-handed archer rolls

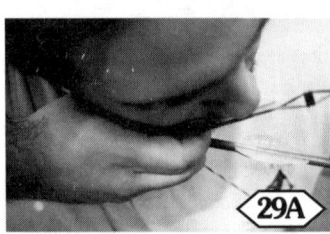

Hand cupped

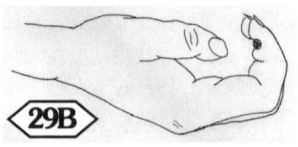

Shallow Hook

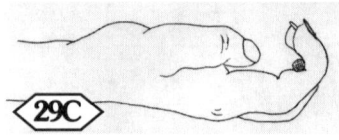

Deep Hook

Idiot Proof Archery

the string counterclockwise as he starts to draw the bow. They then contact the arrow at the inside of the first joint of the middle finger, *lifting the arrow*. The combination of "rolling" and "lifting" causes the arrow to slip off the left side of the rest. Also, when the hand is cupped, the middle joints and the

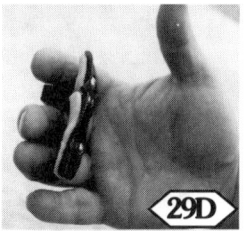

Can't Pinch Tab

knuckles of the fingers are not straight and relaxed, which can crowd the fingers around the nock, causing the arrow to be "pinched" off the rest. The remedy is to hook deeper *(see diagram 29C)*, in the first crease or midway between the first and second crease of the fingers, so the back of the hand can be flat, relaxed, and not cupped. When an archer comes to full draw, the "V" created by the string angle will naturally "pinch" the fingers together. You should allow the middle finger to have some space (about an $1/8$") below the nock, and the index finger should have the same space above the nock. Or, use a "can't pinch" type of tab *(see photo 29D)* that has a spacer built into it to alleviate pinching the nock. Also using a longer axle to axle bow (more than 41") can help relieve this condition.

30. **Plucks The String** Plucking the string is an exaggerated conscious effort to try and get the fingers out of the way of the string, as opposed to a continuous pulling motion, until the fingers *simply lose control* from being pulled or ripped backward toward the shoulder. The hand should fly back naturally, in line with the arrow, usually touching the drawing shoulder or the back of the neck, which are the most popular conclusions to the followthrough. When "plucking the string" the archer does not use back tension and, as the "pluck"

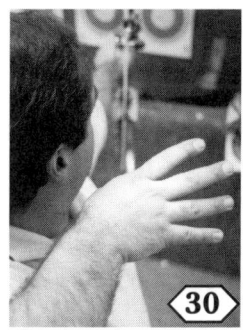

Bernie Pellerite

happens, the fingers come out away from the face, causing excessive string oscillation and exaggerated side-to-side arrow paradox. If the draw elbow *drives* straight back far enough (because of back tension), the fingers (the index finger or ring finger) should stay close to or, better yet, keep *in contact with* the face all the way back to the back of the neck or the draw shoulder.

The Mechanical Release

31. Punches The Trigger

(Trigger Too Light or Too Much Travel) Punching the release is really a symptom of target panic (which is a mental problem, as are the next three form flaws.) But, they all have physical manifestations that violate the principles of good form. As far as punching is concerned . . . if the trigger pressure is too light, you are unable to wrap the tip of your index finger around the trigger and start pulling with the elbow using back muscles. Therefore, you can't get an unanticipated or surprise release or "get into your back muscles" before the release goes off. The same is true of a thumb release set up too light or with too much trigger travel. Most archers who shoot these "fast" releases "pump" the finger up and down on the trigger or try to "touch it off" at the *moment the sight is on the target.*

Even if the trigger is firm, but has too much travel in it, the brain can detect the movement, anticipate it, and therefore try to control it. When "punching," the conscious mind is trying to monitor both the *movement of the finger on the trigger* and *sight on the target,* at the same time. The end result is an addictive and compulsive pattern and habit that forms in an *attempt to control the millisecond of let-go" while in the exact center of the target.* **Note:** If you shoot

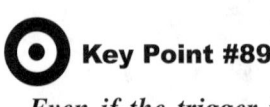

Key Point #89

Even if the trigger is firm, but has too much travel in it, the brain can detect the movement, anticipate it, and therefore try to control it.

Idiot Proof Archery

a standard thumb, index finger, or little finger release, an *essential part* of the cure for punching (also #32, #33, and #34) is *to set up the trigger heavy,* with *no travel (also see chapter 9).* Many pros use releases that require 4-7 pounds (not ounces!) of pressure to set them off, *without any discernible travel* in the trigger which helps to keep them from forming these habits!

32. **Flinches** (another symptom of target panic) This is actually the end result of, and an advanced stage of, punching where *two conscious thoughts* (trigger and target) *very nearly occur* at *exactly the same time,* as mentioned in #31. As I just said, the human brain cannot process two conscious thoughts at the same time, but flinching is about as close as you can come. Our minds flash back and forth from the target to the trigger (or release hand). Most of the time, the two thoughts come into the brain separated by a millisecond. But occasionally, both thoughts will try to enter the brain *exactly* at the same time and the two thoughts "crash" into each other: "Target . . . trigger . . . target . . . trigger . . . target . . . trigger . . . trargertrigget . . . D'oh! (A Homer Simpson-ism!) Physically, it looks like you were shocked by electricity or startled by something. Two "things" can be *done simultaneously* . . . IF one of them is a *programmed action on the subconscious level* (the release) while the other *is a thought* or mental picture that remains on the *conscious level* (aiming). The way to cure flinching is on the empty bale and/or with a bow simulator by developing a correct and trusted shot sequence, so the program to set off the release (or release the string with the fingers), runs on its own, after being *started* by the conscious mind, but *without conscious supervision.* Then, all the conscious (thinking) mind has to do is *aim* . . . until the "program" finishes (subconsciously).

Key Point #89

The human brain cannot process two thoughts at a time.

Bernie Pellerite

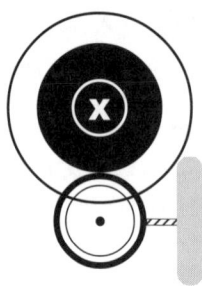

33. Freezing below the spot is a common symptom of target panic

🎯 **Key Point #91**

You can only release an arrow under three conditions . . . while arriving on target . . . while staying on target . . . or while leaving the target

🎯 **Key Point #92**

Most archers are over-analytical, risk taker, or control type personalities who won't trust the subconscious to run the "let-go" program without constantly meddling, monitoring, analyzing, assisting, and controlling it with their conscious minds.

33. Freezes Off (or On) The Target This archer cannot move the sight into the middle. He freezes above, to the side or, more commonly, below the aiming spot, and tries to jerk the sight into (or through) the center while attempting to release (this can be caused by a lack of mental commitment). The second type is *freezing on target*. Here the archer cannot release until the sight is moving *away* from the middle. Remember, you can only release an arrow under three conditions . . . *while arriving on target . . . while staying on target . . . or while leaving the target*. Again, the way to cure both of these freezing scenarios (also #31, #32 and #34) is on the empty bale or bow simulator and reprogram the shot sequence, as in #32. Then, *do a bridge program* like the "21-Day Program" and/or "Rotational Aiming" *(see chapter 10)* so that the archer trusts the new shot sequence.

34. Snapshooting – Doesn't Settle Into The Bullseye (You guessed it . . . another symptom of target panic!) Before releasing, the archer cannot settle into anchor and/or cannot let the sight settle into the bullseye and *remain there* to aim for 3 to 4 seconds. As soon as the archer touches his anchor, the sight touches the center or sometimes even just touches the *edge* of the target, the string is released, *involuntarily*. This "shooting on arrival" scenario is caused, once again by trying to "do" two things at once (like #31, #32, and #33) and must be reprogrammed on an empty bale or

Idiot Proof Archery

bow simulator. *The real reason target panic is so widespread is that most archers are over-analytical, risk taker, or control type personalities who won't trust the subconscious to run the "let-go" program, because they have never programmed it correctly. Therefore, they constantly meddle, monitor, judge, analyze, assist, change, and control it with their conscious minds (see chapter 2).*

35. **Drops The Bow Arm (Quits On The Shot.)** In an effort to see the arrow fly or see where it hits the target, the archer drops his bow arm prematurely . . . one of the major causes of low and low-left arrows (for righties). The cure for this is to *keep* or *hold your position* until conclusion. Conclusion, for example, can be *seeing* the  arrow hit the target (which wouldn't be a good one in this particular case), *hearing* the arrow hit the target or (the most popular), your hand will come back and *touch* your shoulder. All these, and any number of other conclusions, happen *after* the arrow is out of the bow. This will eliminate this type of movement of the bow before the arrow has cleared the rest and riser.

36. **Heels The Bow Upon Release** As the arrow is leaving the bow, the archer tries to "help" a low arrow into the middle by putting a sudden and inordinate amount of pressure or push on the bottom portion of the bow handle, with the heel of the hand. This can cause high arrows and is a conscious effort to move the sight and therefore, the arrow . . . *as it leaves the bow*. Obviously, the archer should relax the bow hand and let the bow shoot "through" the hand toward the target into the sling without "helping it."

Bernie Pellerite

37. Pre-Loaded Torque - Bow Jumps Sideways This is

usually caused by incorrect hand position on the bow handle that puts rotational force (left or right) on the bow. When the shot is released, the bow will immediately twist in the hand and will cause erratic arrows. A consistent hand position on the bow handle should be found (and marked if necessary) so that when the archer shoots, the bow leaves the hand *straight towards the target*, *before* it moves left and down (for right-handed archers).

38. Pulls Bow to the Right (Right-Handed Archer) This

occurs when the archer pulls *excessively* with the right hand, when trying to equalize the number of pounds at full draw. For example, if John Q. Archer is a "push-puller" or "equalizer," he should have the same amount of weight or pressure in the right hand as in the left. However, if he pulls harder with his draw hand than he is pushing with his bow hand, *or* he creeps or collapses with the left hand . . . the right hand will *pull the bow to the right, causing right arrows.*

39. Pushes Bow Left (Right-Handed Archer) Just the opposite, as in #38, is when the archer pushes harder

with the bow hand than he pulls with his string hand (or his anchor will sometimes creep forward because he loses back tension), the bow will be pushed to the left, causing left arrows. For both of these form flaws (if the archer is convinced he should be a push-puller), he should practice equalizing the pressure in both hands. However, if he finds this too difficult, he

Idiot Proof Archery

could use a technique more widely used by top archers. This technique, once at full draw, is to hold the bow statically with the bow hand and pull with the string hand. This is called being a "puller" *(see Step 9 - Start Motor in chapter 8)*. Another cause of left arrows is when the bow arm is fully extended (usually the draw is too long!), which will cause the bow to "preload" and "jump" to the left during explosion. Also see #26.

40. **Over-Holds (9-15 Seconds)/Releases While Shaking** This is more typical in better shooters. This is an effort to *aim too precisely,* or escape letting the bow down. The archer simply says to himself, "I'll just hold a little longer until the sight picture *looks perfect."* He *mistakenly thinks* the sight has to be in the *exact center* when the shot goes off, i*n order to hit the center. Not so,* bullseye breath! *(See page 91 — Want a perfect sight picture?)* Unfortunately, holding this long usually violates the archer's personal "comfort zone," *(see chapter 12)* which is the physical "window of opportunity" to shoot at our optimum steadiness, usually about seven to eight seconds after *beginning* the draw. Normally, when an archer goes past this time frame, the sight picture will rapidly deteriorate. *A correct shot sequence should have a definite, timed rhythm.* Practice timing your release so it falls within your own comfort zone, or let down if your "time is up!"

41. **Peeking/Pops Head Up** As in #35, this usually goes hand in hand with dropping the bow arm. Frequently, the archer simultaneously pops his head up and drops the bow arm. Peeking is an effort to see the arrow in flight and is one of the causes of low or low-left arrows. The cure for this is to followthrough to conclusion. Practice keeping the bow arm up

229

Bernie Pellerite

and the head in the same position, until you reach your conclusion *(see Step 12 - Conclusion in chapter 8)*.

42. **Creeping** Creeping is losing tension at full draw. The arrow starts moving slowly forward on the rest because the archer is losing tension, either in the bow arm or in the back muscles of the draw arm side, or both, *before release*. This is solved by a conscious effort (at first) to maintain back tension (until it becomes automatic) and/or using draw stops. For finger shooters with round or soft cams, using a clicker (last resort) or a device that causes round wheels to have a definite "dead stop" wall can eliminate creeping. Another device that will cure creeping and #43 collapsing, is my **PanicMaster and Bow Simulator** *(see Appendix)*. This is because of the way the laser works on the device at full draw. If you creep or collapse, the laser light will go off prematurely, warning you that you have lost tension so you can correct it immediately. On your bow, you can also install and *visually check,* two cable alignment marks that come together at the full draw position. These marks should be in the archer's sight line and ensures the archer maintains the exact same draw . . . sort of a *visual* draw stop. However, most people forget to continuously check them. (If none of the above work, you might switch to a bow with a "hard wall.")

43. **Collapsing** Collapsing is done *upon release*. This is different from creeping, which happens *before release*. Collapsing, with the bow arm "giving up" (relaxing prematurely), or the release hand going forward with the string upon release (or both), can cause all sorts of erratic shots. Again, as in #42, a conscious effort must be made (until it's programmed) to maintain back tension, or you can use draw stops, cable marks, my bow simulator or a clicker for finger shooters.

44. **Not Letting Down** This is very common in most archers and separates the champions from the near champions. Most good tournament archers will let down about one

Idiot Proof Archery

out of every five to ten times *under normal circumstances*. Not letting down is a "control" problem. Most archers don't want to admit (even to themselves) that they ever need to start over. You need to train yourself that if *anything* feels wrong with the shot, or *anything* enters your mind besides aiming after you start your "motor" . . . let down! Isn't it a little arrogant for those of us that refuse to let down to think we "do it better" than the best shooters in the world? They all let down, when it "feels wrong!" Champions *don't gamble* . . . **they only shoot the good ones!** That's one of the reasons why they are champions!

Analyzing Your Flaws

As an example of how to dissect a form flaw, let's look at one of the most common problems — *missing to the left* —and see all of the potential causes, and how you can identify and cure them. A similar approach to any other form flaw will produce similar results.

Causes And Cures

You will need to identify which cause (or causes) apply in your case. You can do this by video taping yourself *(see photo)* and studying the video tape, or by having a buddy (better yet, a coach) watch you while you shoot and make suggestions. The hardest way is to try and "puzzle these things out" by yourself. A little bit of help goes a long way here. Once you have identified the cause, try the cure. **Keep notes**; not all cures work for all people. It is also easy to forget what you have tried and what you haven't.

Here are five *main* reasons why a lot of shooters have so many problems missing to the left. (Bear in mind that the following examples assume the shooter is right-handed. Left-handed people would find the opposite to be true.)

Bernie Pellerite

Over-Holding As we try to aim, especially on long shots, we tend to try too hard to hold the sight in the exact center of the target, instead of letting the sight move around naturally inside the scoring area. We should pay no attention to the sight or its movement . . . *just the middle of the target!* This "natural arc of movement" is normal and you should not be focused on, worried about, or concerned with interfering with that movement while aiming. The archer who fights this arc of movement (besides developing target panic, eventually) tends to over-hold, which tires the bow arm. To try and compensate (so they don't lose tension and start collapsing), they usually start to *push harder* with the bow hand. The longer they hold, the harder they push with the left side unit (hand/arm/shoulder). Then, when the shot goes off, their bow is "pre-loaded" and kicks to the left . . . causing them to miss to the left.

Pushing the Bow A similar situation to over-holding happens when we draw to anchor with our holding weight *unbalanced*. What this means is, if our total holding weight is 20 pounds, we should have the weight evenly distributed between the bow arm unit and string hand unit (theoretically, 10 pounds each side, if we use the push-pull method). This distribution ensures that the bow hand side pushes straight toward the target upon explosion, and the string hand side pulls straight back. For example, let's say you draw to anchor, then collapse with your anchor (bow hand) into the back of your neck or jaw, thereby off-loading or transferring a few pounds of the weight (that your draw hand side is responsible for), to the bow hand. At explosion, the bow arm will push the bow left, because now you are pushing harder with that side. The result . . . left arrows. Vice versa if you pull harder with the string hand.

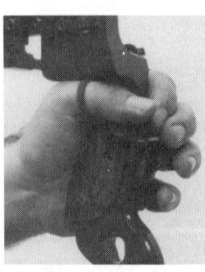

Bad Grip - Too much hand in the bow can cause counterclockwise torque and left arrows

Bad Grip If your bow hand is too far into the grip, you may experience left arrows. This can cause rotational forces

Idiot Proof Archery

(counterclockwise, pre-loaded torque) to the side of the bow handle. Upon explosion, the bow will kick or twist left . . . resulting in left arrows.

Plucking or Punching If you are a finger shooter and you pluck the string (your release fingers move away from your face to the right, taking the string with them), this will result in misses to the left. Shooters who use mechanical releases can also torque or "pluck" the string with a release, causing the string to go right and the bow to go left.

Elbow Out of Alignment If your string arm elbow is not directly behind and in line with the arrow in relation to the target, you may have additional problems. For example, if your elbow is out of line to the right *(see photo)*, upon explosion, the string hand usually flies away from the face to the right, (instead of coming straight back), thus taking the string with it, causing the bow riser to kick left . . . resulting in left arrows.

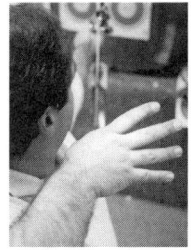
Plucking

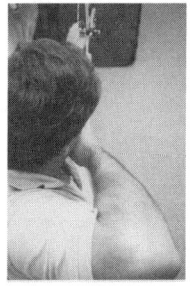
Elbow out of line

Pre-loading Finally, the most common cause of left arrows is because the draw length is too long. This causes the bow shoulder to be "super-extended" and upon explosion, the *left arm swings instantly to the left.* This happens because most shooters overextend their bow arms and they don't have any room left for the bow arm to punch forward *with* the bow as it expends its stored energy. So instead, the bow *immediately* kicks left because of the ball socket in the shoulder. Ideally, the shooter's left arm should be "low and locked" but relaxed into the shoulder socket, so as the release occurs, the bow

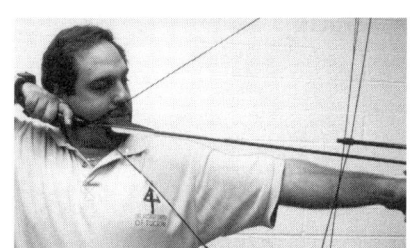
Overextended bow arm.

233

Bernie Pellerite

arm and shoulder unit push straight forward, toward the target. As this is happening, the arrow clears the bow, *before* the arm reaches full extension . . ."hits the stops." The ball joint in the shoulder socket then causes the arm to swing to the left and down, as the followthrough is completed.

Most shooters that persistently miss to the left or have a built-in pre-loading problem as mentioned above, will have a "telltale sign," such as the sight pins are to the left of centershot. This is because when they miss to the left, they have to move the sight pins to the left to bring the arrows back into the center. Depending on how much they "pre-load" the bow *today*, they *may chase* the groups with the pins, back and forth, left and right, from day to day or week to week.

Check the above situations and previous form flaws to see if you fall into some of the categories. If you don't know exactly what the problem is, try video taping yourself shooting, find a qualified coach or attend a shooter's school to help you with your problem.

Chapter 12

Shooting Inside Your Comfort Zone

There are actually two different types of comfort zones . . . one is a physical comfort zone and the other is a psychological or mental comfort zone. The physical comfort zone is largely indicated by the *amount of time at full draw* the average person has to *execute the shot comfortably*. The mental comfort zone is the score or shooting level your ego or subconscious will *allow you to shoot at comfortably*.

The Physical Comfort Zone

Every person has a particular time span or "zone" that he or she needs to shoot within, in order to maximize the chance that the arrow will be launched at the calmest possible moment. As you draw the bow to anchor, you should inhale and settle in. As you do, you exhale part of the breath (usually a third to one half), and hold until the explosion. The average person has to do all of this (from the *beginning of "draw to anchor" through "conclusion"* of the shot) in about an *eight second time span*, because after he or she has drawn and held the bow at full draw for about eight seconds and held their breath for about five or six seconds, their form will usually start to physically deteriorate, and their sight picture will start to disintegrate.

Gold medalist, Darrell Pace, once wrote a paper about comfort zones (for

Key Point #93

Every person has a particular time span or "comfort zone" that he or she needs to shoot within, which is where they are holding the steadiest.

Bernie Pellerite

 Key Point #94

Gold Medalist Darrell Pace said... *if you draw and fire an arrow between one and four seconds, it is called the "Danger Zone." If you draw and fire an arrow between four and eight seconds, it is called the "Comfort Zone." And, if you draw and fire an arrow in eight seconds or longer, it is called the "Lost Zone."*

recurve shooters). He defined it like this . . . if you draw and fire an arrow between one and four seconds, it is called the "Danger Zone." If you draw and fire an arrow between four and eight seconds, it is called the "Comfort Zone." And, if you draw and fire an arrow in eight seconds or longer, it is called the "Lost Zone." This, of course, is based on recurve shooters, who have no letoff, so it would be a little different for compound archers. The average shooter's comfort zone will vary two to three seconds either way, depending on a person's muscularity, athletic ability, lung capacity, age, physical fitness, etc. You should check your comfort zone for duration and consistency, shot to shot. A few professional compound shooters in top physical shape, can have comfort zones from twelve to fourteen seconds, but this is the *extreme exception*. Most compound shooters need to shoot sometime from seven to nine seconds.

After the shot, you also need to rest your bow arm and "stand at ease," for about fifteen seconds, between each shot. This "recharges your batteries" to 100% again, before you draw the next arrow (more on this in chapter 13 — Perfect Practice).

Once you hold your breath beyond your particular physical comfort zone, oxygen deprivation can cause chemical changes in the brain and your visual acuity and/or mental perception of the target can change. Concurrently, lactic acid begins to build up in the muscles, which causes them to fatigue, and the resulting tension will cause the sight picture to deteriorate fairly rapidly from this point on. That's why it's important that your shot have a consistent and *predictable rhythm* and be *timed out* with a stopwatch. Ideally, it should be something like this: pre-aim and inhale as you draw to a point about four to five inches above the bullseye. As you relax, come rapidly down into the *top of the spot* (or aiming point on a McKenzie target, etc.). Put on the

Idiot Proof Archery

brakes! Don't allow the sight to *drop into the middle,* or especially out the bottom of the spot you want to hit. At this point you should be in the top one half of the spot. Slowly *re-relax* your bow arm and shoulder unit, and allow gravity to take you *slowly down* into the center. You should be simultaneously exhaling one third to one half of your breath . . . this varies with the individual. From the time you first started to draw the bow, until you start to hold and aim, is usually three to four seconds for the average shooter. From this point, the remaining four to five seconds of the eight seconds, is for back tension and aiming inside the bullseye.

Your shot should have consistency and a predictable rhythm and be timed out.

Do not draw down from *way above the bale* and especially, *do not draw up from the floor!* It is a waste of motion and precious seconds that should be used for aiming. Furthermore, if you come *up* on the target, you will have to *use muscles* which *will cause unnecessary movement.* Most shooters waste precious time coming in too high or from the floor, then wander around searching for the center for five or six seconds. When they finally get into the bullseye, they only have one or two seconds of their comfort zone left. The shot then starts to deteriorate, so they punch the trigger as the sight starts to rapidly weave in and out of the spot (drive-by-shooting). Also, don't draw directly onto the spot because, as you settle in and relax, your sight will probably drop out the bottom of the aiming spot and you'll have to spend valuable time, or recruit muscles in the bow shoulder (that cause tension), to raise your bow again. *Let gravity work for you* . . . come in from above and you will have a much more relaxed and steady sight picture.

The Mental Comfort Zone

The second type of comfort zone is the psychological or "mental comfort zone." Your psyche has a mental picture of "who you are" and your *self image* and ability as an archer,

Bernie Pellerite

that it is comfortable with. It is stored "in your ego," somewhere way back in your subconscious. Your subconscious will only allow you to perform within a certain scoring range *comfortably.* If you approach a score that you have never shot before, this *violates your comfort zone.* Now, your subconscious will do its best to *keep you down* to the "scoring level" or zone that you have been used to and therefore, are comfortable performing at. As an example, let's say you are normally a 295 out of 300 indoor shooter. When there is a chance that you might shoot a 296 or 297 or even higher, your psyche will kick in and say to you, "You aren't that good!" or . . . "You'll probably blow the next two shots!" This causes you to miss, which keeps you in your comfort zone. Eventually, if you accidentally shoot a few 296s or 297s over a long period of time, your subconscious will gradually become *"comfortable" with that,* and *"allow"* you *to stay* at that level. That is why, when we do improve, it is usually a slow and frustrating process that can take years, instead of months.

Key Point #95

Your subconscious will only allow you to perform within a certain scoring range comfortably.

There are several ways to expand your mental comfort zone. All of them have one thing in common. You have to "sell" or "con" your subconscious into believing that *you are better than you really are.* These techniques can help to *pull you up to a higher comfort zone.* Jay Barrs explains these methods extremely well in his video, **The Mental Game** *(see Appendix).* He discusses self-hypnosis, self-relaxation techniques, and subliminal audio tapes, but the two most popular and interesting methods discussed are positive affirmations and positive mental imagery.

Positive Affirmations

A positive affirmation is a form of "brainwashing," so to speak, that helps us raise our comfort level or zone. In its simplest form, it is a *mantra* or *"wish list"* that you repeat over and over, to sell or convince your subconscious mind of something

Idiot Proof Archery

it currently doesn't believe! One typical system is accomplished with 3" x 5" index cards. First, you list things that *you want to accomplish*, in the order you want to accomplish them, one on each card. (Jay also suggests that you hand write them.) As an example, let's say you are a 295 shooter. You would write on the card, "I am perfectly comfortable and at ease shooting 300 by May" (90 days from now). Or, if in the past you have been second or third at the state championships, you might write, "I am perfectly comfortable and at ease winning the State Championship, next spring" (three to five months from now). The important point here is, the goals you write down must be *reasonable, realistic* and *attainable, within the period of time you have chosen*. In other words, if you are only a 275 shooter, it won't do any good to write a card about becoming a 300 shooter next week. First, you can only stretch your comfort level about 10% or 15% at a time. Secondly, this method doesn't have a chance to work in only one week. After you have written out your cards (5 to 15 affirmations), keep them with you at all times. Take them out four to six times during the day, and read them *out loud* to yourself (don't let anyone catch you . . . they may put you in that little white canvas jacket, with r-e-e-a-l-l-y long sleeves!). After three or four weeks, your subconscious will start to believe what you have read . . . just like watching TV commercials work on your subconscious, after many hundreds of repetitions. A good example of this was Billy Mills, winner of the Gold Medal in the 5000 km run in 1964. Billy spoke his *single affirmation out loud* (that he would win the gold medal) *many thousands of times*. He was the only person who believed he could win a race that no American, let alone a Native American, had ever won. He was right!

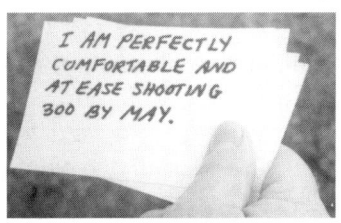

Positive affirmation

Key Point #96

You can only stretch your comfort level about 10% or 15% at a time.

Bernie Pellerite

Another method I have heard great champions use is putting one affirmation in five or six common places like the steering wheel of your car, on the bathroom mirror, your desk at work, etc., and read them while you visualize them every time you go from one place to the other. Do that for three weeks, skip a week, then change all the cards to another affirmation for another three weeks, etc.

Positive Mental Imagery

Another way to raise your comfort level is through *positive mental imagery*. Right before you draw to anchor, run a little "commercial" in your head. You should see yourself running through your entire shot sequence . . . drawing to anchor, settling down, relaxing everything, starting your motor, calmly aiming in the center, executing the shot perfectly, reaching your shot conclusion, and finally you visualize the arrow going *right into the center*. This all takes less than a second (it's part of #5 in my shot sequence). Then, you actually perform the shot the same way, while it is fresh in your mind. This is a common tool used by many champion athletes. Competitive divers will visualize themselves striding to the end of the board, executing the dive perfectly and entering the water with no splash. Most professional athletes that perform disciplines (and archery is a discipline) such as driving a golf ball, shooting foul shots in basketball, etc., find this technique helps them to perform consistently at the championship level.

There are other ways to help raise your mental comfort level. You

Positive mental imagery.

Idiot Proof Archery

can visit your local library, book store, or the internet, and look for books, videos, or audio tapes on mental management, self-relaxation techniques or self-hypnosis. These techniques can help you learn to *relax, concentrate* or *focus longer*, etc. You can also check out some subliminal audio tapes. My wife and I quit smoking using one of these tapes, so I can vouch for their effectiveness. If you are serious about your shooting, try one of these. You'll be surprised by what can be accomplished.

Ron Herbert, Lakeport, MI, writes, "I started out in the 260s out of a possible 300 60X indoors. I asked everyone I knew how to shoot better but no one would help me. So I got some of your videos (Volume 1-6) and watched them several times. With their help, my scores rose to 300 and 50 plus Xs with a high of 59 Xs. I couldn't seem to reach the illusive 60X 300 mark. So, I took your shooter's school at JR Custom Archery in Ypsilanti, MI. Four or five months after taking the school and making changes to my mental game, I finally reached the 60X mark in a league in Port Huron, MI. With practice, I finally started averaging 57 plus Xs and have shot a number of perfect 60X rounds.

Shooting outdoor field rounds, my average is up to 545-550 on the field and hunter. I have won the Michigan State Field and Hunter Championship, the North American Field Archery Championship, Shooter of the Year AA Freestyle in the Michigan State Archery Association, shot a 1089 at the MI State Field Championships and tied for first but lost in a shoot-off. I also shot a perfect 60X 300 at the Canadian Indoor Nationals."

Thanks for the help,
Ron

Bernie Pellerite

Joe Hicks of White Settlement, TX, writes:
Dear Bernie,
    I first heard about your class in November of 1996. My girlfriend, at the time, asked me if I would like to take the class the following February as a Christmas present. It was the best gift ever!!!
    Before attending your school I was barely shooting 300s. After taking your class, shortening my draw length 3 inches, and applying your techniques, I'm now shooting consistent 300s and in the upper 50Xs. Since the class I have won several local tournaments, the State Outdoor, the State Indoor (600/113Xs) and the Indoor Southern Sectionals (600/118Xs). Thank you for helping me see more of the center!!!!

                                    Thanks again,
                                      Joe Hicks

P.S.: That girlfriend is now my wife of three years.

Chapter 13

Perfect Practice
The Do's and Don'ts
of An Accelerated Learning Curve

Consistently hitting what you aim at with a bow and arrow is really hard to do! This "predictable accuracy" that eludes so many of us is an attainable goal, but it's never really achieved or maintained without endless hours of practice. For those of you who would rather "pray for luck," here's an old archery saying . . . "It takes a lot of luck to succeed with a bow and arrow . . . the more you practice, *the luckier you seem to get!*" It follows that if we're going to have to practice, we might as well make it count. Like most good archers eventually discover . . . practice does *not* make perfect . . . perfect practice makes perfect!

The best way to do that is to have a qualified coach keep you on track. By the way, besides teaching the shooter's school, I also do private and group lessons at my home (see Appendix for details).

The following is an outline of a uniquely productive and *accelerated practice regimen*. These "super sessions" are for serious bowhunters and target archers only. With the proper dedication, these **do's and don'ts** will greatly accelerate your learning curve and your level of understanding and accuracy with a bow and arrow.

Key Point #97
It takes a lot of luck to succeed with a bow and arrow . . . the more you practice, the luckier you seem to get!

Key Point #98
Practice does not make perfect . . . perfect practice makes perfect!

Bernie Pellerite

- **DON'T** try to practice while you are worried about a piece of equipment that is about to fail or is not in order . . . you have enough to think about! Fix it first!

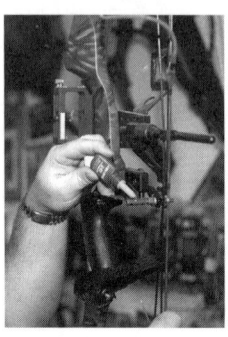

LocTite™ all nuts, bolts and screws that don't have to be moved frequently.

Record your bow and arrow's vital statistics because it will save you, if you have to re-cable or replace a string.

- **DO** make sure your bow *is tuned properly* (or as good as *you think* it should be), your arrows are *matched* to the bow and are *identical*, and nothing is loose. Silicone, rubber cement, or LocTite™ all nuts, bolts and screws that don't have to be moved frequently.

- **DON'T** spend hours timing, tuning, and making adjustments at home, only to have something move or fail at a tournament or in a treestand, and have no idea how to put it back, *exactly* the way it was before (now, let's see . . . how far was the peep from my nocking point?).

- **DO** keep a *log book!* A small 3" x 5" spiral notebook will do. Record your bow's poundage, axle to axle length, brace height, tiller measurements, nocking point position on your bow square, distance of the peep sight from the nocking point, arrow speed in feet per second, arrow weight, total and individual pin gap (trace them if possible), and your exact draw length. Sooner or later a string or cable on your bow will break or stretch, your serving will separate, unwind or break, or your peep, pin sights, or rest will move. When it happens, you can *avoid a disaster* by referring to your log book. You can repair or reset the affected part back to its original specs without altering performance or wasting hours retuning or sighting in your bow again. This same farsightedness should also be standard for other critical adjustments. For instance, marking the position

Idiot Proof Archery

of things like limb bolts, overdraw, arrow rest, peep site, pin sights, center serving and cam roll-over position with correction fluid (Wite-Out®) can save you, by quickly identifying and correcting one or more items that might move from their original position, for one reason or another.

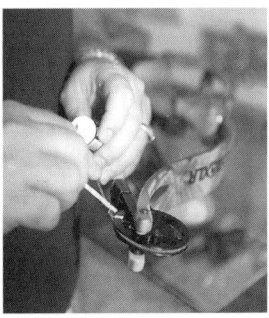

Marking the cam roll over point can tell you instantly, when something moved or stretched.

- **DON'T** try to pull your bow (especially heavy poundage), when your muscles are cold. Not only will this start the wrong set of muscles into action (usually shoulder, arm and chest muscles), which gets you off track immediately with a shaky sight picture, but you are asking for tendonitis or possibly rotator cuff surgery later. Try using an exercise band to warm up.

- **DO** stretch and warm up your muscles with a length of rubber tubing or rubber stretch band. This lower stress start-up allows you to key on your back muscles (*rhomboids*), and allows the arms and shoulders to relax, which facilitates a much steadier sight picture, from arrow number one.

Stretch and warm up your muscles with a length of rubber tubing or rubber stretch band.

- **DON'T** start shooting a small target at 20 to 40 yards right away. You're often so intent on hitting the target, your form goes to pieces right from the start. Your "tip off" to this condition is, for example, when you're hitting in the middle on Monday, Thursday you are shooting to the right and on Saturday you are shooting left. This, among other things, can be caused by a lack of "muscle memory." At the beginning and intermediate level, usually the very first arrow we shoot in a

Bernie Pellerite

practice session sets up our subconscious and short-term muscle memory, for a "first impression" of *how the shot should feel*, and therefore be executed. Since we're so preoccupied with "trying to hit the target," we usually don't maintain good form, and shoot a "bad first shot." It can sometimes take hours or dozens of shots to straighten out this bad first impression that we gave our subconscious.

- **DO** shoot the first few arrows at five or ten yards, so you don't have to worry about missing. This enables you to concentrate more on *perfect form* . . . and *perfect feel* . . . which sets up the right "first impression" for our subconscious to try and duplicate. (This is like a golfer, tennis or baseball player taking a few practice swings to *re-educate their muscle memory* about a good swing.) If you can, *close your eyes* after you come to anchor, and shoot several shots at three to four yards with no target, or use my bow simulator. This lets your subconscious experience how a good shot should feel. If you are really serious, schedule a *whole practice session* each week on an empty bale or with the bow simulator. Shoot for half an hour with your *eyes closed*, and a half an hour with your *eyes open*. With your ego "unplugged," scattering your arrows and *no target*, you can completely explore, experiment with or absorb whatever part of your form or timing you wish, one at a time . . . without caring where the arrow went. If you can, video yourself shooting the *first shot with your eyes closed,* and compare it with a *20 yard, eyes open, first shot* from another session . . . they should look the same, form-wise. Most people are surprised at the huge difference. If there are differences, you can

Bernie's PanicMaster and Bow Simulator is great to set up how a good shot should feel.

Idiot Proof Archery

then work on getting them to look the same . . . which is the whole key to good form.
- **DON'T** waste time practicing scenarios that won't happen. If you are going bowhunting for whitetail this November, from a treestand in zero degree weather, you won't be very well prepared by shooting at a 3-D target on level ground, in shorts and a t-shirt in August.
- **DO** try to duplicate whatever situation you are preparing for as closely as possible. You may not be able to duplicate the weather conditions, but you can duplicate most of the other factors. Practice from the same kind of treestand, at the same height. Wear the same clothes, shoot the same arrows and broadheads, shoot at dawn and at dusk (under low light situations), shoot in the rain, shoot your backup bow, shoot from a sitting position, etc., etc. If you are a bowhunter, don't shoot at the kill zones on 3-D animals. Most are not anatomically correct at the present time. Pick a spot, where the *real* vitals are, and aim at it. Find out what you and your equipment will do under the above conditions . . . *before* you find out the expensive and hard way. You may have to shoot straight down, or pull your bow back while twisted around or sitting down. Or, you may have to draw and shoot after running to cover after a long stalk. *Be prepared!* Take an egg timer and a magazine with you into the treestand. Set the timer for fifteen minutes and read the magazine until the timer goes off. *Shoot one shot . . . then climb down!* Do the same thing the next day! I'll bet the second day *you'll take more time!*

    If you are a 3-D or target archer, simulate the stress of a tournament as closely as possible. Shoot against your buddies. Shoot the same number of arrows as you have to in the tournament, and score them as they will be scored. Put some pressure on yourself! Shoot for a Pepsi or dinner, or the registration of your truck . . . whatever gets you stressed or your adrenaline flowing! (More on this in chapter 14.) If you are a bowhunter or 3-D shooter, practice with a good rangefinder. Set your sights with it, and use it to double

Bernie Pellerite

check your results. If you don't check the yardage *after* you shoot and miss, you'll never know whether you've misjudged the distance, or you executed the shot badly.

- **DON'T** try and shoot a dozen arrows at the target in two minutes. This is generally an attempt to overcome anxiety about missing by not taking the time to *think each shot through*. The shooter tries to put his subconscious on *automatic* through quick repetitions. He therefore tries to accomplish two things . . . "get in the groove" of hitting the center while "avoiding responsibility" for missed arrows. He'll usually try to con himself or spectators . . . "Well I missed because I didn't really take my time. I could have hit it if I wanted to . . ." Yeah, right! Of course, the more arrows he shoots at a time, and the longer he shoots (sometimes two to three hours), the more tired he gets . . . and the more he misses. It's a vicious circle. If you are practicing on a 5-spot target for example, and you are missing on the last one or two arrows most often, there is probably a good reason. Other than possibly building up anxiety, most people experience this problem because they *shoot too fast*. Your muscles are like rechargeable batteries. Shooting an arrow expends a certain amount of energy. The muscles *need some time and relaxation to fully "recharge."* This keeps them in their "comfort zone," as we just discussed in chapter 12. Most archers don't allow enough time between arrows. A typical scenario might go something like this . . . you have 100% energy level when you draw your first arrow. By the time the first arrow is drawn and shot, your energy level is down to 85%. If you shoot too fast, by the time you shoot your second arrow, your energy level is only back up to 90%. Once again, if the third arrow is shot too soon, your energy level may only be up to 80%. And, when the fourth arrow is shot, it's only recharged to 70% . . . and the fifth arrow is only 60% . . . and so on. No wonder your last arrows are not as good as your first! After each shot, you should put your bow in a bow holster or, if you shoot a long stabilizer, rest it on the ground, and let your arms (and the rest of you)

Idiot Proof Archery

relax completely. Your muscles that are involved in the shot need to be completely relaxed for a sufficient period of time (usually 15 to 20 seconds). The length of time will vary for each individual, depending on age and physical condition. In any case, you must allow your muscles to *recharge to 100%* after each shot. *Your last shot should feel exactly the same as the first shot!*

Key Point #99

You must allow your muscles to recharge to 100% after each shot. Your last shot should feel exactly the same as the first shot!

- **DO** shoot each arrow as if *it is the only one you are going to shoot today!* "Relax . . . reflect . . . and recharge" between shots for fifteen or twenty seconds. You'll win more often if you try to shoot *sixty "one-arrow tournaments"* than if you try to shoot *one "sixty-arrow tournament."* Remember how you eat an elephant . . . *one bite at a time!* If you practice putting all your concentration and effort into every shot, not only is it more likely to hit the target, but when that record book buck is standing there broadside, or it's the last shot of a tournament, you'll find that the "subconscious well" that we all try to draw from under pressure, is only full of *good shots.* Stress *quality, not quantity!* Shoot only five or six arrows at a time, fifteen seconds apart, and if any shot doesn't feel right, *let it down and start over!* If you get tired or can't seem to focus as well as you should, stop for the day. *Don't reinforce failure!* If you're doing well, practice a little longer. Try to put yourself *totally* into each shot. *Thirty to fifty carefully shot arrows* per session will do more good than 300 arrows shot quickly and casually.

Key Point #100

You'll win more often if you try to shoot sixty "one-arrow tournaments" than if you try to shoot one "sixty-arrow tournament."

- **DON'T** randomly fire arrows *without a purpose, a system, a rhythm* and *a sequence.* If you don't shoot every one the same way, or if some are flying differently than others, or you have no particular purpose to accomplish on a given

Bernie Pellerite

 **Key Point #101**

Work on one problem area at a time until it is no longer a problem.

session, then you are probably just wasting your time. For example: "I'm going to shoot 30 arrows at an empty bale, and watch my bow hand, to learn to quit grabbing the bow." Work on one problem area at a time until it is no longer a problem.

- **DO** record your shot sequence, and number and chart your arrows. *Use your log book to triple your progress!* Number and enter the steps of your individual shot sequence in your log book: Example: #1 Nock arrow, #2 Hook release (or fingers) on string, #3 Set bow hand, #4 Pre-aim, #5 Draw to anchor, #6 Center target in peep, etc. etc. Some people will have five steps and some have fifteen steps, but it's important you record yours, so you can *systematically analyze and improve* any one of them, if you need to. Video yourself if you can, so you can compare what you look like shooting well with what you look like when you are in a slump. It will get you back on track, if you inadvertently start changing something. You should also number your arrows . . .

You don't want to know the number of the arrow you are about to shoot.

but don't put the numbers where you can see them while you are drawing the bow *(see photo)*. For instance, this could cause you to *start to anticipate* or *predispose* that #2 arrow will hit high right . . . *because it did the last two times*. You will then start to *subconsciously favor* holding low left on the target for the #2 arrow.

Draw the scoring rings, representing the target, on the pages in your log book, or make reduced copies of your targets *(see diagram, next page)*, and record *where each numbered arrow hits the target* . . . put the

Idiot Proof Archery

number where the arrow hole was. Example: #3 hit 6 o'clock in the 5-ring; #6 hit 1 o'clock in the 4-ring; #8 hit the center of 5-ring, etc. At the end of five sessions or so, take your log book and *chart the results* on a "bar graph" or "pie chart." You will probably notice certain patterns developing. Maybe, for example, 70% of your misses are low left. Now, *this is valuable information!* This could mean you are dropping your bow arm or maybe popping your head up. Or, you might discover that 62% of your misses are on the last two arrows. This could mean you are not resting between shots and are getting tired. Or, you may be over analyzing and trying too hard to shoot a perfect end . . . holding *way too long*, thus making you shoot outside your comfort zone. Or maybe you find out that your #4 arrow, always shoots high. This could mean it is hitting the rest, weighs less than the others, is bent or you need to check the fletch and/or nock alignment. This type of *accelerated practice session* can put you years ahead of your competition in just a few weeks or months.

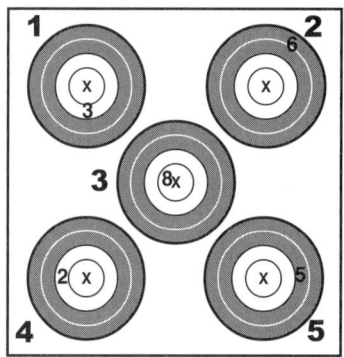

- **DO** run what I call, "instant replays." What this means is, as soon as you shoot an arrow, "replay" in your mind where the sight was (or more important, where your *mind was!*) . . . at the instant of release. For instance, if the sight was at 6 o'clock, one inch below the bullseye, and *your mind followed it down there . . .* and then the shot went off and the arrow landed at 6 o'clock . . . then you shot a good shot! You will usually find that, if you think in the middle . . . the sight *and* the arrow will go where you think!

Key Point #102

You will usually find that, if you think in the middle . . . the sight and the arrow will go where you think!

Bernie Pellerite

Write it down in your log book. Record the shots that felt bad or were aimed off target, and you will be surprised at the results. If you have access to a video camera, use it in your practice sessions. Record yourself from a side view and then, from behind and from the front. When you shoot a good or bad shot . . . *tell the camera* what you think. Then, tell it what you did right or wrong *immediately*, while it's still fresh in your mind. Hold up a target for the camera and point to where that arrow hit. By talking to the camera on *bad* and *good shots,* later when you watch it, you can analyze this "instant feedback" . . . which is invaluable for self-coaching. By recording your practice sessions, you can discover and analyze patterns and flaws . . . to learn *why and when you miss most often.* Then you can overcome anything that arises, before it becomes too serious or *ingrained into your form.* You can also put an inexpensive ($5) bathroom mirror under the camera, leaning against the tripod, to show a profile view of your form. As you come to full draw, peek out of the corner of your eye and look in the mirror at your form . . . are you leaning back? . . . is your elbow too low? . . . is your draw shoulder up or down? If you see something wrong . . . let down and start over! This will help you stop a lot of bad form *before it takes hold,* if you are willing to apply yourself.

Use a video camera, in your practice sessions. Put a mirror under it and look at it occasionally to see if your form is okay!

- **DON'T** pressure yourself into trying to beat the local "hot shot" or into trying to shoot a perfect 200 on a 3-D round, if your personal best is only 174. Only a fool expects to shoot twenty bullseyes in a row in a tournament, when he has never shot more than eight in a row in practice.

Idiot Proof Archery

- **DO** set realistic and attainable goals. You should have three types of goals. Your *immediate* goal should be to shoot only **this** one shot today . . . in the exact center of the target. Your *intermediate* goal should be to beat your previous best score. Your *long term* goal may to be to win the world championship . . . but that one is up to you! You should only compete, in any given tournament, with *your last best score*, not the local hero. Pay no attention to your competitor's scores . . . you can't change them. The only thing worrying about them will do is change *your* score! Your goal should be *one point higher than your best previous effort!*

If you want to greatly improve your accuracy in the woods or at a tournament, then you must be more *astute, organized, analytical,* and *intense* in your practice sessions than you've ever been in the past. Remember . . . "If you continue (in practice) to do what you've always done, you'll get what you always got (in tournaments)!"

Key Point #103

Your goal should be one point higher than your best previous effort!

Key Point #104

Pay no attention to your competitor's scores . . . you can't change them. The only thing worrying about them will do is change your *score!*

Key Point #105

You must be more astute, organized, analytical, and intense in your practice sessions than you've ever been in the past.

Also, don't forget the **Rule of 6 P's —**
Persistent **P**erfect **P**ractice . . .
Prevents **P**oor **P**erformance!

You'll get worse before you get better

If you do decide to bear down and "take the cure," remember this: you'll get worse before you get better . . . accept

Bernie Pellerite

it! Normally, it takes sixty to ninety days for your score to return to normal . . . and then to steadily increase. The reason for that is, as you try parts of the new "idiot proof" form, each shot will be part your new way and part your old way. Until you totally ingrain the new form into your subconscious, it's still *not yours*. That's why we recommend not shooting a target . . . just an empty bale or a bow simulator. Gradually, the new form will completely replace your old way and you won't even be able to remember how you used to do it. Don't give up! Stick with it . . . it will pay off in the end. Just ask any of my students who are scattered throughout the book! Stay away from targets. They will only slow down or kill your progress. Remember you can't learn while you're aiming.

Here's an idea that a lot of pro shops and clubs have adopted that will help make empty bale shooting less boring. I call it "Empty Bale Night." One night a week (usually just an hour), is set aside for anyone who wants to work on their form, release or whatever. All shooting is done up close to the bale with no targets. Anyone who comes in shoots up close or not at all. This way, you can help and remind each other what everybody might need to do. You can ask your buddies to watch you (and you them) to make sure you're correctly doing whatever it is that you are working on. It's fun, because the competition (the target) is taken away and you can relax and feel like you're actually accomplishing something.

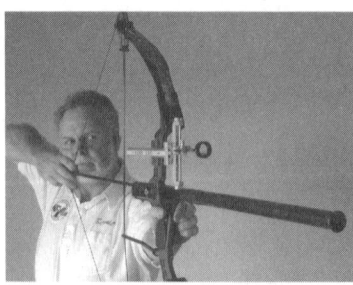

Shooting the **Laz-Air Shot Trainer** allows you to ingrain the shot sequence and the laser gives you a visual reward.

Shooting with your eyes closed transfers the feeling into your muscle memory.

Idiot Proof Archery

Chapter 14

Tournament Nerves
Choking Under Pressure & Shooting in Adverse Conditions

Tournament Nerves

Unless you are one of the very few archers that have mastered it, shooting under pressure has always been a major problem for all of us. When the "moment of truth" arrives on the tournament circuit, most of us are ill-prepared to perform the way we should. The ability to properly execute the shot while nervous, anxious, afraid, or excited, is not a natural situation for any of us. We must *practice it!* Think about it! . . . how can you expect to do something in a tournament that you have never practiced?

Most of us think that simply shooting arrows until we get fairly consistent at hitting the center of the target is practice. It *would* be, if all you wanted from your practice was recreation. We must remember our individual reasons for practicing in the first place. If your reason is to be competitive in tournaments . . . *you are doing it wrong!* To get used to the nervousness created in high pressure situations, we need to understand how it works and how to deal with it.

When we practice (if we are doing it the same all of the time), we

Illustration by John Rios

255

Bernie Pellerite

🎯 **Key Point #106**

We must remember our individual reasons for practicing in the first place. If your reason is to be in competitive tournaments... you are doing it wrong!

eventually develop a shot sequence (as I covered in chapters 7 and 8). We nock an arrow, then we grip the bow handle, hook on to the string with fingers or release, etc. If done correctly, with a lot of repetition, we eventually start doing these steps to the shot without having to think about it. We should now be able to *concentrate totally on aiming*. The body is operating the equipment *subconsciously,* while the *conscious* mind is immersed in aiming . . . remember, this is the key to "*predictable accuracy.*" Even beginners have experienced a few shots that "sort of just went off by themselves." This happens on more of a regular basis as we progress into the intermediate and advanced levels of archery. Eventually, when we can perform at this automatic level consistently, we are ready for the "big time" (or so we think)! But we soon find out that, to some extent, the winners are usually determined by who can *control their nerves* and *handle the pressure,* on that particular day. However, if you think about it, being

🎯 **Key Point #107**

The body is operating the equipment subconsciously, while the conscious mind is immersed in aiming . . . this is the key to "predictable accuracy."

1987 The Vegas Shoot . . . are you ready for the big time? That's me!!! . . . the only guy in shorts . . . in January!

Idiot Proof Archery

nervous at an important event is *perfectly normal*. It is part of the human equation, and happens to all of us. It is *how we handle it* that separates the winners from the rest of the field.

Why Being Nervous is a Problem

Understanding what pressure or nervousness causes us to do is the key to the solution. When we are nervous, we tend to not execute subconsciously anymore . . . because we don't *trust* our "let-go" system. We interrupt mental aiming and start trying to *control* the shot execution ("let-go") with our conscious minds and aim, simultaneously (just like in chapter 10). We become more deliberate and cautious so as to *not make* "mistakes!" Not understanding that we've become more careful *(go on defense)* and that it violates the offensive second half of our sequence *and* our "comfort zone," is a huge mistake! We erroneously calculate that we have a better chance at executing a perfect shot (and we'll settle for nothing less!), if we bring all of our senses to bear while we're under pressure. Because we alter our pre-programmed *(natural)* shot sequence and shot timing, and are no longer immersed in aiming at the moment of execution, we have little *chance to succeed*. Keeping our conscious mind out of the shot and on aiming was the *key in practice* . . . and it is *still the key under pressure!* How can we execute a "surprise" release when our total concentration is consumed by thoughts like . . ."*It's almost in the middle . . . get more pressure on the trigger . . . not too much! Oops! It's going back out . . . ease off the trigger . . . force it back in. Hurry! My elbow is starting to shake! . . . Should I let down? Nah, I can hold a few more seconds . . . Get ready, it's coming back . . . Get more pressure on the trigger? It's **perfect** now . . . where is the trigger? Why hasn't it gone off? . . . Squeeze harder! . . . Hurry up! . . . Uh-oh, It's going to drop out! . . . I'd better help it . . . Shoot it now! . . . Punch it,*

Key Point #108

When we are nervous, we tend to not execute subconsciously any more, because we don't trust our "let-go" system.

Bernie Pellerite

NOW! . . . Darn, I missed! . . . I knew I should have let down!" Sound familiar? I hope not, but if it does, you are in the same boat as most others . . . *that forget* how to shoot when the "heat is on!" The key here is to recognize your weaknesses and prepare for them.

How to Perform Under Pressure and Stop "Choking!"

If you **think** you are probably going to "screw up" or "choke" under pressure . . . you will! However, to overcome it, there are a few key things you must understand. **First key:** admit it! It's okay! It's perfectly natural! Denial is the worst thing you can do in this situation. **Second key:** the pressure or nerves you feel and the thing that is moving your sight around is really just a higher adrenaline level. **Third key:** if you expose yourself to pressure often enough, eventually you will get used to it! Unfortunately, most of us practice *practicing* so much that we eventually become really good in *practice* . . . and hopeless in tournaments. Instead, set up your practice sessions so you can *raise your adrenaline level* to simulate those high pressure situations as closely as possible. For instance, shoot against your buddies and, if necessary, give them a handicap. Make it tough to beat them. Bet dinner on the outcome . . . or the loser has to wash the other guy's truck. Make yourself shoot while you are excited or nervous and in front of as many people as you can. Have the "hyperactive neighbor kid" bang a drum, or have your buddy scream at you while you shoot. (This is actually done by the French national team! Their elite shooters try to shoot at ninety meters, with a "drill sergeant" screaming at them.) Play bad music at really loud levels, especially music you find distracting. Another good *pressure practice*, if you shoot at home, is to have your wife keep score. Bet her that if you don't shoot your average (let's say it's 295 out of 300), then you'll clean up the garage (or *mow the lawn*, etc.) . . . *tonight!* Now *that's* pressure!

 **Key Point #109**

If you expose yourself to pressure often enough, eventually you will get used to shooting with high adrenaline levels.

Idiot Proof Archery

Do whatever you can to create distractions and pressure, so you can *practice running your shot program subconsciously while **really focusing on the target** . . . in the face of pressure and distractions!* I have designed a drill that will help you get your adrenaline level up to tournament levels and help you to simulate pressure situations. This drill gets progressively harder toward the end (to simulate pressure), and it will also teach you to *focus* and *stay "hooked up," aim longer* and *aim finer!* This is what you do . . . get a regular 5-spot indoor target *(see page 33)*, and take it down to your copying center. Tell them to reduce the original and make several copies at 87.5% the original size. Also make several copies at 75%, 62.5%, 50%, 37.5%, and 25% of the original size. This is how the drill works: Take the smallest target (25% size), put it on the bale and go to the 5 yard line. Adjust your sight so you can hit the middle at 5 yards. As you look through your sight, the X-ring will be extremely tiny, but will look *exactly* like the X-ring on a normal sized 5-spot target at 20 yards. (Remember, you are at 25% of the distance, looking at a target that is 25% of the normal size.) The drill gets increasingly more difficult as the distance increases, but the target *always looks the same,* because the percentage of size is keyed to the same percentage of distance from the target. Shoot five shots, pull your arrows, and shoot five more from the 5 yard line (one arrow at each X-ring). *You must hit the X-ring all ten times, or you will have to shoot all ten shots over again* which at close yardage (5 to 15 yards) is fairly easy to do. Next, you move back to 7½ yards and shoot at the 37.5% size targets for ten shots. This too, will look like the normal 5-spot target at 20 yards through your peep sight. But like the 25% target, it will be easier to hit because your sight movement is less perceivable, at the closer yardages (5 to 15 yards). This gives you more confidence, like shooting a rifle while braced on a bench rest. You must hit all ten Xs before moving back to the next position, which is 10 yards and the 50% size targets. Continue moving back in 2½ yard increments and put up the next larger target. (At 12½ yards you will shoot the 62.5% target; at 15 yards you will shoot the 75% target; at 17½ yards you will shoot the 87.5%

Bernie Pellerite

target; and finally, at 20 yards, you will be shooting the normal sized 5-spot target.) *If you miss* any of the ten shots at a particular distance, you must *shoot all ten arrows again*, before moving to the next distance. Also, if you are an indoor tournament shooter, use a timer to add another element of pressure. If you want to make it even tougher, just shoot five arrows at each of the seven distances *but*, if you miss *any* Xs, you must go *all the way back to the shortest distance and start over!* Now, that will get your adrenaline going! As time passes, and you get better and better, challenge yourself to shoot ten arrows at each of the seven distances (70 arrows) without missing any, and without starting over. This method will put pressure on you and help you to discover how you react to it! This drill can be modified, depending on the shooter's ability and practice time available. It should teach the shooter how to handle an adrenaline rush and the benefits of precise concentration on the exact center of the point of aim, all the way through followthrough . . . to conclusion. It will teach you that you can only think about one thing at a time. So, you can't choke unless you *think* about it!
Fourth key: if you're thinking about aiming until conclusion, that's all your mind can handle at one time!

Pay close attention to two things: 1) What do I *think about* under pressure? and 2) Do I have a *pattern* under pressure? First, you'll probably realize you don't really concentrate on the target . . . from the "aiming moment" through conclusion. Your mind is probably wandering back and forth, *trying to control* the physical parts of the shot that you have already mastered in practice (to the subconscious level). But now you won't let them function, because you don't *trust* them . . . because this shot is *really important* (as I said six or seven times before)! You MUST learn to *trust* that once you commit and start your motor, it will continue to work on "automatic" until the shot goes off (without thinking about it). Again, the

Key Point #110

Remember, you can only think about one thing at a time. So, you can't choke unless you think about it! And, if you're thinking about aiming until conclusion, that's all your mind can handle at one time!

Idiot Proof Archery

Key Point #111

The conscious mind needs to be constantly occupied, from the aiming moment through conclusion! If it's left to it's own devices the conscious mind will interrupt aiming to think about choking!

conscious mind needs to be constantly occupied during this period (the aiming moment through conclusion). If it's left to its own devices, *the conscious mind will interrupt aiming* and the "choke thought" can then replace it. Be sure you understand this fully and the battle is nearly over. Most top shooters talk themselves through it . . . "Aim, aim, continue to aim . . ." and so on. Some challenge themselves, "Aim . . . aim . . . I can aim better than this . . . aim . . . aim . . ." Whatever works for you, use it. The next time you are under pressure, try it. You'll eventually understand the **Fifth key:** nervousness or anxiety is simply a thought process . . . a state of mind that *releases extra adrenaline which causes you to shake.* You'll eventually find the final **Sixth key:** *you can't think* about choking or being nervous or losing if your mind is *focusing 100% on aiming.* The reason is, of course, because you can only think of one *thing* at a time! . . . and that's the *"thing"* you'll probably get accomplished! So, out of the above: 1) choking 2) being nervous 3) losing 4) hitting the center! . . . PICK ONE! . . . *good choice!* See, that wasn't so hard, was it!? ANY QUESTIONS!?

Another technique used to succeed under pressure is recognizing your behavior patterns. Instead of going to tournament after tournament and just taking your lumps . . . learn something from your mistakes. Keep a "shot log" of your performance under pressure. Buy a small spiral notebook *(see photo)* to keep in your quiver and note where your arrows hit in the target, after you shoot. After two or three tournaments, you'll have a lot of information. There is probably a visible pattern of either low, high, left or right

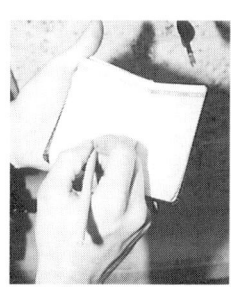

A log book can give you five years of experience in three months, if you understand how to use it!

Bernie Pellerite

arrows that are shot under pressure. If you record all of your misses, you can recognize your weaknesses and correct them. Burley Hall explains this method in his video, **Winning at 3-D** *(see Appendix)*. Burley says, his records showed that 90% of his misses in pressure situations were to the left (probably from holding too long). Now, when the pressure is on, he holds slightly to the right. Remember, you can't expect your mind to perform well under stress, if it never *practices* under stress and knows what to expect!

 **Key Point #112**

Remember, you can't expect your mind to perform well under stress, if it never practices under stress!

I'm confident that if you apply these principles to your own situation, you will find shooting competitive archery a lot easier in the future.

Shooting in Adverse Conditions

Some of the toughest things to do with a bow and arrow includes shooting while the wind is blowing, while it's raining, or while you're shooting uphill, downhill or on side hills. Because I have produced over three dozen archery videos with over a dozen world and national champions, I have been able to "pick their brains" and discover their techniques for shooting in these conditions. Also, because my wife and I spent six years shooting competitively in Hawaii where the wind blows almost constantly, we got a lot of experience practicing these "do's and don'ts of playing the wind." And since then, I have picked up some additional tips that make up a fairly comprehensive "arsenal" against wind, rain, and on hills that I now teach. Since the conditions are so different, we'll look at each separately — the following should better prepare you to make the best of a bad situation.

Shooting in Wind

Don't Practice In The Wind If you shoot a compound bow with a release, *you cannot effectively practice while the wind is blowing you all over the target.* It will also cause most people to start punching the trigger of the release (or worse!). If

Idiot Proof Archery

you shoot fingers (without a clicker), you can end up plucking the string or snapshooting.
Rule #1 The wind never blows consistently. **Rule #2** *Practice is, by definition, a controlled environment in which we try to duplicate excellent archery shots.* We do this to ultimately absorb those techniques and/or feelings into our "muscle memory" (subconscious program). **Rule #3** You can't (effectively) practice shooting a stationary target if you're in a row boat during a storm, or while riding a bucking horse, or shooting in an unpredictable wind . . . *without causing more problems than you solve. Consistency* is the key. But by all means, go out on a windy day and *try out* or *test* the following "wind systems" once you've practiced learning them under *controlled* conditions. This will give you a *feel* for what or how shooting in the wind affects your head and your system . . . but don't try to *learn* your system in the wind! Practice on a calm day and *log your results.* Finger shooters with clickers (which dictate *"let-go"*) *may* be able to get *some* benefits practicing in the wind. But for the majority of us, especially those with, or on the verge of, target panic . . . it's *a major no-no!*

Aiming In The Wind There are only two ways to aim in the wind . . . bad and worse! Just kidding! You can *aim off* to one side of the bullseye and let the wind blow the arrow into the center (pray it will) . . . or *cant your bow* to one side . . . and aim in the center. Whichever method you choose, don't expect to hold rock steady or get perfect results . . . it won't happen!

Aiming Off is not recommended for most personality types. This is because your subconscious mind is always trying to *put your sight in the middle of the target* . . . *naturally!* Remember the self-centering subconscious? You are now trying to *contradict that natural tendency,* and very few people can do it effectively. Some shooters who focus or *concentrate on their apertures* rather than on the center of the target can do this more effectively. But, most of them don't hold as long at full draw and/or they aren't using telescopic sights (scopes) that

Bernie Pellerite

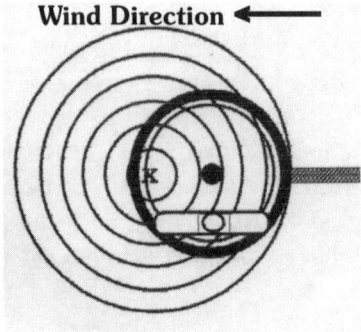

Aiming Off

magnify movement. These archers are usually ex-rifle or pistol shooters that are *more comfortable with focusing on the sight*... and not the target. These individuals may find it more effective and easier to aim off *(see diagram)*, than to cant the bow.

Canting The Bow I have found that this is the method that works best for most people. Simply tilt the top limb of your bow *into* the wind . . . 3, 4, or 5 inches (or 5, 10, or 15 degrees, etc.) off normal (or plumb), and aim in the center of the target. The cant (or tilt) automatically casts the arrow away from the point of aim in the direction of the cant. For example, you might ultimately find that, if you cant the top limb 5" (or X degrees) to the right into a 10 m.p.h. crosswind (right to left) from 30 yards . . . then your arrows will end up close to the middle. You can practice this method on a calm day by aiming in the middle and canting the top limb different amounts, to find out how far left or right your bow shoots the arrows at different distances. If you have a level mounted on your bow or sight, practice using the bubble in the level. For example, at 45 yards with all of the bubble to the left of center (top limb canted to the right), your arrows might hit 6 inches to the right. Record this information in your logbook. At 50 yards, you may be 8 inches to the right. Record this also. Next, practice at different yardages with ¾ of the bubble off center, then ½ of a bubble, etc. and record your results. Get as much information as you can. *If you practice on a calm day when you know your shots are*

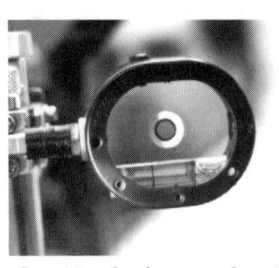

Canting the bow to the right (from the archer's perspective) casts the arrows to the right.

Idiot Proof Archery

being consistently executed, you can trust the results! Then, take all of this information to the range on a windy day. Try out what you have discovered against the wind, and record your results. This logbook could save you at the next tournament.

Don't Over-Hold Shoot in the wind with the *same timing* as you do on a calm day. Let down and start again, if you can't get the shot off with your normal timing. One of the most common mistakes is to try and hold longer (and therefore better). This is wrong! If your natural shot sequence is 8 seconds and you try to hold an extra 3 to 4 seconds . . . you'll probably stay in trouble because of the wind. Over-holding causes several bad things to happen. Your muscles (and therefore your sight picture) will start to shake from oxygen deprivation and fatigue, if you try to hold past your physical comfort zone. Because the wind is blowing your sight around anyway, this is aggravated by the shaking from muscle fatigue. Even worse, over-holding causes your mind to leave the target . . . and go to the release (where it should *not* be), in an effort to time the shot, causing all kinds of fear, anxiety and panic to build. This situation can cause you to start punching the trigger or plucking the string, causing bad shots and bad habits to form. Also, the longer you tend to hold, the greater your tendency will be to push excessively with your bow arm because you start to feel it collapsing, or in an effort to "help the shot." In right-handed archers, this will cause left arrows.

Don't Over-Control If you try to "muscle the bow" into holding steady, that will only make it worse. Again, recruiting muscles causes movement! *Relax, and let the sight move around* . . . it's going to, anyway! Also, focus on the spot you are aiming at . . . not the sight, and shoot the best shot you can. Shoot through it . . . don't alter the shot sequence or timing!

Add yardage (maybe) You will probably find you have to add yardage to the shot because the crosswind will "kill" some of the arrow velocity, *causing it to drop low* . . . even if you canted or held off *correctly!*

Consider Adding Mass to Your Bow You will find it much easier to hold steady in the wind if you *add mass weight*

Bernie Pellerite

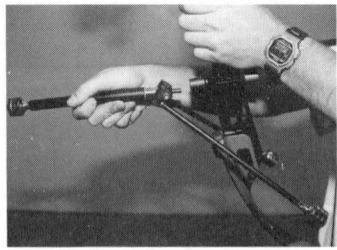

Consider adding mass to your bow with a back weight or v-bars. Either could make your bow steadier in the wind.

to your bow. You might add a heavier stabilizer or a set of V-bars or a back weight. Any of these can make a big difference on a windy day. It will also make you steadier when the wind *isn't* blowing! **Caution:** Make sure to keep the added weight *close to* and preferably, *below* your hand. And, don't just add the weight when the wind blows! The extra mass weight changes your shot dynamics and your physical comfort zone, so work up to the heavier weight slowly in practice (so you don't injure yourself) and record the results in your logbook, so you know what to expect when you shoot on tournament day.

Set Realistic Goals As with normal shooting, it is important not to set your expectations past a point that you can reasonably expect to reach. *Don't expect miracles!*

Remember, all these methods will vary from shooter to shooter, bow to bow, and arrow to arrow, depending on the speed of the wind. It is *not an exact science!* What they will do is give you that few extra points that your opponent won't get! You'll *have a plan* and are *much less nervous* and *afraid* . . . because you are more *aware of and prepared for* what is probably going to happen when the wind does blow.

 **Key Point #113**

You will get a few extra points that your opponent doesn't get, because you have a system and a plan for the wind.

Shooting in the Rain

If it is raining and you absolutely have to shoot, there is *no magic*. Most people who shoot, don't shoot well. But, there are a few factors to consider that may help you. The "air resistance" is greater when the air is loaded with humidity and/or drops of water. This can slow down the arrow, or the arrow and fletching

Idiot Proof Archery

can pick up moisture which can cause it to weigh a little more, and therefore hit slightly low at longer distances. You are better off in this situation with plastic vanes, rather than feathers. If you absolutely must shoot arrows with feathers, *weatherproof* them with Scotchguard™ or one of the commercial waterproofing treatments. Whatever you shoot, keep your arrows dry. Put a plastic bag over your quiver, covering your arrows. Also, you should use a scope cover to avoid getting your scope wet.

Try adding a yard or so on longer shots to compensate for the lower arrow speed. Since there are so many bow-arrow setups and so many different kinds of rain, the more you practice and experiment with your equipment in the rain, the better your results will be. You don't have to worry about developing snapshooting or punching in the rain, because it doesn't usually move your sight around violently and unpredictably like the wind does.

Shooting Up and Down Hills

Most shooters learn the hard way . . . that up and down shooting angles cause a new set of problems. A lot of people don't know, for example, that as you draw to anchor on a downhill or uphill shot, you need to *bend at the waist* and *maintain the top "T formation"* of your upper body *(see diagram)*. If you don't, you will find that it's real hard to get your front sight in the middle of your peep, among other things. Another problem arises if you draw normally and then elevate your bow for an uphill shot. If you put excessive "heel pressure" on the bow handle to elevate your bow, when you release the shot, the bow will kick up because of the pre-loaded torque on the handle and you'll probably miss it high. Good shooters, especially if they shoot a round wheel or soft cam bow, put alignment marks or

Bernie Pellerite

tape on the cables at near-peep-sight height so they can check it at full draw. These marks ensure that they are at the exact same place at every draw. They check these marks first before aligning the front sight in the peep. They realize, unlike most people, that if you are shooting uphill, *your draw length gets slightly shorter*. When shooting downhill, *your draw length gets longer*. This is because of the draw angle and arc, and also the shoulder and arm position of the shooter.

Also, you will soon discover that your sight marks may be off when shooting up or downhill. As a *general rule of thumb*, when shooting above or below level: 1) make no corrections from -10 to +15 degrees. 2) for targets higher than +15 degrees or lower than -10 degrees, shoot as though they were about one yard closer. 3) For uphill and downhill shots, the amount of correction needed increases with range. Slightly more corrections are needed when shooting downhill. For example, at severe angles, such as 45 degrees, you have to shoot a 30 yard target for 22 yards, and a 60 yard target for 44 yards. These tests were done at 250 f.p.s., with aluminum arrows. Lesser corrections for carbon arrows are necessary. This information was furnished to me by Freddie Troncoso, who stresses that your *tests may vary*, because of differences in draw weight, draw length, arrow fletch, and other factors. Therefore you need to experiment with your own equipment, to find out what works for you.

Shooting on Side Hills

If for example, you are trying to shoot a target on the side of a hill and your back is to the hill, you will notice that most all of the holes in the target are on the *downhill side* of the target. This phenomenon is caused by *pre-loaded torque* via *gravity*. As you try to draw, gravity wants to force you to lean downhill to keep your balance. The normal course of action in this circumstance is to come to full draw, and then try to *force the bow* to an upright position in order to level the sight. This will be rather hard to do, as gravity tries to pull you the other way. As you release the shot, the bow is now pre-loaded to the downhill side and, in this example (for a right-handed archer),

Idiot Proof Archery

will torque to the right upon explosion, causing you to miss to the downhill side. So here's the secret for defeating this phenomenon . . . before you draw the bow, try *leaning* a bit *toward the hill* which, in this example, would be back on your heels . . . and *tilt the top limb* of the bow *into the hill* (to the left in this example) as you draw. Then *level up from left to right*, thus eliminating any body or hand torque that gravity would have caused. When you release a good shot, it should go in the middle.

The above techniques should help you immensely when trying to shoot under pressure or in adverse conditions. But remember, you will have to adapt these to *your style* and/or system and *practice* or *test them* until you are comfortable with them.

Larry Boone *of Pinckney, MI, a graduate of the shooter's school, broke the world record at the IFAA World Championships (Senior Division) with a perfect 600 and 96Xs. The old record was 594 with 92Xs. He also finished 4th overall at the NFAA Indoor Nationals in Tulsa. Larry credits several tips he learned at the shooter's school ". . . total focus on the X (not the sight) and to shoot sixty one-arrow tournaments, not one sixty-arrow tournament . . . which is the way to get in the winner's circle."*

Thanks Bernie,
Larry Boone

Bernie Pellerite

Jamie Martin, is a 3-D shooter from Point Pleasant, NJ. A week after attending the shooter's school, he competed in his first indoor tournament, the Atlantic City Archery Classic (2nd biggest in the U.S.). After two days, he was in first place in the championship flight . . . until the last five arrows! Then, the pressure finally got to him and he shot three 9s and two 8s and finished second. That's still not bad for your first time!

Usually your scores go down temporarily when you incorporate something new into your shot sequence ... but not in these two cases.

Patty Sickler and PSE Pro Staffer **Mike Tokolics** demonstrated the knowledge passed on to them by the NFAA Shooter's School Master Coach Instructors Bernie & Jan Pellerite.

Both attended a school at Neil's Archery in Endicott, NY. Two weeks later they attempted the near impossible, shooting two tournaments in one weekend. At the first tournament, Mike and Patty won the PA State Archery Assn. 3-D Championship in St. Thomas, PA. The second tournament was one day later where Mike won the NY Field and Bowhunter 3-D Championship, and Patty placed 2nd. This tournament took place in Chemung, NY. (NOTE: The distance between the two events round trip was 784 miles!)

Mike says, "It pays to attend a class AAA+ school and gain the knowledge and tools to achieve your personal goals."

Thank you both so much!
Mike and Patty

Idiot Proof Archery

Chapter 15

3-D and Estimating Yardage
"Legal and Illegal"

A lot of people think there is no connection between shooting marked-distance targets indoors or outdoors, and scoring well on a 3-D animal in the woods. Wrong again, "McKenzie breath!" If you think the only secrets to winning at 3-D are having the highest chronograph readings and estimating yardage, you have a long walk back to the clubhouse! I'm constantly bombarded by 3-D shooters, hoping I'll tell them (what they want to hear) . . . that the secret is this new bow, or this little known release, or this secret 3-D decoder ring! They are all looking to *buy* the magic bow or magic arrows. Well I am, too! I've had them on order for a long time, but they haven't come in yet . . . I think they are back ordered!

After producing thirty-seven instructional videos, owning a pro shop, coaching thousands of archers, and picking the brains of every pro . . . *that had a brain to pick* (and would let me pick it), I've pretty much narrowed it down. The real secrets to winning (legitimately) at 3-D are . . . estimating distance, consistent shooting form, and a mental program that doesn't fold up under pressure. Arrow speed helps *just a little,* but is not nearly the be all and end all, as Burley Hall proves in his video, **Winning at 3-D** *(see Appendix).* He proves that even at 310 f.p.s., you have to be nearly perfect on estimating the yardage to get the big bucks. Even if your yardage is right on, your form or

Key Point #114 ⊙

The real secrets to winning (legitimately) at 3-D are estimating distance, consistent shooting form and a mental program that doesn't fold up under pressure.

Bernie Pellerite

nerves can (and will!) kill you, if they are not razor sharp and rock steady. You can literally give the actual distances to all of the targets to most 3-Ders, and they still can't beat most pros . . . because they can't *execute* the shot. The 12 ring on a 3-D animal is about 1¾" in diameter and the 10 ring is about 5". Most 3-D shooters can't hit a 5" bullseye at a marked 40 yards *consistently* under pressure. Hardly any can consistently hit a 1¾" circle at a marked distance of 20 yards under pressure, let alone trying to hit it at an unknown distance of 35 to 50 yards. One of the main reasons for 3-D popularity over dot or target shooting in the first place was that you could shoot fairly well, even with target panic, on a 3-D animal. This is because there was no *visible* spot or target that you had to hold on. It was sort of like shooting at a blank bale. *No dot . . . no panic!* Target panic, in case you haven't learned by now, goes away when you remove the aiming dot! You are not trying to get a perfect rifle sight picture with the sight in the exact center of the target, because you can't *see* the exact center . . . which removes the fear of missing. I did an experiment back when I came up with the *Archery Festival* concept in 1994 (which is now widely used). The concept was to have many different types of shoots at one huge tournament or festival . . . 20 yard indoor, 3-D marked, 3-D unmarked, field round, novelty shoots, etc., etc. I took a look at the scores from the people who shot both the marked and unmarked 3-D events at a national tournament that I helped organize. On the marked range, there were stakes with posted yardage. There was also a 1" orange dot in the middle of the McKenzie 10-rings on the targets. On the other 3-D range (which was very similar), there was no yardage marker or dot . . . just a stake to shoot from, as with most unmarked 3-D tournaments. After polling the scores of over 100 shooters that competed on both

You can still shoot 3-D with target panic because there's no visible target/dot.

Idiot Proof Archery

courses, the results were absolutely amazing. On average, the scores were *20 points lower on the marked range* . . . go figure! Why do you suppose that was? The answer may be astounding to some but as I discovered, it is one of the main reasons that 3-D was popular in the first place. If you have target panic, and 99% of the shooters do (punching, freezing, flinching, snapshooting or tournament nerves), your symptoms don't show up on an empty bale or any target medium that *doesn't have a visible aiming spot*. After all, you don't have *shooting panic* . . . you have *target panic!* So, when we put the orange dot in the center, you were then *obligated mentally* to have to hold the sight in the *exact* center and try to execute the shot, both at the same time . . . and you can't do that with target panic. A lot of people wonder why 3-D popularity has waned recently . . . going the same route target shooting has been going for years. The real reason, in my opinion, is that there's always been, and always will be, way too much difference in the scores between the 99% that punch, freeze, flinch or snapshoot . . . and the 1% that don't! After a while, the 99% get tired of getting the crap kicked out of them by the few robot-like, super human, ice-water-in-the-veins, no-heart-beat and no-pulse shooting machines that completely dominate the winner's circle. The real problem is that most of this 99% don't know (or don't want to know) that their *problem* has a name (see chapter 10). And, as long as they have it, *they can't win* . . . *they can only play!* They live in denial and play the gadget game, in hopes of finding (buying) that magic whatchamacallit or speedburner bow!

However, draw lengths of 33" and 340 feet per second arrow speeds hardly ever take home the money. Just ask Shannon Caudle, who shoots much slower and wins at IBO and ASA. Or Bobby Ketcher (one of the shortest pros on the tour), who shoots under 280 f.p.s. and does pretty darn good. (He shot a *perfect* 400 IBO round at the Bedford 15th Annual Classic in 2000.) Other top pros like Randy Chappell and Randy Ulmer have given away up to 40 feet per second to faster bowed competitors, but still managed to win. Remember, *they pay you for where it lands* . . . *not how fast it got there!*

Bernie Pellerite

 **Key Point #115**

Remember, in 3-D, they pay you for where it lands . . . not how fast it got there!

I once did an unofficial survey in my area. I asked some average 3-D shooters to keep a log of the next two or three tournaments they shot. They were to keep track of their misses, as to whether they were up or down, left or right. The results were amazing! They missed the 10-ring left or right an average of six times per round, which translates to 12-15 points. They had the yardage okay, but their form and execution weren't there and they blew it left or right. It's funny though; they never seemed to remember those, when they were recounting the reasons (excuses) they didn't score well at the tournaments. It was always . . . "Gee, if it wasn't for that 5 I took on the 42 yard turkey on target #12" or . . . "That X (zero) that I took on the javelina on target #19 got me! Jeez, do you believe that darn thing was 48 yards?" Sound familiar? Unless they were shooting in a wind storm, they might need to work on their shooting form and their release. And where do you suppose they could test their shooting form under pressure? *Not on a 3-D course . . . of course not!* (Pun intended!) Too many variables and too many excuses! Try tracking *your* left and right misses the next two or three shoots. You'll be surprised! A famous 3-Der, Burley Hall said, "If your misses are up and down, work on your yardage judging. If your misses are left and right, work on your form."

Competing on indoor target and outdoor field rounds will make you much more confident, accurate and tournament ready. 3-D pros like Randy Ulmer, Randy Chappell, Bobby Ketcher, Susan Thompson, Jesse and Ginger Morehead, and dozens of others tested and honed their form and tournament nerves in marked yardage tournaments and it paid off when the pressure was on . . . just ask them. When it came to shooting up and down hill and shooting in the wind at the 2000 IBO World Championship at

 **Key Point #116**

Competing on indoor target and outdoor field rounds will make you much more confident, accurate and tournament ready when it comes to 3-D.

Idiot Proof Archery

Snowshoe Ski Resort, most of the NFAA and target-trained archers out-shot the other shooters. Marked distance target, field, and 3-D rounds are the best way to learn professional level form under pressure. If you don't have form, you don't have much. So, the next time there is one of these tournaments in your area, give it a try. But be forewarned . . . *it' can be habit forming!*

3-D Rangefinding Systems

Several years ago, while attending major 3-D tournaments, I had the opportunity to talk to numerous exhibitors, tour-

Bernie shows pro 3-D star Randy Chappell the secret to having a "low, locked, and relaxed shoulder." Randy, who gave up 40 f.p.s. to some speedsters, was the first pro ever to shoot a perfect 400 at an IBO tournament.

nament organizers, amateur and pro shooters about a subject of growing concern at the time. I discovered, to my amazement, that a surprising number of amateur and professional shooters had been using *"framing systems"* to tell the exact distance to a 3-D target, instead of "guessing" or "estimating" yardage (in the traditional sense). There are many different framing techniques which we will discuss later, but a hypothetical situation might be . . . to align your 40 and 50 yard pins with the top of the back and the bottom of the belly of a McKenzie small deer target (at full draw) then tape-measure the distance from your sight to the target . . . let's say, for example, it's 45 yards. Every time you see that particular type of target . . . and the 40 and 50 yard pin "frame it" *(see Figure A, pg. 276)*, it will *always be 45 yards away!* If the pins are just barely inside the animal it may be, for example, 43 yards or vice-versa if they are just outside the animal, it may be 47 yards. I discovered that "framing" has been around in international field competitions for many, many years, and it somehow found it's way into high

Bernie Pellerite

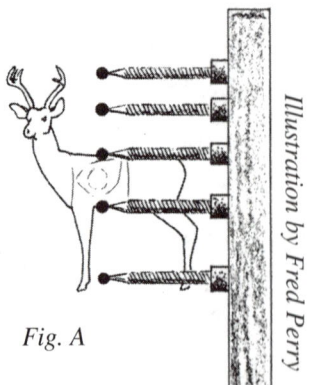

Fig. A

Illustration by Fred Perry

level 3-D competition several years ago. This subject seems to have been "political dynamite" in the archery community and a total taboo on the national 3-D circuit from 1992 to about 1998. People have different opinions on whether it was legal, moral or ethical. But, we'll discuss that later.

I debated over writing about this because it's not "politically correct." You see, there's an unwritten rule in archery (I guess it's written now!) that says . . . you can't talk or write about the negative things in our sport, *because it might be bad for archery*. Some people that subscribe to this rule have adopted a "don't ask – don't tell" philosophy about this, and other controversial subjects. Many of you, who know me personally, have already figured out by now that I've never been political or "politically correct." Furthermore, I have always been a "tell it like it is" and an "in your face with the naked truth" kind of guy. I guess I'm sort of like Andy Rooney on CBS's **60 Minutes**. I tend to *notice a lot of little things that other people don't*, and I ask a lot of questions . . . *"Didja ever notice* . . . Billy Bob Big Shot sure does let down a lot when he's shooting the large deer and the antelope targets, doesn't he! And when he finally does shoot, he always gets a 10 (or 12) . . . *Why is that?"* Do you suppose, 1) He knows something we don't, 2) He is just particularly good at judging yardage on those two animals, or 3) This is all just pure coincidence. Well, maybe this chapter will help some of you answer that and many other questions about the subject.

I try to stress in my videos, articles and coaching that "All problems have solutions!" However, with some extremely difficult problems like this one, *a lot of people don't want to hear the solutions*. Many others don't even want to hear about the problem! As one well-known manufacturer/shooter said to me in 1995 when I told him I was thinking of doing an article

Idiot Proof Archery

on "framing systems," he said, "So, you are going to spill the beans on us, huh?" Well, I guess I did, but I was by no means the first. As I understand it, this method was being taught by at least one shooting school and at least two top level coaches in the early 1990s. I was first exposed to it in a book by NFAA National Champion, Kirk Ethridge, called ***Professional Archery Technique***. This is a great book, by the way. You may want to get a copy *(see Appendix)*. Kirk is a very focused (Type B) shooter (who was the first to shoot a *perfect score* of 600 with 120 Xs at the NFAA Indoor Nationals . . . which he has since done twice). He is also a very intelligent and articulate writer and author. Among other interesting subjects, Kirk devotes an entire chapter to "Debunking Range Estimation." It describes in detail a few of the methods I will be explaining later. I will outline several methods of framing that I have observed, read about or have been told about by others . . . some at the top of the national 3-D tournament circuit. I will attempt to relay the reasoning some have expressed for thinking it's okay and just part of the sport. I will also give you the rationale for why it should be illegal and some possible ways to stop it or catch people doing it. Because of my original article (and others like it) most of the major 3-D organizations have changed their rules (since 1995) to make it more difficult to use framing systems (although a few shooters are still trying, and probably succeeding, to do so).

Framing Methods

A "framing method" is defined as using two or more fixed reference points (usually on your bow, accessories, or body), to visually span or "frame" two or more reference points on any given target of known dimensions. This can be used as a "rangefinding" method to determine the distance to the target. In order for the "framing system" to work properly, the first two references (like the gap between two pins) must be held at the same distance from the eyes, and the targets must be of standard size. It is important to note that most framing systems are being employed to *supplement* the archer's genuine ability to estimate

Bernie Pellerite

🎯 **Key Point #117**

Most framing systems are being employed to supplement the archer's genuine ability to estimate yardage. To place "in the money"... you must be able to judge yardage pretty well on your own.

yardage. To place "in the money" or near the top using one of these systems at most 3-D shoots, you must be able to judge yardage pretty well on your own... especially up to 30 yards or so. Beyond that is where most people have trouble. Therefore, the people who use a "framing system" generally set it up at 35 to 50 yards. Please understand that if they are terrible at estimating yardage, *this system won't make them top shooters.* But, if they shoot in the high 180s out of a possible 200 on an IBO course for example, a good system can easily put them in the mid to high 190s. Now they are usually in the money at the amateur level and can even be very competitive as a pro. Most of the following techniques can get them within two yards, or closer, of the exact distance to the target, which is usually close enough.

Here's an example: if they use a pin sight as a rangefinder, generally they prepare their shot using their "best guess" first, then when they are at full draw, the correct yardage is revealed (by aligning two known fixed points on their sight, with two known fixed points on the target). This system often merely verifies that their "best guess" was correct, but when they are not correct, it can mean the difference between scoring a 5 and a 10. As you can imagine, a pin shooter can design a fairly complete system for rangefinding by using the 14 vertical gaps between the pins and/or the pin guard *(see Fig. B)* and/or the horizontal gaps between the pin guard and different points on the pins *(see Fig. C).* They can adjust these pin gaps for every 5 yards like 35, 40, 45 and 50 yards or every 4 yards like 35, 39, 43 and 47 yards, or whatever progression they choose. They then move the whole set of pins up or down so their 20 yard pin is accurate at 20 yards. They may have to move their peep or bend the pin *tips* up or down a little, to make them work at the correct yardage. If the target is not broadside and is angled, they can use the vertical pin gap system, (top of the back to the

Idiot Proof Archery

bottom of the belly), and if it is tilted forward or backward, they use the horizontal pin guard gap system (hip to chest or hip to head section seam). As Kirk points out in his book, ". . . you may want to set one of these vertical gaps . . . to fit a specific target size's maximum distance. For instance, you could choose to adjust this gap to fit perfectly the 3-D McKenzie small deer at 45 or 50 yards. For the other size deer or animal targets, simply note where your pin appears on the animal at its maximum shot distance."

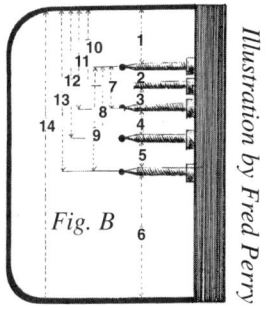
Fig. B

As they advance toward the target, the bottom pin progresses up the deer's abdomen. The same is true if they are using the horizontal pin guard gap, except as they advance, the pin tip progresses inside the hip

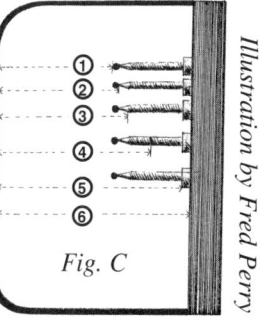
Fig. C

or chest, depending on which way it's facing. They can then make notes as to where the pin tip falls at five yard increments, for instance, on different size targets. If they practice using their notes enough, they will eventually memorize them and get very proficient at "estimating distance."

Once they have memorized three or four distances on, let's say, the McKenzie large deer, they move on to another. **Note**: There may be other targets that have the same or nearly the same back-to-belly, chest-to-hip, or hip-to-head section seam measurement as the one they just memorized, so they take good notes. If this sounds hard or time consuming, you're right, it is! For that reason, some shooters only have two or three distances on one or two popular animals memorized. Those distances may have only come into play (in the 1990s) two or three times on a range with 20 targets, but if they thought, for example, that a grazing deer was 36 yards and the system reveals it is

Bernie Pellerite

really 40 yards, depending on how fast the bow is shooting, they would have scored a 5 or an 8 instead of the 10 they got with their system. If they do that only twice per round, they'll gain 4 to 10 points they wouldn't have had without the system. Since most big shoots have 40 targets, multiply 4 or 10 x 2 = 8 to 20 points extra. Where would that put them? If they are even more sophisticated or ambitious in their systems and practice, you can imagine what can be accomplished. The key is to avoid shooting fives . . . you can't win shooting fives.

The key is to avoid shooting fives; you can't win shooting fives.

Key Point #118

Other Popular Framing Systems

Scope Shooters Scope shooters can achieve similar results by horizontally framing the outside of the hip section of an animal target with the housing of the scope and noting where the dot in the scope falls on the target *(see Fig. D)*. They can also use the vertical gap between the dot and housing, or the bubble and the dot, to frame the distance between the top of the back and the bottom of the belly *(see Fig. E)*. They may adjust the sight bar in or out to get the necessary sight picture. This and "special binoculars" are the methods used most by Olympic-style shooters who shoot unmarked FITA rounds using target faces with circular scoring rings of known dimensions, and is where framing originated *(see Fig. F)*. The NAA (National Archery Association, see Appendix) has currently legalized, or I should say has decriminalized, this practice (except for the special binoculars), apparently because almost everyone had some kind of system anyway. Refer to current NAA rules for details.

Miscellaneous Techniques

Although using the gaps associated with pins and scopes *were* the most popular ways of rangefinding, there are many more. Using the width of the sight adjustment knob, or the end of the sight bar, or the width of any piece of equipment in (or near) the sight line will work just as well. The shooter simply

Idiot Proof Archery

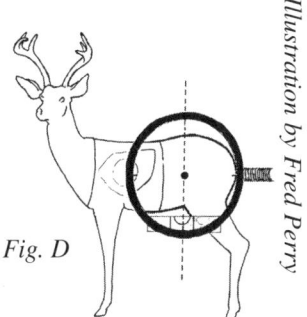

Fig. D

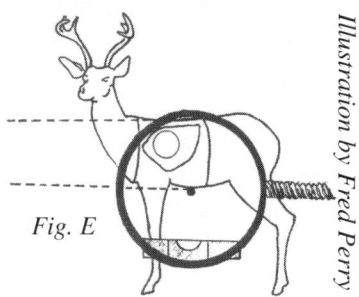

Fig. E

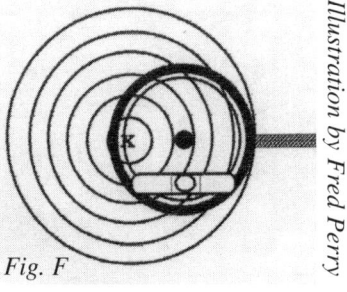

Fig. F

frames the intended target at full draw with the chosen fixture, or the gap between two fixtures, then moves the sight onto the bullseye (using the correct pin), and shoots. In the case of a scope sight, he holds a little high or low from his original "best estimate" sight setting, based on what he "learned" from framing the target, and then shoots with the confidence of "knowing" the correct distance. The other method is to frame the target and then let down and change the sight to the correct yardage setting. This practice is now illegal in most of the major archery organizations. So, now they have to let down, redraw, and mentally re-sight on a different spot on the target, to compensate for the misjudged first setting.

Another very popular technique that was easily observed, is putting the bow in a bow holster, or resting the bottom cam on their belt with their arm fully extended and the top limb conveniently positioned between their eyes and the target *(See Figures G and H, pg. 282)*. Using the limb tip or the gap between the cam and limb tip is an excellent method, as long as they make sure that the limb tip is always the same distance from their eye. Speaking of fully extended arms, did you ever see anyone in this position *(see Figure I)* pretending to count to

Bernie Pellerite

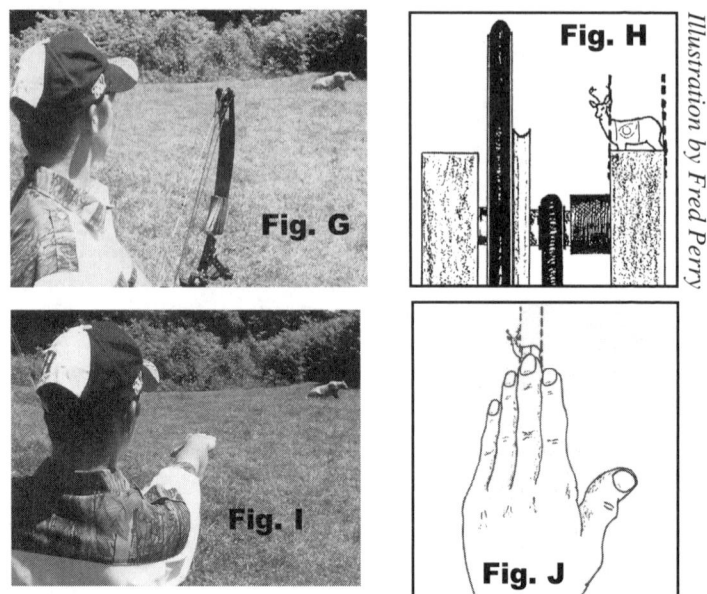

themselves, " . . . 20, 30, 40," etc. They are usually faking the first two or three arm positions for your benefit. The one that really counts is the last one, where the finger tips are pointed directly at the target *(see Figures I and J)*. They are secretly framing the target's horizontal width, using the width of the end of their fingers or the width of their fingernails. There are four different finger widths and therefore four different yardages in this method.

Other methods include marks or incremental scales on the inside tip of the bill of a baseball cap, so when they tip their head down a little, they can line up the target between the marks. Shooters have been known to point to the target and let their thumb ring dangle and frame inside the ring, or use the two natural creases on the inside of their palm at the joint of their thumb, to frame back-to-belly of the target. There are a few more I'm sure, but as you can see the possibilities are unlimited.

By far, the most popular method now is using "special binoculars!" An acquaintance of mine confessed to me that he

Idiot Proof Archery

used his binoculars at ASA tournaments as a rangefinder. First he focuses them on the first target. Then he sets his sights, using his "best estimate" . . . then shoots. While walking to the target, or back from the target after scoring, he steps off the correct distance. Let's say he shot it for 37 yards and when he steps it off, it is actually 40 yards. He then goes to the next target *knowing* the binoculars are correctly focused at 40 yards (he also has hash marks or lines drawn on the focus adjustment knob). On the second target, when he looks through the binoculars, if he has to turn the focus adjusting knob one line to the *right*, he knows it's farther (1½ yards, for example) than 40 yards. If he has to turn it two lines to the *left*, he knows it's 3 yards less then 40 yards. **Note**: This only works with a few types of binoculars, usually the real **long** and expensive kind ($1000 to $3000, especially 10x50 or bigger, and particularly if they have a zoom feature). Some of these binoculars are so critical that they will focus clearly on a 41 yard deer target, and if you step back *one yard* . . . it will be slightly out of focus! I'm told that most cheaper models have a greater depth of field and/or have less critical focal length with a shorter focusing barrel, and may look the same at 35 and 40 yards, thereby making them worthless.

    A few more obvious techniques include a set of pictures with kill zones outlined in white that a shooter pulls out and looks at, just before he or she shoots. They may or may not look through their binoculars first. If you get a chance to look close at the animal pictures, you may discover marks or scratches (probably coded) on the pictures that shows the archer where the pin or scope dot falls at different yardages on the target. In the past, looking at pictures during shoots may have seemed normal. But, now that binoculars are legal in IBO, ASA and NFAA shoots, making kill zones quite visible, there's really no reason to even possess these pictures. **NOTE concerning binoculars:** Currently IBO has a .5 power limit and most organizations don't allow marks on the focus knob, etc. Therefore you should always check with tournament officials beforehand concerning what equipment or methods are legal or illegal, as rules may vary from one organization to another.

Bernie Pellerite

The Bad News/Downside In order to be able to frame with your sight, a shooter needs *good vision*, the ability to *hold steady*, and a *good memory*. For example, if you see blurry pins out in front of you, it's hard to tell exactly if the sight and the animal incorrectly. Also, if your sight is shaking or moving continuously, this system is worthless! And finally, if you confuse "framing" the 30 and 50 yard pin around the *small* deer at 41 yards, with the *large* deer at 46 yards . . . you're dead! Plus, the skill takes six months to a couple of years to develop the ability to do it correctly. Also, in recent years, the proliferation of new and different targets, especially McKenzie's and Rinehart's, makes it even more difficult to keep all of the necessary information in your head. There *used to be* only six or seven different animal targets. Now, there are over thirty different ones!

How to Spot Shooters Using Framing Systems

Before 1995, there were a lot more people at 3-D shoots who used framing systems at one time or another. Now, under the new rules with all the different types and sizes of targets, there are very few. However, if you suspect you're dealing with one of the unrepentant, here's a few ways to catch people at it. Currently, most of the shooters that are still determined to *cheat you* in order to *beat you* are using "special binoculars." They usually have nearly invisible marks on the focus knob to calibrate distance, or for example, they only have one scratch or dent on the focus knob that lines up with another scratch on the case at, let's say, 40 yards. Then they line up their 40 yard mark and look at the target. If they have to move the focus knob four lines or

Expensive binoculars with long focal barrels and marks on the focus knob make good rangefinders.

Idiot Proof Archery

clicks to the right to focus it, then the target is 44 yards, etc. But, just because you see some of these signs *doesn't necessarily mean that shooter is framing.* Remember, not everyone who uses one of these methods is trying to cheat you . . . but everyone who is trying to cheat you is using one of these methods.

Key Point #119 ◉

Remember, not everyone who uses one of these methods is trying to cheat you . . . but everyone who is trying to cheat you is using one of these methods.

Is This Cheating?

Some organizers I've talked to about this have taken the "don't ask – don't tell" position. (It's a bit like being homosexual in the armed forces; if you admit to it, they'll kick you out. But if you don't say anything, they won't ask.) These same organizers were also hoping I would not write about this, because they didn't want to deal with the consequences.

First of all, let me explain that I've got my own personal convictions about the issue of whether it should be legal or illegal, but that's another story. Second, it's not my job to decide, and I can live with either decision, as long as *everybody knows the options* and it's not kept secret by the few . . . to win the money . . . from the many. **Let's just level up the playing field!**

At a national championship shoot in 1994, I was positioned fifteen or so yards in front of the shooters and well off to the side, video taping the three or four shoot-offs. Low and behold, right in front of me and hundreds of other spectators, up steps a top-ranked shooter (from the east coast), who took his time glassing the target and placing his bottom cam (after several attempts) into the *exact position* he wanted on his shooting belt. He then proceeded to extend his arm fully, closed one eye and sighted across his limb tip at the target. Before he finally let an arrow go, he had to let down *three separate times* (and each time looked at his laminated animal target cards hanging from his belt). The three other competitors walked up to the stake, glassed the target, set their sights and shot. They didn't take more than 20 seconds each. He took probably two minutes . . . and he won the shoot-off! Afterward, I approached him

Bernie Pellerite

and asked which part of the limb he used for framing. He turned white as a sheet, started stuttering, and finally said, "Uh . . . well, I don't really use it for that purpose. All I was doing was checking to see if the target was angled." He then hurried off. A couple of years later, he supposedly admitted to a close friend, that *his system* was accurate to within one yard. He later went on to win numerous tournaments and thousands of dollars. *I don't know if he still uses a system or not*, but I'm convinced that a lot of others in the pro and amateur divisions *wouldn't even think about* using a rangefinding system to help them win. And, I'm sure there are others who have probably tried some methods and found that they didn't work for them, or it wasn't worth the trouble, so they don't use a rangefinding method.

I certainly don't want to paint a picture that all of the winning amateur and pro shooters have a framing system. It's not for me to say how many were, at one time, using some framing system or another. I'll leave that up to you. By now, most organizations have been forced to take steps and change some rules, and most of the shooters now are doing it, *without framing*. So, obviously, there had to have been a big enough problem that they *had* to change their rules! But if you think someone is using a framing system and if you want to do something about it, take your concerns (make sure you are right first!) to the tournament officials. Ask for a ruling! Is this legal or not? That's the only way to get some of them to take *a more visible position on this* problem.

Legal 3-D Techniques

Head yardage

My wife Jan and I have been lucky enough to pick up dozens of little "secrets to 3-D success" and pass them on in our videos and shooter's schools, and now in this book. Lots of them were shared with us by 3-D legend, Burley Hall in his video, **Winning at 3-D** *(see Appendix)*. Because this video is chock full of inside tips and info, it is one of our more popular

Idiot Proof Archery

videos for 3-Ders.

Regarding yardage estimation, one of Burley's more innovative techniques is *head yardage*. This refers to setting your sight pins to the way you over or under estimate yardage, rather than by setting them to actual, tape measured 20, 30, 40, and 50 yard increments.

By logging each and every miss as to whether it is high, low, left, or right at your next few tournaments, you can go back and check your log to see where all your misses were. There is usually a pattern. If your misses were left or

Burley Hall shares his secrets in his video, **Winning at 3-D**

right, at 9 o'clock or 3 o'clock, then move back to close yardage and work on your shooting form. If your misses were high or low, at 12 o'clock or 6 o'clock, you can adjust your pins to how you over or under estimated the yardage. This is called *head yardage*.

As an example of what happened to Burley, he says, "On 400 point courses, I was consistently shooting 388 to 394. I couldn't seem to get those few extra points. I started keeping track of my misses, and after about 6 shoots, I found out that 99% of my misses were out the bottom of the 10 ring. What I did was set my pins to the way I underestimated yardage, which ended up being about 3 yards short. Now my top pin (20 yard pin) is zeroed in at 23 yards, because when I look at a 23 yard target . . . *my head tells me it's only 20 yards* . . . so I put my top pin on it. I also made my 30, 40, and 50 yard pins about 3 yards "hotter." For example, if I think it's 40 yards (it's usually really 43 yards) but I use my 40 yard pin . . . except now it's zeroed in for 43 yards and will automatically compensate for my *average under-estimation*. Now my sight settings are about 23, 33, 43, and 52. (On the long end, I didn't add quite as

Bernie Pellerite

much.) After setting my pins up this way, I kept track of my scores. I shot perfect scores on 6 or 8 different ranges."

That's how it works for Burley. For you, exact yardage may work, or you may always shoot out the top, but set your pins to how your "head" estimates yardage and give it a try. It might make a big difference!

Key Point #120
You can set your sight pins to the way you over or under estimate yardage (head yardage!).

Traditional (Legal) Techniques for Judging Distance

The most traditional method is through *vast experience* . . . trust the *computer in your head* or trust your *gut reaction*. I call this your best guess or "gut feeling method." To practice this in a less time consuming way, walk around your range or in a woods typical of what you hunt in or shoot 3-D tournaments in, and take a laser rangefinder with you to check your guesses. Keep notes of your tendencies in your log book. For example, "I tend to be long, over forty yards, and short, under forty yards."

Another technique, explained to me by Steve Ruis (Editor of **Archery Focus**), is to use *visual parallax* or the "owl method." Use a twig or branch midway to your target (that you can gauge the distance to easily) as a rangefinder. Move your head several inches to the right, then to the left. If the twig seems to move a lot in comparison to the position of the target, the target is far off. If the twig moves only a little bit, the target is probably closer to the twig than you are to the twig. Like all of these methods, you have to practice. They all have strengths and weaknesses. This one is good if you can't see the ground past the twig, for example.

Another method is to break down the distance to the target into pieces (halves, thirds, quarters) until you find something you can estimate fairly well. For example, if you see a spot that is about halfway to the target and another spot that is about halfway to *that* spot (one quarter of the way to the target) . . . which is 15 yards away . . . then the target is 4 x 15 yards, or 60 yards away.

Idiot Proof Archery

Another way is the 20 yard method. Most indoor shooters are very familiar with 20 yards, so they simply find something 20 yards away, then find a spot 5, 10 or 15 yards *past* the 20 yard spot, and then add up the distances.

Key Point #121

You have to practice these estimation methods. They all have strengths and weaknesses.

Most pros use a three-method, averaging system. For example, they might walk to the stake and use the "gut feeling" method and estimate, for instance, that the target is 38 yards away. Next, they walk 5 or 6 yards off to the side of the stake and use the 20 yard method. In this example, let's say they guessed 40 yards. Then, they go 5 or 6 yards to the other side of the stake and use a third method, like the half way method. This time they guess 21 yards to the half way point, which they double, to get 42 yards. Now they do an average of all three estimates . . . 38, 40 and 42 yards. They get 40 yards, as an average. Now they *have to commit to 40 yards and not second guess themselves.* They can't keep changing their minds, i.e., "It's probably a little more like 42 yards. I think I'll hold a little high on the shoulder and play it safe." Playing that game will kill you in the long run. Once you decide on a yardage, *don't second guess yourself and change it!*

Marvin Hundley of Fairfield, Ohio won $1,000 at the Easton Eagle Eye Championship Shoot-off at the 1999 IBO World Championships by beating 292 other shooters. Marvin said, "Bernie taught me a relaxed bow shoulder and how to really focus on aiming while the release goes off by surprise."

Bernie Pellerite

But, no matter what method you use . . . you can be fooled by certain types of non-typical terrain or optical variations in normal terrain or lighting. Judging distance can be complicated by any number of factors. Here are a few to watch out for (and practice!).

You Will Be Inclined to Judge A Distance Too Long When—
- You shoot from a brightly lit area into a place that is much darker.
- You are shooting at a downhill target.
- You have to shoot across a ravine, small valley, or over small hills.
- You have tall trees along both sides of your shot path.
- You can't see all of the ground between you and your target.

You Will Be Inclined to Judge A Distance Too Short When—
- You shoot from a place that is dark into a brightly lit area.
- You are shooting at an uphill target.
- You have to shoot across open water or a wide open field.

Bobby Eyler, Dundee, Michigan attended a shooter's school and then went on to win the MBO class at the IBO World Championships at Peek n' Peak, NY.

Idiot Proof Archery

Chapter 16

Hunting With a Bow

Hunting Gurus

For most of us, when 3-D season comes to an end, our thoughts turn immediately to bowhunting. We daydream about the excitement of that "moment of truth," when we face the ultimate test of our mettle. We ponder whether or not six or seven months of practicing on "extremely patient McKenzie's" will translate into that once in a lifetime, monster buck mounted over the fireplace. As we make that transition from foam to flesh, we must make a lot of changes and trade-offs, or so we've been told! A lot of us have become pretty spoiled all year by shooting 280 to 320 f.p.s. on the 3-D or field courses, with no wind planing and comparative pinpoint accuracy. Now, we think we must slow everything down, get bigger, heavier arrows, bigger fletch, and screw on broadheads that dip and dive and veer off course. A lot of us believe that for *only one reason*. It is because we've been bombarded for years with bias articles by various "hunting gurus" that spend 90 to 120 days each year in the woods. They go to ten or fifteen countries and spend tens of thousands of dollars to prove that their "pile of dead animals" is higher than those of us that hunt five or ten days each year. Then they get to tell the rest of us exactly how and what we can and cannot do in the woods, what kind of bow to shoot, how much penetration we'll get with this or that broadhead, how to hold the bow, how fast the arrow should go, whether or not to shoot fingers or release aids, to shoot aluminum or carbon arrows, how far away we should shoot, to shoot an overdraw or not, and on and on *ad nauseam*. Why is that?

Bernie Pellerite

If you think about it, most of these gurus (and I'm not trying to take anything away from their successes) have been hunting professionally for twenty years or more and have maybe twenty to sixty record book animals on the wall, and probably another one hundred that fell short. Well, I think that's great, but that translates hypothetically, to 1,800 to 2,400 days in the woods, with only 120 to 160 animals harvested. That translates to one animal for every eleven to fifteen days in the woods (a 6% to 11% success rate). And, factor in that most are *sponsored* totally or in part for these exotic hunts. They *almost never go* on the inexpensive local whitetail hunts on public lands (as most of us are forced to do). If you think about it, most above average hunters, given the same time and money to spend on trophy hunting, wouldn't have too tough a time succeeding 6% to 11% of the time.

Don't get me wrong . . . I believe we can learn a lot from some of these gurus about scent, tactics, camo, planning, and general hunting strategies. But, I'm just tired of reading articles that try to dictate proper shooting form, setup, and technique (one way . . . usually *their* way . . . fits all!) to already proficient target or 3-D shooters who also hunt. They criticize and prejudge high-tech equipment such as overdraws, release aids, carbon arrows and expandable broadheads, etc., when most of them have never tested or used them. In most cases, these gurus have *zero credentials to coach anyone* on shooting form, anyhow. One guru in particular was quick to point out in a magazine article that target and 3-D shooting experience has little, if any, value in a hunting situation. Of course, the same fellow has preached overdraws are too critical, releases too slow and cumbersome, carbon arrows won't adequately penetrate, and expandable broadheads aren't dependable or lethal enough for a "real hunting situation," blah, blah, blah!

You Don't Have To Change All That Much

This kind of self-righteous, self-serving (sponsor-serving) narrow-minded, "if you don't do it my way (and use my sponsor's stuff), it's no good" mentality does not belong in

Idiot Proof Archery

archery or bowhunting publications, no matter how high their "pile of dead animals" might be. In the early 1990s, when heavy arrows were much more "politically correct," this kind of shortsightedness got me so wound up and angry that I set out on a mission to prove it was all bull . . . and that's exactly what I did! I had not hunted for fifteen years because I was busy competing in tournaments, coaching, and producing instructional videos. But, I took to the woods to prove that if you hit where you aim, you can harvest practically any size animal with all the equipment they said would never work. I took my 3-D bow (set at between 54 and 63 pounds, depending on the game I was after), complete with overdraw, mechanical release, very light (307 grain) carbon arrows fletched with 2½" offset vanes, shooting at 284 f.p.s. and two blade expandable 65 grain broadheads. These "puny little knitting needles," as some heavy arrow advocates have called them, crashed completely through ½" thick plywood and stuck into the excelsior bale behind it at 100 yards; a feat my conventional three and four blade heads failed to accomplish at ten or twenty yards. (Their tips barely protruded out of the other side of the board.) I've tested some of these non-windplaning expandable heads and found that a *few of them* (not all) have *25% to 100% more penetration* than the average three or four exposed blade head. There are many more, much improved, expandable heads on the market now (some better than others), so don't judge them on their *previous reputation* (be it good or bad). Buy some and test them yourselves. You'll probably be surprised.

We've also been "sold" several ideas such as a fast bow is always noisy, and therefore worthless in the woods . . . that carbon arrows penetrate fine in 3-D targets, but not in live animals . . . overdraws are fine for 3-D, but are too radical for a hunting arrow, etc., etc. First of all, in recent years new technology has produced several models of extremely fast and quiet bows, even when shooting light arrows. (Always check the AMO chart for minimum recommended arrow weight.) Second, for those of you who think I just sit home and shoot at plywood, I put 14 animals in the **Safari Club International Bowhunting**

Bernie Pellerite

European Red Deer taken with 307 grain arrow made #2 in the Safari Club International Bowhunting World Record Book

World Record Book in just four years. Of course, I spent lots of money doing it and had a really great guide that could get me to within 250 yards, or closer, to the animal to start with. I'm not exactly the best hunter in the world but, as I set out to prove, if you can put the arrow where you want, you don't have to shoot 600 grain arrows with big broadheads to succeed. I put ten of the fourteen in the *Top Ten in the World Record Book,* for non-indigenous animals taken with a bow. The Rocky Mountain Elk (7X7) and the European Red Deer *(see photo),* weighed approximately 750 pounds and 600 pounds, respectively (both placed #2 in the Top Ten in the World in their categories). They both had opening wounds in excess of 2½" with these *puny mechanical broadheads.* In the case of the elk, the "knitting needle" penetrated a ¾" rib bone and protruded out the other side when shot at 45 yards.

All fourteen of these animals were harvested with a *two* blade expandable broadhead. The arrows were 25½" Easton 3-28 ACCs fletched with 3" offset vanes, and shot off a Golden Key-Futura TM Hunter rest. Total arrow weight was 307 grains. Please don't get me wrong. *I'm not saying that everyone should go elk hunting with a 307 grain arrow.* And, unlike my "heavy arrow" opponents, I'm *not* suggesting that my method is for everyone. I did it to prove a point and because I knew it would work. The point here is, if I can do it with a 307 grain arrow, then you can load up a 375 to 450 grain arrow with complete confidence, as long as you have good shooting form and a good, sharp, straight-flying broadhead. I think you should use what

Idiot Proof Archery

works for you, but I have put together what I consider to be a unique hunting setup that is more or less "idiot proof." It's based on the premise of a fast, quiet bow at medium poundage . . . arrows with minimum weight and maximum velocity that have target arrow trajectory and accuracy with minimum drag . . . and broadheads that don't drop or wind plane and have maximum penetration. An *oversimplification* would be to put camo on a quiet, fast and well-tuned 3-D bow, silence your rest, screw on non-planing expandable broadheads on your 3-D arrows and go hunting!

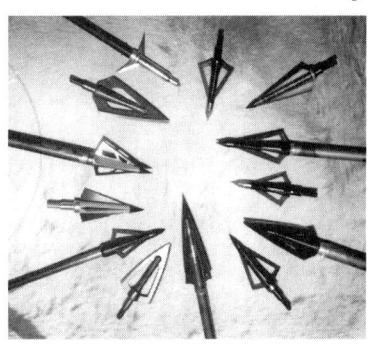

There are plenty to choose from. I used the expandable one (top left). You should use what works for you!

If you get aggravated at spending time and money tuning your broadheads, continually readjusting your sights, misjudging the distance with your slow bowhunting setup and losing game, try this one. You may be amazed at the results!

The Truth About Kinetic Energy And Penetration

As I mentioned above, for many years we have been bombarded by articles delivering the message and reinforcing the notion that heavy aluminum hunting arrows penetrate better than lighter (carbon) arrows, especially if you want to harvest a large-bodied animal over 300 pounds. "Light carbon arrows just won't deliver enough energy," they used to claim. One of the more popular advocates of the heavy arrow even coined a new phrase . . . *"penetrating energy,"* inferring that energy, all by itself . . . penetrates! This philosophy is grounded in what I call, "the heavy bullet theory." Many advocates of heavy hunting arrows (500 to 600 grains) point to the fact that like bullets, the heavier the projectile, the better the penetration and/or the more damage they cause. Their primary argument is that a heavy arrow "will always absorb and carry more kinetic energy from

Bernie Pellerite

the bowstring," than a light arrow. It then logically follows that if your arrow has more energy (directly off the string), better penetration has to follow. Since kinetic energy of a given arrow is relatively easy to check with a chronograph and a grain scale, you can prove their theory for yourself. There has been tons of articles that show you how; simply shoot three or more well-executed shots through a good chronograph to get an average arrow speed, and use the following formula:

$$\frac{\text{mass x velocity x velocity}}{450,240} = \text{kinetic energy (in foot-pounds)}$$

Anxious to test this formula myself, I gathered some arrows I found in the garage of the extremely light and extremely heavy variety i.e., 307 grains (my hunting arrows) and 567 grain aluminum arrows. Both were of sufficient spine to shoot from my 60 pound Browning Mirage hunting bow (now an antique, but was among the fastest in 1990), set at 27¾" draw and equipped with a short overdraw. My 307 grain 3-28 Easton ACC's (cut to 25½") with 65 grain tips, tuned well through paper and came out of the bow at a very respectable 282 f.p.s. The heavy arrows I used were 2512s, nearly full length with heavy tips to help reduce the spine enough to tune well out of the same setup as the light arrows. All I had to do was change the nocking point about ⅛" higher when shooting the 2512s. The 567 grain arrows went through the chronograph at 218 f.p.s. That is 64 f.p.s. slower than the light arrows. By the way, in case you are wondering . . . no, my bow is not noisy with the light arrows and no, I'm not "nearly dry-firing the bow." I've shot setups much the same for years (before it became fashionable) and never broke a cable, limb or string, and have yet to have an animal "jump the string" because of excessive bow noise.

Contrary to popular belief, the Archery Manufacturers and Merchants Organization's (AMO) minimum recommended arrow weight is not a flat 6 grains per pound. It varies greatly, depending on draw length, bow weight, and type of cam. The chart varies

Idiot Proof Archery

from a low of less than 3 grains per pound (54 pounds at 25" with round wheels) to a high of over 9 grains per pound (75 pounds at 33" with speed cams — *see chart on next page)*. I don't advocate shooting below AMO recommended minimum arrow weights. So, after checking with Marlow Larsen, then the design consultant at Browning, Don Rabska a technical expert at Easton, and also consulting the AMO chart, I determined my equipment setup just barely meets the AMO minimum for 60 pounds at 27¾" draw using speed cams. You should always use this chart to prevent injury to yourself or damage to your equipment.

Having said that, let's try to determine which arrow will penetrate the best. Using the "more energy = more penetration" theory, it's no contest. The heavy arrow will always win because it absorbs more energy from the bowstring. For example, my 567 grain arrow multiplied by 218 f.p.s. squared, divided by the conversion factor of 450,240 yields approximately 60 foot pounds of kinetic energy, or "60 ft.-lbs. of penetrating energy," as our heavy arrow expert would say. My 307 grain arrow placed a respectable second place, with 54 ft.-lbs. That is a difference of 10% of kinetic energy which logically proves that the heavy arrow will have better penetration, right? Well, if you buy that logic, then you'll surely buy this logic, too . . . If you place a grasshopper on a tabletop . . . *remember* the grasshopper in chapter 4? Like the grasshopper experiment, the "more energy = more penetration" theory fails to consider all the variables that affect penetration of a hunting arrow in a given target medium. Let's explore some of the *more important* and *often overlooked variables of penetration,* as to the cause and effect.

Configuration, Size, and Number of Blades If the blades are angled to facilitate spinning of the shaft in flight, this could cause the head to try and "screw" itself into the intended target, thus creating much more *resistance* and less penetration.

Bernie Pellerite

AMO Minimum Recommended Arrow Weight Chart

Actual Peak Weight (lbs) / AMO Draw Length (inches)

Minimum Recommended Arrow Weight (in grains)

Recurve Bow	Round Wheel	Energy Wheel	Speed Cam	25"	26"	27"	28"	29"	30"	31"	32"	33"
33	32	29	27	150	150	150	150	150	150	150	150	150
34-41	33-38	30-35	28-32	150	150	150	150	150	150	150	151	165
42-46	39-43	36-39	33-36	150	150	150	150	150	163	179	195	211
47-52	44-49	40-44	37-41	150	150	150	167	185	203	222	240	258
53-58	50-54	45-49	42-46	150	163	183	203	224	244	264	285	305
59-63	55-60	50-54	47-50	172	195	217	240	262	284	307	329	352
64-69	61-64	55-59	51-55	202	227	251	276	300	325	350	374	399
70-75	65-71	60-64	56-60	232	259	286	312	339	365	392	419	445
76-81	72-76	65-70	61-65	262	291	320	348	377	406	435	463	492
82-86	77-81	71-74	66-69	292	323	354	385	416	446	477	508	539
87-92	82-87	75-79	70-74	322	355	388	421	454	487	520	553	586
93-99	88-94	80-85	75-80	352	387	422	457	492	532	581	629	676

Idiot Proof Archery

Also, the larger, wider, or more numerous the blades are, the more *resistance* is created. Generally (all else being equal), two blades penetrate better than three, three blades penetrate better than four, etc., because of *resistance*. Even the heavy arrow advocate won't argue this one!

Type of Point For instance, two blade heads, sharpened to the tip *generally* penetrate somewhat better than those with nose cone or chisel point. Why? Less *resistance!*

Angle of Arrow Entry The flatter and smoother the trajectory, the more energy is directly behind the point. The more erratic (fishtailing, porpoising, etc.) the trajectory, the more the back portion of the arrow wants to plow up, down or sideways on impact, which causes more *resistance*.

Initial Energy Versus Impact Energy The heavier and slower arrow's initial kinetic energy, velocity and trajectory diminished with distance more rapidly than the lighter, faster arrow. Why was that? Could it have been *"more resistance"* through the air? Is there a pattern developing here about *resistance* or is it just my imagination? Even some of the heavy arrow advocates are starting to admit finally that at 20 yards, the difference in impact energy diminished to only about 2% to 3% in some cases. In my particular experiment, the difference in *initial kinetic energy* (60 foot pounds versus 54 foot pounds, measured one foot out of the bow) was 10%, while the difference in the *impact kinetic energy* at 20 yards (approximately 52 foot pounds versus 50.5 foot pounds) closes to only about 2½%. And, by the way, to get the heavy arrow to hit in the same spot as the light arrow at 20 yards, I had to use the 50 yard pin. The *velocity difference* of the two arrows was now increased from 64 f.p.s.

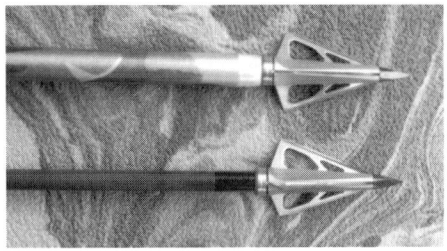

The heavier slower arrow's initial kinetic energy, velocity and trajectory diminished with distance more rapidly than a lighter faster arrow with the same broadhead.

Bernie Pellerite

to 70 f.p.s. in favor of the light arrow, because it lost less velocity down range. As I continued to move back to 25 yards and tested both arrows again, the energy difference was now only 1%. Finally, at approximately 29 yards, they both produced nearly the exact same amount of kinetic energy. The 307 grain arrow at 269 f.p.s. equals 49.34 foot-pounds. The 567 grain arrow at 198 f.p.s. equals 49.36 foot pounds of energy. The light arrow maintained 91% of its initial energy and about 95½% of its initial velocity, compared to the heavy arrow that maintained only 82% of its initial energy and 91% of its initial velocity, at 29 yards. This will vary depending on equipment, arrow weights, fletch, etc. But obviously, over thirty yards, the lighter arrow was delivering more energy (and going 71 f.p.s. faster!), maybe because of less *resistance* through the air. Go figure!

Total Surface Area of Resistance is the total resistance that any arrow and broadhead combination meet when attempting to pass through a given target medium. In my kinetic energy experiment, the heavy arrow had substantially more surface area than the light arrow (approximately 63% more). This drag (or *resistance)* varies from arrow to arrow, but is a *key factor*, often overlooked in predicting penetration (all other factors being equal).

The Spine (Stiffness) of the Shaft Most of us have heard about or seen slow motion pictures of arrows shot from bows and know they go through all kinds of contortions . . . bending and buckling around the bow riser. This bending can be called *arrow cycling* or *paradox* (which are entirely different). However, most people are not aware that as the arrow strikes the target, it also bends and buckles (more or less, depending mostly on how stiff the spine of the arrow is). Therefore, the stiffer spined arrow bends less and (like a straight stiff nail hit with a hammer), it offers less *resistance* to penetration than a weaker spined arrow, which acts like a similar nail made from a softer metal that bends more, when hit with the hammer.

The Shape and Diameter Of The Ferrule The ferrule (the part of the broadhead that the blades are fastened to) has more to do with penetration (especially on bone) than the blades!

Idiot Proof Archery

That is, if all other factors are equal and the broadheads are the same. I believe that this is the most often overlooked factor in predicting penetration. Consider this logic — no one argues that any arrow penetrates better with a field point than with any broadhead. Why? You got it! Less *resistance!*

Key Point #122

The ferrule has more to do with penetration, especially on bone, than the blades!

So, if everything is equal (except the arrow shaft and fletch) and we are using the same broadhead on both test arrows, we can accurately predict the percentage of difference in the penetration of the two different shafts by removing the blades and shooting the arrows. For instance, if the lighter, smaller diameter shaft penetrates 23% more without the blades than the heavier, larger diameter shaft without the blades, then it will still have 23% more penetration when you replace the blades and test again. Since the blades are identical, they cause the same extra *resistance* when added to either shaft, so if we remove them from both, we merely remove an equal amount of *resistance* from both.

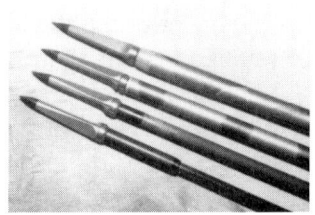

The shape and diameter of the ferrule is more important to penetration than the blade

What we are really testing is the *resistance* on the total surface area of the ferrule, shaft and fletch and the ability of the ferrule to produce a hole for the rest of the shaft and fletch to pass through, which is more critical than you might think. For years, we've all been spoon-fed the notion that the blades on a broadhead somehow cut a clear path for the rest of the

*Nearly all ferrules are larger in diameter than carbon or carbon aluminum shafts, thus making a larger diameter hole for the thinner shaft to pass through . . . creating less drag or **resistance.***

Bernie Pellerite

shaft and fletch, and that there is practically no drag because of the "gaping hole" it cuts. First of all, the blades don't make a "gaping hole," they make thin slits the same thickness and width as the blades. The hole in the center is made by the ferrule. Consider this . . . nearly all ferrules on nearly all broadheads are larger in diameter than the diameter of most carbon or carbon/aluminum shafts. They therefore make a larger diameter hole than the diameter of these skinnier shafts and therefore, encounter a minimum of drag or *resistance* while passing through this "hole." Conversely, nearly all ferrules are smaller in diameter than nearly all heavier aluminum hunting shafts. *Creating a small hole* for the *larger shaft* to try to pass through, will create considerable and often *insurmountable resistance.* Remember, in my experiment, there was 63% more total surface area with the heavy arrow.

What's The Point? Don't get me wrong. I'm not against heavy arrows and I'm not saying everyone should shoot light carbon arrows. I'm just tired of reading articles that don't tell the whole story or preach that carbons won't do the job in a hunting situation. Remember, most arrows with most any broadhead will pass completely through whitetails at close range (15 to 20 yards) *if the shot is placed properly.* So, if you hit every one where you want to, and don't misjudge the distance because you only shoot 15 to 20 yards, there is no advantage to 20-70 f.p.s. increase in speed and better penetration. In this case, you won't need carbons! If you prefer aluminum arrows, you can also greatly increase velocity if you change to the Ultra-lite series. (Consult the Easton arrow chart.) But, if you are like me, and want to extend your effective shooting distance by 10 to 15 yards and want all the penetration you can get in case you hit a big bone or get a *marginal hit* (which is all we're really talking about here), you might want to give carbon arrows a try.

The above seven variables are

Key Point #123

Remember, most arrows with most any broad-head will pass completely through whitetails at close range (15 to 20 yards) if the shot is placed properly.

Idiot Proof Archery

just some of the lesser known factors to consider (besides kinetic energy) when trying to predict the penetration of one arrow versus another. Remember, *it's not kinetic energy that results in penetration . . . it's the efficient use of kinetic energy that does. Resistance, or the lack of it, is always key!* Here's another example: if I took that big heavy arrow and put a 4" x 4" block of wood (½" thick) on the end, and shot it out of a 100 pound bow (that theoretically produced 100 pounds of kinetic energy), and I took a 35 pound recurve and shot a small carbon arrow tipped with a field point (that produced 30 pounds of kinetic energy) . . . which one will penetrate better? A final example: take two nails the same length; one thin and one twice as thick. Try to drive each into a 2" x 4" board with the same stroke by letting the hammer "drop" straight down from the same height, creating approximately the same energy. Even though it's not too scientific, it is obvious, isn't it? Even though technically the thicker heavier nail supposedly absorbs more energy from the hammer (like the heavy arrow), it's much easier to drive the thinner nail into a 2" x 4". Hmmm . . . must have something to do with *resistance*. Well, I guess we could have combined some of these experiments . . . what if we hit that grasshopper (from Tiller Tuning in chapter 4) with the hammer? Ah! Logically that would prove . . . oh my God; it boggles the mind, doesn't it?

Key Point #124

Remember, it's not energy that results in penetration; it's the efficient use of energy that does. Resistance, or the lack of it, is always key!

Using Mechanical Releases in the Woods

As with most shooters who choose to bowhunt using mechanical release aids, most soon find that the selection and operation are not without their problems. The first problem the average shooter faces is that the advice they receive can often be very confusing and sometimes conflicting. One guy says, "You need this thumb model." Another says, "You need an index-finger caliper with a hair trigger." Still another says, "You need a wrist strap rope release if you want accuracy," etc.

Bernie Pellerite

There always seems to be plenty of disagreement as to which type is really the best. So, here is my two cents worth about the "do's and don'ts" of selection and execution of the mechanical release.

Selecting a Release It's important to understand that most release aids have certain advantages and disadvantages, depending on the situation. For example, if you shoot target or 3-D, you'll find that releases activated by back tension keep you from anticipating the release, and are therefore more consistent if properly used. However, in the woods, these could prove slow and cumbersome to load in front of a buck at the moment of truth. Therefore, most hunters prefer "clip-on-the-string" type caliper models. Caliper releases generally are easier to load and fire quickly under pressure. But with wrist strap, molded hand grip or concho models to choose from, which is best? In my opinion, the best hunting release is the one you feel most comfortable with and can operate with the most consistency. For me, that is a good wrist strap caliper with trigger travel adjustments. The reason I say this is, for years I used my rope target model, not only for 3-D and target, but also for hunting. I put a lot of trophies on my wall and I felt I could load it as fast as anyone until one day, when I fumbled around in front of a record book red stag (about three seconds too long), and watched him trot over the hill and out of sight. Luckily, the next year I came back with a much quicker to load, wrist strap caliper and put him on my wall, and in the SCI record book. There are other reasons I strongly recommend this type of release for hunting: 1) It's hard to lose or misplace a release that's always tied to your wrist. 2) Concho and molded grip types cause you to bend your wrist at anchor. They also promote string torque and oscillation which will cause wind planing with most exposed blade broadheads. This is opposed to a relaxed,

Key Point #125

Most hunters prefer "clip-on-the-string" type caliper models.

● **Key Point #126**

The best hunting release is the one you feel most comfortable with and can operate with the most consistsency.

Idiot Proof Archery

straight and in-line wrist position that comes straight back upon execution, as with wrist strap models. 3) Wrist strap models allow you to relax the fingers on your drawing hand (because the weight is on the wrist) and you are more likely to duplicate the same execution if the hand and fingers are not under pressure from the holding weight of the bow.

Solving Caliper Release Problems There are a few possible problems associated with shooting a caliper release. Some calipers, especially those with ball bearings in the jaws, tend to prematurely wear out monofilament center servings. The cure for that is to serve a ½" long nylon second serving over the monofilament center serving, where the caliper jaws contact the serving *(see photo)*. Some bows, especially short axle-to-axle bows with longer draws (29" and up) have a tendency to un-nock some types of arrows at full draw. The problem here is that either the nock is too tight and "pinches" off the serving at full draw, or the nock throat is not deep enough to stay hooked on to the string at extreme angles. There are three remedies available. One is to get nocks with a deeper throat. Second, install an Eliminator Button (a rubber button that fits over the string between the nock and the release - *see photo)* between the nock and caliper jaws. This usually puts enough pressure on the under side of the nock to keep it on the string at full draw. Third, for more severe cases, install a "string loop" made from nylon cord or release rope that is knotted above and below the nock. So, at full draw, the severe angle is flattened out . . . like pulling back the string with one finger over and one finger under the nock. Installing this loop, which Burley Hall details in his video, ***Winning at 3-D*** *(see Appendix)*, can have several advantages. 1) It aligns the peep sight

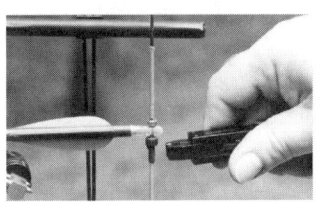

"Eliminator Button" with a second serving under it.

String Loop

Bernie Pellerite

Joella Bates of Waverly, TN spent the "Weekend at Bernie's" (movie title pun intended) for private lessons. Joella is a five-time world 3-D champion and two-time National 3-D champion. She is also the first woman in the world to ever kill an African Cape Buffalo with a bow! She travels all over the U.S. doing dealer clinics and shooting exhibitions for children and adults.

automatically, thus eliminating the need for the rubber tubing that straightens your peep at full draw. **(NOTE:** Slow motion film reveals that rubber tubing distorts the string . . . *pulling the nock up* as the bow string is released). 2) The loop eliminates "up-pressure" or bend in the arrow that can happen to some archers at full draw. 3) It will keep arrows from falling off the string at full draw, or when you let down and draw again. 4) It eliminates wearing out the center serving with the jaws of the release. 5) It prevents string torque caused when a shooter doesn't pull straight back, or twists the head of the release, thereby torquing the bow string upon release. However, it's not without maintenance problems. It can stretch out and it can pull through the knots *if not put in properly*, so you need to pay close attention when adding one to your setup.

Proper Execution Be sure that whichever model you choose, the trigger is set at heavy tension (3-4 pounds) and has *no discernible* travel in it. As I said before, *travel causes anticipation* that leads to punching the trigger, or worse. Heavy triggers will give you the confidence to put your finger on the trigger (and pre-load it) without worrying about "losing the shot" before you are ready. Conversely, excessively light triggers will promote fear or anxiety about touching the trigger and setting off the release prematurely. This sometimes will cause some shooters to set up at anchor with their finger completely off the trigger, and then suddenly punch or slap at the trigger at the last moment, which yields inconsistent results *(see chapter 9).*

Idiot Proof Archery

If you are having trouble punching your release, consider trying my invention, **Bernie's Can't Punch™ Release**. This release (see photo) has a second stationary trigger (in front of and below the real trigger) that requires you to pull through the shot with your back muscles (see diagram of Can't Punch on page 169 and also in the Appendix). You can't punch this release! You can use it to shoot target, 3-D or *hunt* with it (several people have sent me letters and pictures of game they have harvested in the U.S. and Africa, using the Can't Punch). It will help you defeat punching, freezing, snapshooting, flinching and the other forms of target panic. When **Ted Nugent,** bowhunting rock star, first saw **Bernie's Can't Punch** he said, "This release is as important as Fred Bear's personal guidance . . . assisting me through my Target Panic!"

Bernie's Can't Punch™ Release

Whichever release you choose, let me offer one last word of caution when analyzing the correct way to set off your release. Be *super-conscious* about your trigger finger (whichever that may be on your particular release) and its position at anchor in relationship to the trigger itself. For example, if you shoot an index finger model, make sure you don't have to extend your index finger, i.e., have to *reach* for the trigger to set off the release and barely catch the trigger with the end of the finger. This promotes a down and back jerking motion which, as you can imagine, is not very consistent. Conversely, you should not have too much finger wrapped around it, so that you can put the second section of the index finger on the trigger. This will kill most any chance you had of shooting with back tension (for more on this, see chapter 9). At anchor you should be able to just barely reach the trigger with the *first crease of the index finger,* so the tip of the finger can bend down, pointing straight to the ground. Slowly squeeze off about half the trigger pressure, then stop squeezing . . . increase your back tension and "tow"

Bernie Pellerite

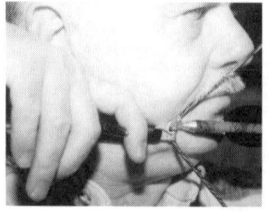

At anchor you should be able to just barely reach the trigger with the first crease of the index finger, so the tip of the finger can bend down, pointing straight to the ground.

the trigger rearward with your back muscles. In about three or four seconds the release will occur; your hand will fly directly back toward your release elbow, your results will be much more consistent, your groups much tighter and your hunts will be more successful. Good luck!

*Whitetail hunting legend, Myles Keller, who shortened his draw length over 3" and cured his target panic as a result of the shooter's school says, "I'm holding **twice as steady now** and I'm shooting groups so small, I'm hitting my own nocks at 25 yards." When Myles first came to Bernie's school, he said, "I'm freezing so badly that I can't hit a 12" paper plate at 20 yards! Four months later, he could hit a tennis ball at 50 yards (with broadheads)!*

Post Script

Jan and I hope that you will gain something from this book that will positively affect your perspective, your enjoyment, your success in the woods and your score in tournaments in the months and years to come. If I can add something to your experience with a bow and arrow, invoke a smile from time to time, help you find your way when you are lost or keep someone from quitting the sport we all love . . . *I have hit the middle of my target!* . . . Let me hear from you!
 **Keep aimin' in the middle! . . . And remember . . .
 HAVE FUN . . . THIS IS JUST A GAME!**
Bernie Pellerite . . .

Appendix

Robinhood Video Productions, Inc.

1036 Arcaro Dr., Gahanna, OH 43230 USA
Phone 614-933-0011 — Fax 614-933-0010
Email: AskBernie@aol.com   www.robinhoodvideos.com

Robinhood Videos is the **world's largest producer of instructional archery videos** with 37 titles marketed into 34 countries. They are well known for the innovative method of marketing their video tapes, as they are almost always done in series. They can be purchased at a discount by buying more than one, or they can also be bought individually.

International customers: Most of the videos are available in European PAL format. Please contact Robinhood Videos for price and availability. There is a slight additional charge for each PAL video.

The NFAA Shooter's School Video Series
By Bernie Pellerite

This phenomenally successful mobile shooter's school is presented in 6 volumes and is the most advanced, comprehensive, and popular school in the world today. It was designed for intermediate to professional level archers by  school creator and Master Coach, Bernie Pellerite, who is also an accomplished target archer and bowhunter with over 75 tournament wins and 8 state titles in 3-D and target archery. Bernie also has 10 animals in the Top Ten in the World of the Safari Club International (SCI) Bowhunting World Record Book. Bernie's no-holds-barred and "tell it like it is" attitude make for 7 hours of exciting, fast paced and in-depth discussion of over 200 topics, from Shooting Form and Target Panic (Volumes 1, 2, & 3) to Tuning Tips (Volume 6). High tech teaching methods such as slow motion video, overhead shots, and actual laser sight pictures of the students enable his insightful shot critique and comparative analysis. This is supplemented by personality profile analysis, shooting drills and lots of hands-on coaching to transform the average student, who by the school's end, can hold at least twice as steady and shoot with confidence.

This series was shot live in an actual Shooter's School with uncensored, unsolicited and unrehearsed responses from the students and Bernie.

#501 VOLUME 1: PERSONALITY, PROFESSIONAL FORM AND THE SHOT SEQUENCE — (80 min.) Defining and understanding the part your personality plays in how you shoot tournament archery, your predisposition to target panic and your natural aversion to disciplines. Analyzes: controller, analytical, focused and risk-taker personalities. Also, the **first seven steps** to the physical and mental shot sequence, "Idiot Proof" bone-to-bone form, from stance to anchor. This is the *first of three tapes* for curing target panic or reprogramming your shot sequence. (intermediate to professional level)

#502 VOLUME 2: PROFESSIONAL FORM AND THE SHOT SEQUENCE— (65 min.) The **final five steps** to physical and mental aiming and shot execution. This is the *second of three tapes* for reprogramming your "let-go" system, the rest of your shot sequence and for curing target panic. This tape covers the offensive part of the shot execution including: release techniques for finger shooters and all major types of mechanical releases. Also discussed are: how to achieve back tension, mental and physical aiming, natural arc of movement and more. (intermediate to professional level)

#503 VOLUME 3: TARGET PANIC AND THE SHOT ANALYSIS — (55 min.) Tape *3 in the series of 3* for reprogramming your shot and curing target panic. Methods and shooting drills to cure all forms of target panic. PLUS: Personal shot critique and diagnosis of students, in freeze frame/slow motion. Also, actual laser aiming patterns of students with freezing, snapshooting and punching problems. Analysis includes overhead and profile views, critiques of shooters and a before and after comparison that shows a 50%-200% improvement in holding and aiming abilities in just one day! (intermediate to professional level)

#504 VOLUME 4: HOLDING TWICE AS STEADY AND SHOOTING UNDER PRESSURE - (50 min.) This video also covers: accelerated learning programs; perfect practice tips; pressure drills to desensitize your reaction to anxiety and fear of missing, shooting inside your physical and mental comfort zone; understanding the effects of tournament nerves and adrenaline on the body; how to stay focused and execute under pressure, and how to shoot the same scores in tournaments as you do in practice plus more. (intermediate to professional level)

#505 VOLUME 5: JUDGING YARDAGE, RANGEFINDING SYSTEMS, AND SHOOTING UP AND DOWN HILLS - (50 min.) ALSO: Exposing illegal rangefinding techniques in 3-D tournaments, professional techniques for judging yardage legally, plus how to keep from being fooled by your surroundings when estimating distance, the formula for shooting up, down, and on hills, plus the secret to shooting in the wind such as holding off or canting the bow, equipment setup and much more. (intermediate to professional level)

#506 VOLUME 6: FACTS AND FICTION TUNING TIPS - (65 min.) Exposes the myths and the magic about bow setup and design, including the difference between a forgiving and efficient setup. Analyzing the difference between the techniques that actually help your score and those that just help your head. Including: tiller tuning, timing, sight and bow leveling, powder and paper testing, loops, F.O.C. balance, spine, arrow tuning, speed, arrow paradox, rest clearance, matching your arrows, fletching, bare shaft testing, group testing, carbon vs. aluminum arrows and much more. (intermediate to professional level)

The Master Coach Seminar Series - 9 Videos

These nine tapes were shot live at a Master Coach Certification School. The four Coaches that conduct this video series are: BERNIE PELLERITE who has 2 videos, LEN CARDINALE who also has 2 videos, ED ELIASON has 3 videos, and LARRY WISE has 2 videos. These 4 Master Coaches share the most in-depth and advanced level information ever captured on video.

Information on these next two videos has been added to the Shooter's School Series as an update.

#601 44 FORM FLAWS - (77 min.) Bernie guides you through identifying, analyzing and correcting 44 of the most common mistakes and misconceptions of shooting form. He'll help you achieve professional "Idiot Proof" form, a much steadier sight picture, and a solid shooting platform with a logical step by step analysis and critique of the most common shooting form defects. This includes: alignment, bow hand and grip, anchor, bow arm, finger and mechanical release and more. (intermediate to professional level)

#602 TARGET PANIC AND A DISCIPLINE CALLED ARCHERY - (75 min.) Bernie analyzes our natural aversion to discipline, explores the shot sequence, and examines the different predisposed personality types and their susceptibility to target panic. He guides you through the subconscious programming available to conquer target panic and mentally construct a successful shot. This is also an abbreviated version of the first three Shooter's School Series but also contains **plenty of new information**. (intermediate to professional level)

The next two videos are by **Len Cardinale**, Bernie's good friend and personal mentor. He is an internationally respected coach and archery analyst with no equal in matters of the personal shot blueprint, training methods, and the cause and effect psychology of the excellent archery shot. Len has worked with several international archery teams, and he was an instructor in the P.A.A.'s (Professional Archery Association) School. He has owned and operated his own pro shop, Butts & Bows, in Belleville, NJ, for over 36 years where he gives private and group lessons. Len is also a contributing editor for Bowhunter Magazine and is a member of the Bowhunting Hall of Fame. He is available for seminars and private coaching and can be contacted at Butts and Bows, Belleville, NJ, (973)751-2223 after 5 p.m.

#608 MENTAL KEYS THAT UNLOCK TARGET PANIC - PART 1 - *By Len Cardinale* (67 min.) The first video covers an in-depth discussion and analysis of vital aspects of the shot sequence and the archery discipline including: concentration, attitude, using the empty bale, anticipation and all of its eventualities, defining target panic and its symptoms plus much more. (intermediate thru professional level)

#609 MENTAL KEYS THAT UNLOCK TARGET PANIC - PART 2 - *By Len Cardinale* (65 min.) The second video covers aiming mentally vs. calibration, execution, bridge programs from the empty bale to the target, physical and visual anchors and Len's personal shot blueprint, which includes the essential principles and 7 steps to the shot. These two videos are a great supplement to the Shooter's School Series by Bernie Pellerite. (intermediate thru professional level)

313

Easton Arrow Seminar - 3 parts
By Ed Eliason

Ed is a 7-time world champion and one of archery's all-time good guys. His phenomenal energy and attitude makes him a favorite at seminars and clinics worldwide. **NOTE:** Although this **technical seminar** was designed for Easton dealers, as reference about customers indicate, coaches and advanced archers that are **extremely detail oriented** can also benefit greatly from this information.

#605 PART 1: ARROW SELECTION - (55 min.) Ed explores the difference between several types of arrows, importance of spine and weight, shaft size, selection charts and introduces you to Easton's Arrow Flight Simulator computer program. (intermediate thru professional level.)

#606 PART 2: PREPARATION AND ASSEMBLY OF COMPONENTS - (54 min.) Ed explains proper selection and installation of nocks, points, inserts, and uni-system. Also choosing the proper glue, helical, offset and straight fletching, repairs, re-fletching, pros and cons of vanes vs. feathers and much more. (intermediate thru professional level)

#607 PART 3: ARROW TUNING METHODS - (50 min.) Ed discusses tuning variations, including paper testing, fine tuning, the French method of tuning, bare shaft tuning, impact and visual tuning, fletch clearance, effects of weather on arrow flight and much more. Also included is some exciting slow motion footage from Easton. (intermediate thru professional level)

Larry Wise is a professional archer, author and master bow technician who writes for several archery magazines.

#603 PROFESSIONAL STRING MAKING - (70 min.) Professional archer and master technician Larry Wise covers how to create quality strings, material selection, length, how to make center and end servings, split yokes, and one cam cables. Discussion includes installation and adjustment, tying in nocking points, peep sights, loops and much more. (intermediate to advanced level)

#604 1 CAM vs. 2 CAM BOWS; BEYOND TUNING - (73 min.) Professional archer Larry Wise illustrates and compares the differences between one cam, round wheel, and 2 cam bows. Discussion includes tuning differences and how to plot force draw curves, determine percentage of bow efficiency and calculate kinetic and stored energy. (intermediate to advanced level)

OTHER VIDEOS

#301 THE 3R's OF 3-D - (42 min.) Right Form, Right Tuning, & Right Distance. Larry Wise, world champion, author, and master technician steps you towards competitive 3-D shooting, dispelling the myths & revealing the secrets of the 3R's of 3-D; Right Form, Right Distance, and Right Tuning. Includes Larry's own practice tips on trajectory, speed, push-pull aiming, shoot testing, effective muscle groups, cam synchronization and judging yardage. (beginner thru intermediate level)

#302 SUPERTUNING YOUR 3-D BOW - (37 min.) Tuning techniques for the competitive 3-D archer. Go beyond the basics as Larry Wise, world champion, author and master technician, simplifies the tuning process for the high tech competitive 3-D setup of two cam bows. Topics include: draw adjustments, force draw curves, cam synchronization, factory and dynamic pre-bend, rest tension, powder and paper testing, group testing and long range adjustment. (beginner thru advanced level)

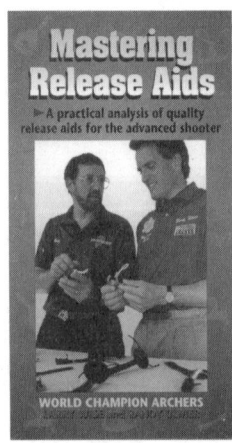

#305 MASTERING RELEASE AIDS - (43 min.) A practical analysis of quality release aids for the advanced shooter. World champions, Randy Ulmer & Larry Wise show you how to enhance your shooting skills through the selection, adjustments, anchor, mental and physical execution of some popular high tech releases. Includes: back tension, push-pull, pressure vs. movement, muscle memory, subconscious release, punching the trigger, release activation, target panic and more. (intermediate thru semi-advanced level.)

#303 WINNING FORM - (64 min.) Analyzing the components of a good shot, for the advanced 3-D & target archer. Randy Ulmer, world 3-D and target champion, teaches you competitive shooting form, revealing his professional techniques and the vital components of the successful shot. Includes: hand placement, anchor, bow arm, muscular involvement, breathing, back tension, pre-loaded torque, and the secrets of optical, physical and mental aiming. (intermediate thru semi-pro level)

#304 HIGH TECH TIPS - (54 min.) Professional advice for the serious 3-D and target archer. World 3-D and target champion Randy Ulmer reveals winning secrets of a top professional tournament archer. Topics include: judging yardage, practice intensity and detachment, "feeling" the perfect shot, pre-loading torque, practicing on an empty bale, shooting on hills, back tension, aiming and many more. (intermediate thru semi-pro level)

#306 ADVANCED FORM; PERFECTING THE SHOT - (48 min.) An in-depth analysis of the physical shot sequence for the serious recurve or finger shooter, with a master Olympic-style archer, Ed Eliason. He has a positive mental attitude and unique informative point of view. Ed discusses problems of the shot such as: warm-ups, eliminating torque & tension, holding steady, the perfect sight picture, getting past the clicker, release secrets, shooting up and down hill, back tension and more. (intermediate thru advanced level.)

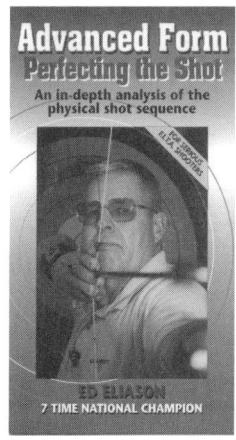

#307 ARCHERY'S MOST ASKED QUESTIONS - (52 min.) Serious answers for competitive archers. Ed Eliason, 7 time national champion and master Olympic-style archer, shares the answers to the most asked questions from his international seminars. This informative question and answer session addresses some fundamental problems for finger/recurve tournament shooting, such as: tournament pressure, positive mental imagery, shooting in the wind, bare shaft and paper testing, arrow spine, F.O.C. balance, fletch clearance, tuning for 90 meters and more. (intermediate thru semi-advanced level)

#308 THE MENTAL GAME - (44 min.) Conquer the gold through subconscious mental programming. World champion archer and gold medalist, Jay Barrs reveals his secret formula for winning the gold. "The Mental Game" instructs you on how to set up subconsciously-activated programs to realize your full potential in competitive target archery. Discussion includes: realistic goals, mental imagery, positive affirmation, alternate mental training methods, comfort zones, subliminal messages, self-hypnosis, practice, tournament application and more. (intermediate thru professional level.)

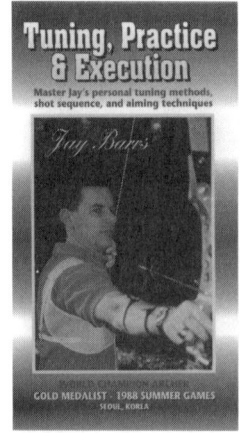

#309 TUNING, PRACTICE & EXECUTION - (41 min.) Hosted by Jay Barrs, world champion and gold medalist. Master Jay's personal tuning methods, shot sequence, and aiming techniques. Jay takes you on a personal tour of the challenging world of a champion Olympic-style recurve shooter. Experience shot perfection with his precise tuning techniques, exacting personal shot regimen & subconscious aiming procedures. Also, equipment setup, powder & bare shaft testing, fine tuning, alternate tuning, shot sequence, practice tips & procedures and mental aiming. (intermediate thru advanced level.)

#401 BURLEY HALL'S WINNING AT 3-D - (44 min.) Secrets of: Speed, Judging Yardage, Equipment Setup & Shooting Form. As 13 time National 3-D Champion, Burley shares the secrets of his personal techniques that captured more first place wins for him than any shooter in the history of 3-D archery. Including: short cuts to timing, steadying your sight picture, tiller tuning, form & aiming, shooting under pressure, gaining extra speed, "head yardage", leveling your sight, advantages of a loop and much more. Also, **Easton slow motion footage** reveals arrow paradox, bow shock, string oscillation & arrow rest interference. (3-D ...intermediate thru pro level.)

#402 THE COMPLETE GUIDE TO BEGINNING ARCHERY - (81 min.) A Comprehensive Training Guide for the Beginner, Age 6 to 60. Larry Wise, veteran pro, author, educator, and star of several other videos from Robinhood Videos, covers the basics for beginners. Larry incorporates dramatic slow motion footage to illustrate key points of interest. Discussion includes: a brief history of archery, types of bows and arrows, accessories, problem solving, glossary of terms, shooter safety, organizations, bowhunting and broadheads, beginners' needs, the steps to good form and much more. (beginner level)

#207 THE BASIC BOW MECHANIC - (49 min.) By Professional archer and master bow technician, Larry Wise. Learn the basic operation, major adjustments and repairs of the compound bow. It is designed for individual or pro shop use and teaches you the basic how, what and why of the compound bow. Larry removes the mystery surrounding cams, steel cables, let-off, draw curves, stored energy and much more. He also simplifies major adjustments and repairs of fast flight systems and steel cables, and re-serving strings to completely re-cabling a bow. (beginner thru intermediate level)

Reprograms your shot like shooting on an empty bale . . . without the bale!

Pro shops and shooters alike can use the **Bernie's PanicMaster & Bow Simulator** to try out new release aids, teach proper release

techniques, check draw length or to identify and deprogram all forms of target panic — like punching the trigger, freezing off the bullseye, snapshooting or flinching. Before the PanicMaster, the only cure for target panic was to re-program

your shot by spending many tedious hours shooting countless arrows into an empty bale with no idea of whether it's working or not, until you're 60 days into the program. Unfortunately, most personalities can't wait that long to see if they are improving, so they quit the bale and start shooting targets to test their programming and *then they go backwards, so they end up quitting the bale!* But with the **PanicMaster & Bow Simulator** they get continuous feedback ... wherever the laser dot went off ... is where the arrow would have gone!

Practice Smart, Not Hard with this fun, new, low-stress technique . . . anywhere, anytime with the feel of your own bow . . . without firing an arrow!

Dave Hryn *of West Seneca, NY, won the Atlantic City Archery Classic, the NFAA Outdoor Nationals and currently holds the world record in Freestyle Limited for the Field Round and the IFAA Hunter Round. Dave says, "Bernie's Shooter's School and personal instruction helped me . . . (reprogram my shot sequence)." Dave credits Robinhood Videos and* **Bernie's PanicMaster & Bow Simulator** *which he used to reprogram all that information.*

Bernie's PanicMaster and Bow Simulator is a **laser-equipped**, multi-function re-training device that simulates your bow's holding weight, mass weight, and balance at full draw. It is the result of combining several high-tech teaching methods Bernie uses in the nationally acclaimed NFAA mobile Shooter's School that he conducts throughout the U.S. and abroad.

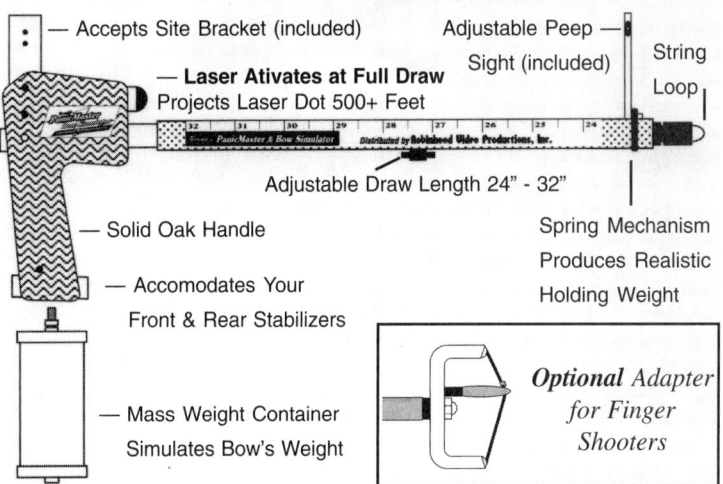

*Ted Nugent, bowhunting rock star, said the following, after Bernie cured him of his target panic, "The only real remedy I know is **Bernie's Detox Exorcism Program** (Ted-ism!) ... this combined with his laser sighted training device, **Bernie's PanicMaster & Bow Simulator**, changed archer's lives across the land."*

*Joe Church of Toledo, OH, had target panic and was snapshooting. He bought **Bernie's PanicMaster and Bow Simulator** on Thursday and won the IBO World on Sunday. The next weekend he won the ASA World in the barebow division. Joe raised his average **15 points in two days** using the Simulator.*

Bernie's PanicMaster & Bow Simulator
... This exciting innovation supplements and enhances your regular practice sessions by accelerating your learning curve & programming you subconsciously, **2 to 10 times faster.**
... Helps evaluate your holding ability, aiming & release.
... You can practice longer because you don't pre-stress your shoulder and arms to muscle past the bow's peak weight.
... "Unplug" your ego and get true quality practice sessions. Concentrate on your release or form without the influence of "Where did the arrow go," *but still know where it would have gone because of the projected laser dot!*

The PanicMaster & Bow Simulator comes with ...
... A built-in laser that activates at full draw and goes off when you fire.
... A rear spring mechanism that can be drawn back to a "wall or valley" to produce a realistic holding weight . . . just like any compound bow.
... The holding weight is approximately 16 to 18 pounds. (Other springs available for heavier poundage)
... The draw length is adjustable from 24 to 32 inches (can be customized much shorter)
... Drilled and tapped to accommodate front and rear stabilizers
... Solid oak handle - fits left and right-handers
... Wrist sling
... Mass weight container (holds 5 pound capacity of lead shot)
... Sight package includes an adjustable rear peep and front mounting bracket to accommodate your own bow sight.
... A training video (choose "44 Form Flaws" or "Target Panic and a Discipline Called Archery" or any Robinhood Video)
... Written instructions on how to make adjustments
... Written programs help retrain your back muscles, execute a subconscious release, and calculate & correct draw length.

Other Accessories Available ...
... An adapter for finger shooters
... 23# or 46# springs
... longer slide for finger shooters
... replacement batteries for the laser (takes 3)

Bernie's Laz-Air™ Shot Trainer

Bernie's Laz-Air™ Shot Trainer is a laser-equipped patent-pending, pneumatic shooting aid that allows shooters to practice by "dry-firing" their own bow without damage. It attaches *without removing the arrow rest or detuning the bow.* The built-in laser projects a red laser dot up to 700 feet. Concentrating on this laser dot keeps your mind out of the release sequence and focused on aiming. It also gives the shooter a mental reward as it shows projected arrow impact and the effects of any bow hand torque (both dynamic or static). As the string is released, the arrow/piston inside the tube forces air toward the end of the tube which turns off the laser dot (this indicates where your arrow would have hit). So, in essence, wherever the laser dot goes off, that's where you arrow would have landed, i.e. if the dot jerked left and then went off, you missed to the left and vice-versa. The laser dot also shows how steady you hold (or not), how long it takes to get in the middle, how long you stay in the middle, and whether or not you are steady in the middle. This laser picture enables the shooter to diagnose any one of a dozen shooting form and shooting sequence problems. This device is excellent for programming shot sequence and curing target panic, i.e. freezing, snapshooting, flinching, or punching the trigger.

See www.robinhoodvideos.com!

This bracket and coupling attaches between the bow and the stabilizer and holds the Laz-Air tube in place.

*Here's what the **Can't Punch** did for these shooters*

Paul Arnold, *Marshfield, WI, writes:*
Dear Bernie . . . About three months after attending your school, my scores started to come up from my old average, then above it . . . 300 with 45Xs, then 55 Xs, and **one day 300-60 Xs** - I shot it with your **Can't Punch Release!** I now shoot carefree archery, thanks to you. Hi, my name is Paul Arnold and I **had target panic!** Thank you, Bernie.

*Riley Cox of Mt. Sidney, VA, is a 14 year old 3-D shooter who had target panic. His dad purchased a **Bernie's Can't Punch Release** for him. He placed 2nd at the 2nd Leg of the IBO Triple Crown at Erie, PA, and, by the way, cleaned the course the first day with a perfect 200!*

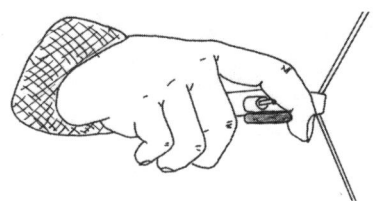 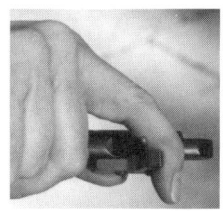

If you try to "punch" this release, the middle section of the index finger goes forward and up away from the Activator, or the real trigger.

All you have to do is hang on with the tip of the index finger, pull and, as your hand relaxes, the second section of the index finger pushes against the real trigger ... a real surprise!

Tommy Ray, Dixmont, ME (age 8) had target panic so bad, he was unable to draw his bow. With the help of **Bernie's Can't Punch Release** he was cured. At the World IBO Championships he finished with 100 points (a perfect score) with 9 out of 10 X's, and a robinhooded arrow! He also went to Africa with his dad and harvested 3 warthogs and an impala with his **Can't Punch Release**.

Mike Martin of Niagara Falls, NY. He won two IBO Indoor Worlds, 2 Canadian National Masters and the CFAA Nationals Team 300 Round Championship (Senior Pro Division) while using **Bernie's Can't Punch Release**.

 **Paul Cybart**, Dunkirk, N Y writes:
Dear Bernie, My form of target panic was freezing. This led me to get ... your **Bernie's Can't Punch!** The second time I used it for 3-D I shot a 288 out of a 300 & ... I Robinhooded my son's arrow which was in the middle of the kill. Thanks again!

You can get the same results as a traditional back tension release with no need for dental insurance. Just pull and aim! It's "Idiot Proof!"

Here's what the pros said when they first saw *Bernie's Can't Punch™*

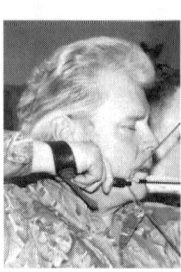

Myles Keller *Whitetail hunting legend (33 P&Y's).* *"This is the darndest thing I've ever seen. You don't have to worry about the trigger ... just aim! This is as good as it gets!"*

Ted Nugent *Rock star and bowhunting advocate.* *"This release is as important as Fred Bear's personal guidance, ... assisting me through my Target Panic!"*

Jackie Caudle *Co-owner of ASA & Top Pro* *"This release definitely has the potential to keep <u>anyone</u> from punching the trigger!"*
Larry Wise *Target Pro & Tuning Guru* *"Really good new idea! ... That will cure punching or target panic by using back tension!"*
Bobby Ketcher *3D Pro Circuits "Little Big Man"* *"Most shooters have some form of Target Panic ... this definitely takes care of the problems."*
Randy Chappell *Pro 3D Star & IBO record holder (1st perfect 400)* *"What a release! Bernie has hit a home run with this idea!"*

    This exciting innovative product was created through the collaboration of two great innovators, Bernie Pellerite and the late Bill Scott.

    Bernie, president of Robinhood Videos, is also an archery analyst who writes for several magazines and is the creator and the Director of the extremely popular NFAA mobile Shooter's School. Through years of owning a pro shop and teaching thousands of archers, most of whom had target panic, Bernie realized the value of the triggerless "back tension release" in curing his students' target panic.

Unfortunately, not everybody had the dedication or patience to master it. Most people took a minimum of 6 months (and a good dental plan!) to master the *old* triggerless releases. I have recently invented **Bernie's Missing Link** and **E-Z Back** to rectify that problem (see page 328 and 329). A very large percentage of the shooters still prefer an index finger release. But, as most people have found, it's nearly impossible for the shooters to maintain a "surprise" release with the index finger activating the trigger. Before long, they're flinching, punching or jerking the trigger, or have some other form of target panic. The back tension release, which cannot be anticipated like the trigger type releases, seemed to be the only answer.

Well, now you're FINALLY IN LUCK!!! **Bernie's CAN'T PUNCH**™ brings you the *best of both worlds* and it is easier and quicker to master. Bernie analyzed the problem with the index-finger/target-panic problem and designed a "CAN'T PUNCH" panic-proof feature, called the "Captivator©," that has been incorporated into the Scott Mongoose, Lil' Goose and Ole Faithful rope head releases.

This release "captures" and deactivates the tip of the index finger. By transferring the entire holding weight of the bow from the index finger to the "Captivator©," it neutralizes the pre-programmed punching reflex. The user must relax and expand the rest of the finger, the back of the hand, wrist, and forearm and squeeze the back muscles together, which causes the second joint of the index finger to flatten out slightly. This then contacts the real trigger, setting off the release, without conscious thought . . . a true surprise release! If the shooter tries to punch it, then the middle joint of the finger actually arches and lifts off the trigger and the release cannot fire! You virtually have to set it off with back tension and a relaxed and expanded draw arm/wrist/hand/finger unit, or it won't go off! The only way to "punch" this release is to take your index finger off the "Captivator©" and consciously punch the real trigger, like any other index finger release. If you do that, you've wasted your money!

We have many, many success stories from people who have been helped by the **Bernie's CAN'T PUNCH**™. Give it a try!

Bernie's Missing Link™ RELEASE

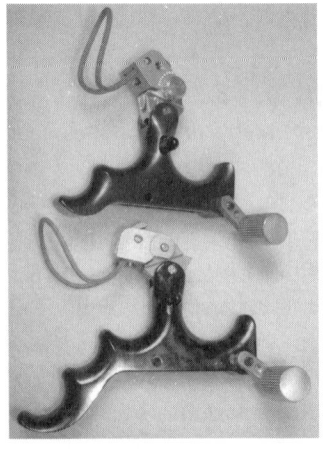

Bernie's Missing Link™ is a pure back tension release and comes in regular and jumbo and 3 or 4 finger versions. It has a new patent-pending **"Link"** between the head and the handle that allows the archer to draw the bow with the handle disengaged from the head. This allows full draw to be reached without worrying about misfires, bloody noses, or dental insurance! Once at full draw, the handle is simply rotated forward until a spring-loaded pin in the handle "links" the head to the handle and makes it fully operational. Once the link is made, back tension is now used to fire the release. The **Missing Link** can be used with or without the special Click Cam™ feature (.010 groove in the edge of the half moon cam).

Both the **Missing Link** and the **E-Z Back** are equipped with patent-pending micro-adjustable **Dial-a-Cam**™ and **Cam-Lock**™ features for easy "Idiot Proof" cam adjustment. This totally eliminates the guesswork of setting "travel" or "speed" of the releases. They both also have a new patent-pending system called **A.R.M.**™ (Auto Return Mechanism) which automatically returns the head to the "ready to load" position after firing.

The problem most back tension release shooters have is that at full draw their elbow is inside (to the left of) perfect firing alignment (see diagram) which causes the bow to break left upon release (and miss left) because the line of force is not directly behind the line of the

Contract rhomboid muscles, string side only. This moves elbow into perfect firing alignment at explosion.

Inside (or left of) line
Firing Position
Click-Cam Position

If the draw elbow is rotated too far behind the head, inside the firing position, this will cause the bow to break left at explosion (left arrow) and vice-versa if the elbow is not rotated enough.

arrow. The reverse is true if the elbow is to the right side; the arrow will miss right in most cases. With both the **Missing Link** and **E-Z Back** the handle is engineered where the shooter's elbow is 5 to 10 degrees to the right of perfect alignment (for a right handed shooter) when the archer reaches the click in the cam. Then, without rotating the wrist or fingers of the release hand, the archer simply contracts the draw side rhomboid muscle (between the shoulder blades) which draws the elbow approximately 3/4" to 1" up and behind the archer's head. At this point the elbow is in perfect alignment with the arrow and the back tension that produced the rotation of the elbow causes the mechanism to release with a total surprise in *perfect alignment*. The **Missing Link** and the **E-Z Back** can be shot directly off a D-Loop or with a rope wrapped around the string.

Bernie's E-Z Back™ RELEASE

Bernie's **E-Z Back**™ comes in regular and jumbo with 3 or 4 finger versions. Like the **Missing Link** this is a pure back tension release that can be shot with or without the **Click-Cam**™. It allows the shooter to draw to anchor with all five fingers involved without fear of premature firing or "bloody noses" which has been inherant with most triggerless releases. Like the **Missing Link** it enables the shooter to draw without having to cock or rotate the wrist, or having to draw with the index finger only, to keep it from misfiring. With the **E-Z Back**, at full draw, simply drop the index finger down from the drawing position to the firing position, release some of the pressure from the thumb hold, and rotate the release until you hear a "click" in the cam. This signals you that the elbow is approximately 1" from perfect alignment of the arrow. Now, using back muscles only, rotate the elbow up and behind your head slowly (which takes approximately 4 seconds) and the cam will disengage and fire, with the elbow in perfect alignment with the arrow (without "cranking" the handle). This gives the shooter a surprise release, one that cannot be anticipated. This frees the archer's mind to concentrate on aiming. The **Missing Link** and the **E-Z Back** are the easiest ways to cure target panic i.e. freezing, punching, snapshooting and flinching for those archers who prefer a hand-held release.

Bernie's "*Control Freak*™" Custom Stabilizer System

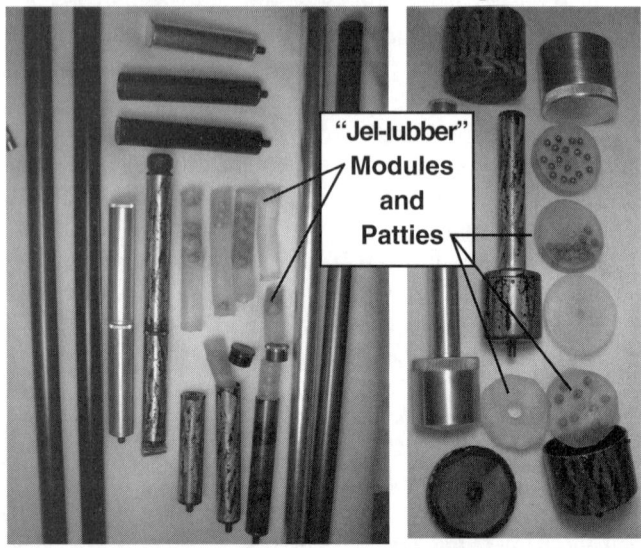

"Jel-lubber" Modules and Patties

Bernie's new patented "shooter controlled" custom stabilizer/dampening system was going to be called the "ShockBlockin-NoiseTrappin-Flubberized-Modular-HoldingSteadylizer" but then he thought, "Nah, I'll never get all that on a tee shirt."

This new "*Control Freak*™" *system* has internal modules made from a secret, patented processed elastomer called "Jel-lubber™" that is as soft as Jello® with suspended weights molded inside them. These variable weighted "Jel-lubber™" modules (some with weights inside, some without) are placed inside the stabilizer by the shooter, who can move them around . . . front to back, back to middle etc., to produce a custom balanced stabilizer. The one inch diameter anodized stabilizers come with screw off caps on one end and are available in 4 inch, 5½ inch, 10 inch and 22 inch. Both end caps have o-ring grooves so they can be joined together with a furnished o-ring between them to make a stabilizer as long or short as the shooter prefers. They will be sent to you with any weight modules you request from 4 ounces to 30 ounces, depending on the module.

Also available is a "canister-type" stabilizer/back weight (see picture). The "can" has a removable top that has a threaded hole on both ends and will accept the 1" diameter *"Control Freak"* stabilizer, or any stabilizer, for that matter. It can also be used as a back weight.

According to Mike Martin, Senior Pro Shooter, "It takes 90% of the vibration out of the shot. It's the best thing I've ever used!" The system works better than conventional stabilizers because the vibration and forward inertia coming from the bow transfers into the suspended weights. The shock and inertia is then dissipated by the jelly-like "Jel-lubber™" compound. These "Jel-lubber™ patties" can be stacked inside the can in any configuration. There is also a patty with all the weights suspended on one side so you can offset the weight of your sight and your cable guard, thus doing away with your V-bars. These "shock blocking canisters" are called the "BossHog," "Chubby" and "Pudgy" and come in 2¾ , 2½ and 2¼ inch diameters respectively and are 2 to 2½ inches tall. The entire *"Control Freak"* line comes in various colors, including camo.

Bernie has also produced stackable stainless steel end weights, offset brackets, and quick disconnects (one regular and one with a 10° drop - see photo below). A lot of pro shooters feel that a 10 degree drop angle on your stabilizer keeps the bow from canting left or right at full draw and makes the bow easier to level up quickly so you don't fight the bubble in the level and overhold the shot.

Bernie's "Control Freak" cannisters can be used as a back weight or used with a stabilizer on the front along with the quick disconnect

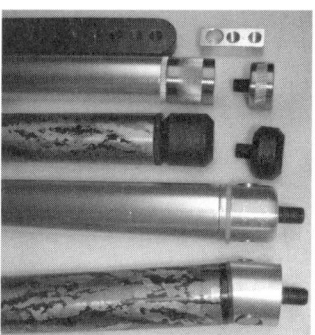

(Bottom to top)
Quick disconnect with 10 degree drop angle;
Straight disconnect;
Stackable black and stainless end weights; Long and short offset brackets.

For more information or to order, call Bernie or Jan Pellerite at **Robinhood Video Productions**, *614-933-0011 or visit their website at* **www.robinhoodvideos.com**.

Private Instruction!
Robinhood Advanced Archery School
"A weekend at Bernie's!"

Private & Small Group Lessons Now Available (1 to 6 people)
Also Available Internationally!

* The most advanced and accelerated archery program in the world today!
* Bernie has worked with shooters who have won over 150 National & World Championships.
* Let Bernie teach you what "Idiot Proof" Archery can do for you!

Certified NFAA Master Coaches
Bernie & Jan Pellerite

Bernie is also the NFAA National Certified Instructor Chairman
Phone (614)933-0011   Fax (614)933-0010

Call for Rates*
*MOST PEOPLE ARE **"CURED"** IN 3-8 HOURS!!*

*Rates include room and board and transportation to and from Columbus, Ohio Airport (if necessary).

Curriculum is an accelerated program for Intermediate to Professional level shooters, and will be customized to your specific needs. **The curriculum could include:** practice regimen, equipment set-up, speed, tuning, holding steady, back tension, mental and physical aiming, professional form, shot execution, tournament pressure, judging yardage, bow torque, problem solving, punching the trigger, penetration, target panic/buck fever, Q & A sessions, and much, much more!

Five-time world professional 3-D champion, Joella Bates came for private lessons and spent "A weekend at Bernie's"

Subject matter may vary from 3-D to target shooting to bowhunting, and would include any or all of the above subjects, based upon request. Students will be videotaped shooting from three angles: overhead, side view, and with a laser sight picture. Later they are personally analyzed in slow motion. Students get to keep their videos for future reference.

Bernie Pellerite is the only **NFAA Master Coach** to achieve the top status of **"Professional Level IV"** since the 3-Tiered Certified Instructor Program was created.

Available for **Seminars, Banquets** & other **Archery Functions** as a keynote speaker, from **1 to 5 hours**
Your choice of subjects:
Back Tension, Tournament Nerves, Target Panic (buck fever), Arrow Penetration, Form Flaws, and dozens more!

Since 15 year old Chris Glass came to Bernie for private lessons, he has set two new world records and regularly shoots 300 with 57-59Xs! Bernie says, "He has the work ethic, maturity and focus that it takes to be one of the best shooters in the sport."

When whitetail hunting legend, Myles Keller, first came to Bernie's school, he said, "I can't hit a 12" paper plate at 20 yards.... I'm freezing so badly! Four months later, he could hit a tennis ball at 50 yards (with broadheads)!

Ted Nugent, bowhunting rock star, was freezing so bad he couldn't put the pin on the chest of a whitetail buck. Bernie's explanation of his proven program helped Ted overcome his buck fever. Ted calls it the "Detox Exorcism Program!"

NFAA Mobile Shooter's School

The following information is current, but is subject to change

It pays to go to Bernie's Shooter's School!

In an effort to enhance shooter education and awareness, the NFAA Shooter's School was created in 1996 by Bernie Pellerite. He approached the National Field Archery Association (NFAA) to see if they were interested. Bernie and his wife Jan are both Master Coaches and spend most of the year traveling around the U.S. in their motorhome (along with their 3 dogs and 2 cats!) coaching serious archery students and certifying instructors through the school. Bernie created and wrote the current Certified Instructor Program and manuals. This unique mobile shooter's school is the most popular in the world and continues to be a huge success . . . just ask anyone who has ever attended!

Curriculum is for intermediate to professional level archers. Topics include 3-D, target shooting, bowhunting, practice regimen, equipment set-up, tuning, holding steady, mental and physical aiming, back tension, professional form, shot sequence and execution, tournament pressure and judging yardage. Problem solving and question and answer sessions will cover topics such as punching the trigger, bow torque, penetration, target panic/buck fever and much more. NFAA membership is not required to attend. Friday afternoon is spent video-taping the students. Each student keeps their own personal video.

School starts Friday at 6:00 PM (or after filming is finished) until approximately 9:00 PM. Saturday and Sunday sessions run from 8:00 AM to 6:30 PM. There is a minimum of 10 and a maximum of 25 students. (Any number less than 10 students must be pre-approved) Students who wish to just audit the course, can only attend one day or are repeating the course, pay a discounted fee. Students get a discount on the 6 Shooter's School videos. Anyone who already purchased the videos will also get a discount on the school. You can also become an Advanced Level Certified Instructor for a small additional fee and one extra hour of class. (Must be 18 years or older and a member of NFAA.) You may join at the school. NFAA members receive one free Robinhood video of their choice. 10% of the fee goes to the host shop or club. Due to the overwhelming popularity of the school and the limited number of open weekends, it is recommended that interested pro shops, clubs or individuals schedule as soon as possible. You can also be put on the waiting list. Available dates always fill up quickly.

For more information, or to schedule a school in your area
Contact either Bernie or Jan Pellerite
Phone 614-933-0011   Fax at 614-933-0010
e-mail AskBernie@aol.com
website at www.robinhoodvideos.com

Also available internationally!

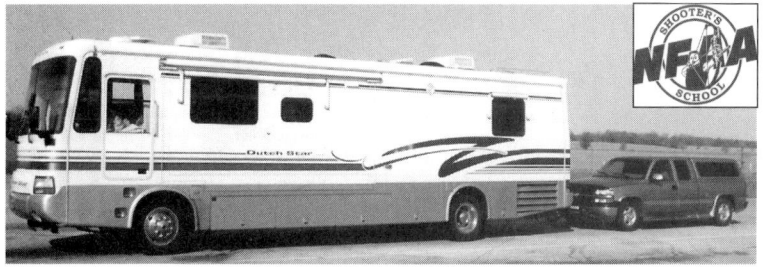

NFAA Mobile Shooter's School . . . have RV will travel!

Professional Archery Technique is still available from Amazon.com or from Kirk Ethridge directly at Different Densities Publications. http://hospice.xtn.net/home.htm

Larry Wise is the author of *"Tuning Your Compound Bow," "Tuning Your Broadheads,"* and *"Step by Step Bow Tuning Basics."* For information contact: Larry Wise, RD #3, Box 678, Mifflintown, PA 17059. Phone (717)436-6629.

Scott Archery Mfg., Inc.
101 Tug Branch Rd., Clay City, KY 40312
Phone (606)663-0344

Easton Arrow Spine Chart available from Easton
5040 W. Harold Gatty Drive
Salt Lake City, UT 84116
Phone (801)539-1400, Fax (801)533-9907
Web: www.eastonarchery.com

Archery Organizations

ASA - Archery Shooters Association
P.O. Box 39, 1301 Shiloh Rd., Ste. 720
Kennesaw, GA 30144
Phone (770)795-0232, Fax (770)795-0953
e-mail: asa@asaarchery.com   Website: www.asaarchery.com

IBO - International Bowhunting Organization
P.O. Box 398, Vermilion, OH 44089
Phone (440)967-2137, Fax (440)967-2052
e-mail: ibo@ibo.net   Website: www.ibo.net

NAA - National Archery Association
One Olympic Plaza, Colorado Springs, CO 80909
Phone (719)578-4576, Fax (719)632-4733
e-mail: info@usarchery.org   Website: www.USArchery.org

Membership application to the National Field Archery Association

Membership in the NFAA includes 6 issues of **"Archery"** Magazine per year, which features instructional and technical articles by yours truly. Also, NFAA Shooter's School updates, Bowhunter News and stories by Tim Atwood and many other features. Also articles by a variety of people on target, 3-D, and bowhunting. It includes schedules for upcoming Shooter's Schools, tournaments, plus International Field Archery Association (IFAA) news.

Any questions you have about joining the NFAA can be answered by calling **1-800-811-2331** or **909-794-2133** fax **909-794-8512** or writing to: NFAA Headquarters, 31407 Outer I-10, Redlands, CA 92373. E-mail: nfaarchery@aol.com. Website: www.NFAA-archery.org

To join by using the attached application, just **MAKE A COPY** of it, fill it in and send it to the above address with the appropriate funds. MasterCard and Visa are accepted.

Join the NFAA!   IPA

Enjoy these Exciting Benefits:
National, Sectional, State & Club Tournaments;
Certified Instructor Programs;
Club & Pro Shop Insurance;
Indoor/Outdoor Leagues; Professional Archery
Subscription to **Archery Magazine**
included. Complete the application and join today!

Name _____

Address _____

City _____ State _____ Zip _____

Phone _____

One year **Individual** membership $45.00
Family Membership $65.00
Junior Membership (under 18) $35.00
Visa and MasterCard accepted
CC# _____ Card exp. date _____

Call toll-free 800-811-2331
National Field Archery Association
31407 Outer I-10, Redlands, CA 92373

It is Jan's and my wish that the information in this book may, in some small way, further the education and promotion of archers and archery everywhere!

**And, remember . . . Play hard!
Aim hard! . . . Help someone!
and Have Fun! . . .**

It's just a game!

Bernie Pellerite